WE MUST BEGIN WITH THE LAND

SEEKING ABUNDANCE AND LIBERATION THROUGH SOCIAL ECOLOGY

Stephen E. Hunt

London, UK
Washington, DC, USA

CollectiveInk

First published by Zer0 Books, 2025
Zer0 Books is an imprint of Collective Ink Ltd.,
Unit 11, Shepperton House, 89 Shepperton Road, London, N1 3DF
office@collectiveinkbooks.com
www.collectiveinkbooks.com
www.zero-books.net

For distributor details and how to order, please visit the 'Ordering' section on our website.

Text copyright: Stephen E. Hunt, 2024

Paperback ISBN: 978 1 80341 585 7
eBook ISBN: 978 1 80341 586 4
PCN: 2024935370

All rights reserved. Except for brief quotations in critical articles or reviews, no part of this book may be reproduced in any manner without prior written permission from the publishers.

The rights of Stephen E. Hunt as author have been asserted in accordance with the Copyright, Designs and Patents Act 1988.

A CIP catalogue record for this book is available from the British Library.

Design credit(s): Lapiz Digital

UK: Printed and bound by CPI Group (UK) Ltd, Croydon, CR0 4YY
Printed in North America by CPI GPS partners

We operate a distinctive and ethical publishing philosophy in all areas of our business, from our global network of authors to production and worldwide distribution.

What People Are Saying About

We Must Begin with the Land

We Must Begin with the Land is a rich and nourishing work written by someone passionate about good food — good for the people, for the planet, for society — and extremely well acquainted to ecological thought and theory. Looking at food and agricultural production through the lens of social ecology, it takes us on a tour from the UK to India, Rojava, Brazil, and back to show how dominatory agriculture has always been tied to forms of violence not only against the land and the planet, but against the people, society, and all beings. This book highlights the ingenuity and generosity of Bookchin's social ecology based around values of complementarity, diversity, solidarity, abundance and quality of life — values embraced by many actors and activists of good food production around the world. It shows how social ecology can help us think in practical terms about food and bring practical solutions to nourish and re-enchant the many places that make our world.
Dr Clemence Scalbert Yucel, Senior Lecturer, University of Exeter

Drawing on rich insights from social ecology, this book offers a reconstructive and revolutionary vision for food, agriculture, and land use. Stephen Hunt takes us on a remarkable journey across 'grounded utopias' and real-world experiences of people who are inventing more just and sustainable food systems outside of capitalism, colonialism, and patriarchy. This is a must-read for social movements struggling for emancipatory agroecologies, radical ecological democracy, and food justice.
Prof Michel Pimbert, Emeritus Professor of Agroecology and Food Politics, Coventry University

Stephen Hunt has written a fine book taking in a multitude of agricultural and ecological stories to inspire and signpost us past the impending multi-crises. This book has a sci-fi quality about it, feeling like a report from the future. It takes in the barely believable as if it were a film, but it actually happened — revolution in Rojava, inspired by Murray Bookchin, whose ideas of social ecology provide the main trunk of this book. The project of democratic confederalism provides an example of what Bookchin's vision could look like in the real world, albeit under the immense pressure of war. Hunt draws out complementary and different themes like Indigenous agriculture and stewardship, the conviviality of a simple meal together, and the potential for a liberatory human-sized technology to prevent scarcity. This is without the bombastic claims of Fully Automated Luxury Communism, and like Bookchin, Hunt is a fierce critic of productivist Marxism. But he does not fall into the liberal trap of looking for the government or the market to save us. He draws upon different ideas of land ownership, property relations, permaculture, and contemporary experiments in collective food production to show some tentative steps forward. This means that *We Must Begin with the Land* can stand alongside and complement the emerging 'degrowth communism' movement, which is providing a similarly rich critique of capitalism but often without the finer details of how we will get there. This book fills that gap.
Steve Stuffit, Trapese Collective

This remarkable book presents big-picture thinking that can truly help to envision innovative strategies and practical pathways to reverse the expanding corporate food system. In the process, Stephen E. Hunt brings the concepts and spirit of social ecology to everyone concerned about the underlying causes of dominatory agriculture. He writes this book with the finest research, accompanied by worldwide stories and grounded experiences, yet easy to understand and captivating. Facing the recent poly-crisis, this timely book stirs us to join the global movement for food and climate justice urgently.
Angus Lam, Board member, Sims Hill Shared Harvest (Bristol)

TABLE OF CONTENTS

Appetiser	1
Hors d'Oeuvre	5

Part 1: Social Ecology and Agriculture   11

Murray Bookchin's Radical Agriculture	13
The Principles of Social Ecology	26
• *Challenging dominatory agriculture*	27
• *Internationalism on the model of democratic confederalism*	27
• *Access to land and usufruct*	29
• *Food sovereignty and abundance through a solidarity economy*	29
• *Regenerative agroecology*	30
• *Respect for ecological integrity*	30
• *Agroecological knowledges*	31
• *Liberatory technology*	32
• *Right livelihoods*	33
• *Quality of production, of consumption, and of life*	33

Part 2: Principles of Social Ecology in Practice   37

The "Sacred Activity": Social Ecology and Food Production in the Kurdish Region	39
• *Insurgent vegetables*	43
• *The defiant trees of Green Tress*	52

Dominatory Agriculture: From Slave Plantations to
  Factory Farming 67
- *Plantations* 67
- *India's colonial food traumas* 70
- *Embattled fields* 73
- *The cages of free enterprise and the rise of chicken power* 74

Internationalism on the Model of Democratic Confederalism 83
- *La Via Campesina* 83

Access to Land and Usufruct 91
- *MST and agrarian reform* 91
- *Kleingärten* 94
- *Access to growing spaces* 101

Food Sovereignty and Abundance through a Solidarity Economy 114
- *Food sovereignty in the United Kingdom* 114
- *Diversification of production* 117

Regenerative Agroecology 131
- *Permaculture* 131
- *The dark alchemy of human manure* 135

Agroecological Knowledges 141
- *Safeguarding Adivasi knowledges* 141
- *Citizen science: Food literacy and democratising research* 147

Liberatory Technology 155
- *Hydroponics and vertical farming* 156
- *Energy gardens of tomorrow* 162
- *Point–Counterpoint: Herbal lays for green gas* 166
- *Radical materials science* 169

Right Livelihoods   187

Quality of Production, of Consumption, and of Life   199
- *Shumei: Japanese natural agriculture the Wiltshire way*   199
- *A party in your mouth: Commensality, or the pleasures of eating together* 203
- *Point–Counterpoint: Farm animals in food production*   209

Part 3: Britain: Lock-in and Unlocking   **227**

- *British Agribusiness: Is it "a great story"?*   227
- *Decolonising food security thinking*   228
- *Ecological integrity and climate change*   233
- *Lock-in and unlocking*   236

Concluding Thoughts   245

APPETISER

To misquote Oscar Wilde, a dish that is not utopian is not worth a second mouthful.

Two kinds of situation compete for attention when I consider the perfect meal. One calls to mind convivial experiences; the other, intimate moments. I think back to a time in Lisbon's Graça district, when the blazing sun eased, and long tables were set up in the streets for neighbourhood dining, followed by live fado music in the local bars. Or idling with friends at balmy summer free festivals, or at social centres such as the Kebele Community Co-op in Easton, Bristol, where food is cooked and eaten collectively to raise money for a cause.[1] Or memorable nights such as those enjoyed by Trees for Life volunteers in an off-grid bothy in Glen Affric in the remote Scottish Highlands. After rising at daybreak to plant the likes of oak, aspen, and goat willow, we would play in the evening. Then we would make use of a gigantic cauldron to share the cooking and serve up platters of wholesome food, before getting out the guitars and playing games that left us convulsed with merriment.[2] More intimately, there were those Christmas meals with extended family. Then, the quieter times with my partner, affording different moments of delight. We once cycled out on a frozen December morning to find a holy well, and came home to cook a winter rhapsody soup. Sharing meals with close friends, such as the sumptuous vegetarian buffets served by Leicester's Asian communities, or cooking on holiday, before putting the world to rights over an ale or two, and then perhaps watching a folk horror film. I hope you will have fond culinary memories of your own. Yet, such simple pleasures are by no means to be taken for granted. World hunger has been increasing for nearly a decade. What follows will make the challenges ahead clear.

So, the indispensable ingredients of the perfect meal are the person, the place, the time, and the space. Meaningful, peak experiences in life frequently involve the cultivation, preparation, and consumption of food, in all their manifold cross-cultural variety. Since nourishment holds a fundamental position in the hierarchy of human needs, the other essential element, therefore, relates to the nutritional and aesthetic qualities of the meal's ingredients. It should be delicious, tasty, and health-giving. To consider the matter holistically, the ethical qualities relating to the circumstances of production are also pertinent. Food needs to be accessible and affordable. Typically, factors such as the environmental and the health impacts of production are discounted as economic externalities. Within the World Trade Organization (WTO), there are longstanding disagreements relating to subsidies and liberalisation in respect to "non-trade concerns," such as the environment, food security, and rural development.[3] According to critics, WTO agricultural trade rules exacerbate efforts to regulate food security and quality.[4] Relatedly, there is the question of whether the production minimises the exploitation of workers, non-human species, or the land itself, however such impacts are understood. Attention to further factors could be added, such as processing and distribution, transport and supply chains, packaging and presentation, and seasonality, provenance, and terroir. For social ecologists, qualitative objectives including ecologically sustainable regenerative agriculture and food sovereignty will not be attained through ethical consumerism, a feature of the market forces deemed to have undermined them in the first place. Grace

Gershuny, for example, argues that the mere purchase of value-added products labelled "organic" or "recycled" is unlikely to "solve the problems created by the market-driven imperative toward increased consumption."[5] Social ecology, therefore, demands a more holistic, transformative, and revolutionary approach. It is at once internationalist and localist, recognising that food is always more than a commodity, since its production and consumption is embedded in social rites as various as harvesting and coming of age rituals, and in many cultures is considered as a spiritual offering or medicine essential to individual well-being and social resilience. Socially, politically, and ecologically entwined in this way, the evaluation of what utopian food might be becomes a complex task. Since this is not a recipe book, the focus in what follows will be upon the production of food, and other grown goods, and their relationships to the conditions of labour and land.

Making high-quality food available can be hugely fulfilling, whether growing across a wide acreage or even in a window box or by foraging. I invite and encourage you to eat or drink something interesting as you read. Try some new recipes, seek out a greengrocer or street market, or maybe revisit something you detested as a child. You never know, one day we may toast cheers and break bread together. I hope so.

Notes

1 Renamed BASE.
2 In particular, a game where you placed a well-known square-shaped mint confectionary on your forehead and then contorted your facial muscles to try to manipulate it into your mouth without using your hands. Who knew that this was a thing and that so many people were adept at it? You had to be there, really.
3 World Trade Organization, "'Non-Trade' Concerns: Agriculture Can Serve Many Purposes" (2004), https://www.wto.org/english/tratop_e/agric_e/negs_bkgrnd17_agri_e.htm.

4. Matias E. Margulis, Kristen Hopewell, and Edi Qereshniku, "Food, Famine and the Free Trade Fallacy: The Dangers of Market Fundamentalism in an Era of Climate Emergency," *Journal of Peasant Studies* 3 (2022), https://doi.org/10.1080/03066150.2022.2133602.
5. Grace Gershuny, *Organic Revolutionary: A Memoir of the Movement for Real Food, Planetary Healing, and Human Liberation*, 3rd rev. and expanded ed. (Montréal: Black Rose, 2020), 208.

HORS D'OEUVRE

Easing the human friction with the rest of the living world is the greatest challenge and responsibility of present generations. The biosphere's flourishing within the Earth's integrated systems is essential for three reasons: to ensure human livelihood and well-being; because other, non-human species have intrinsic value; and for personal self-realisation. Such self-realisation can only be reached through connection and sympathy with other people and living things. The wise John Cowper Powys made the cosmic claim that there will never be a time when you will not have existed; existentially, it matters how we grow and eat, and move and dwell, because if Powys's argument in *The Art of Happiness* is right, our mental life and actions have "eternal significance" for our lives and for all that come after us.[1] Principles of social ecology hold that sustaining ecological integrity within planetary boundaries is impossible without addressing profound social problems embedded in deep history. This entails comprehending and evolving beyond the historic turn towards hierarchy and patriarchy, statism, and capitalism. If the repressive constraints and violence imposed and perpetrated by such dominatory structures can be dissolved, a kind of liberation can be envisaged which could enhance self-realisation by enabling greater personal agency and reducing alienation—that is, collective liberation, not the imagined zero-sum game of individual competition.

Such liberation requires social justice, and justice is absent without the egalitarian impetus to enjoy a fine life, whatever background, ability, stature, or appearance. This enabling notion of equality fosters solidarity and calls for all to embrace care and compassion as a political and spiritual imperative. Audre Lorde is often quoted for her insight that "It is not our differences that divide us. It is our inability to recognize, accept, and celebrate those differences." Such respect for difference has its finest social expression in inclusive participatory democracy. As cultural critic Mark Fisher argued in his final essay, "Acid Communism," after the bloody coup d'état in Chile and global oil crisis in 1973, neoliberalism unleashed a formidable counterrevolution that, in its own terms, successfully repressed the foregoing upswell of emancipatory aspects of the 1960–70s counterculture with its attendant social movements for civil rights, workers' democracy, sexual liberation, and ecology. Today, neoliberalism's destructive and contradictory dynamics are evidenced in multiple ongoing crises. Yet, its hegemony can never be final and absolute. This is because the profit it craves for its sustenance and renewal demands the extra-market experiences, exchanges, and autonomous relationships that produce imagination, ingenuity, and inventiveness, which it represses or monetarises, and the commons of the living world, which it encloses, commodifies, and consumes. Both criticality and a daring re-envisioning of alternatives are called for to reawaken that spirit of what critics such as Michael Löwy, Robert Sayre, and Max Blechman have called revolutionary Romanticism. A transformative paradigm-shift is required to overcome the alienation, insufficiency, and violent pathology of a prevailing ideology that systemically dispossesses people and converts living land into severed zones of monoculture, desiccated and charred wastes, and concrete.

Philosophically, therefore, I am coming from a perspective of social ecology, which I believe offers such a paradigm shift, and of which more shortly. There is another thing I would like to come clean about at the outset: while I was thrilled to be invited to write about agricultural possibilities, my pleasure came with a substantial feeling of impostor syndrome. While I was brought up in a rural town in Wiltshire, and over the years have gardened, kept an allotment, and contributed my labour to Willing Workers on Organic Farms, I can by no means claim to be a farmer. I am, however, at least passionate about food and ideas about food production. And at a time of crisis, food must become a priority for all. So, in what follows, I am going to explore and share some ideas about how a paradigm shift with a social-ecological bent might inspire and help to reframe thinking about food production.

Murray Bookchin (1921–2006), the originator of much social-ecological thought, once proclaimed, "We must begin with the land."[2] Therefore, the first section of this book opens with Bookchin's works relating to "radical agriculture" and an outline of ten key principles of social ecology relating to agroecology. Like the petals of a sunflower, these are intended to give colour, light, and structure to the topical discussions that follow. It is hoped that these topics may eventually seed strategies for change.

Next is a consideration of attempts to implement ideas partly inspired by Bookchin in one of the few living revolutionary territories: the predominately Kurdish region of Rojava, known since 2018 as the Autonomous Administration of North and East Syria (AANES), and since December 2023 as the Democratic Autonomous Administration of North and East Syria (DAANES). Here, there are practical attempts to address significant ecological challenges, while diversifying crops and boosting food sovereignty. The Kurdish freedom movement's ecology initiatives have endured following its militias' defeat of the Islamic State, and despite neighbouring NATO member Turkey's military incursions.

The next sections move on from this discrete and precarious communalist entity to further consider and glean insights from the field of agroecology in multiple international and domestic contexts. Even among social ecologists and eco-activists, consensus is lacking, so there are two noisy interruptions that buffet the main narrative stalk in the form of discursive point–counterpoints considering dilemmas relating to the use of pasture for energy and the place of animals in agriculture.

A social-ecological approach demands a mix of utopianism and pragmatism. Policies affecting food and other grown goods must of course be credible, incorporating practical measures at the local and regional level. Re-envisioning without critique is likely to lead to disillusion. Idealism without a viable pathway to effect change merely perpetuates the dominance of monopolistic business.[3] At the same time, it would seem a highly risky and unwarranted strategy to accommodate prevailing economic and agricultural policies, given current outcomes that include the ecological crisis, cost-of-living crisis, seemingly escalating armed conflict, and the mass displacement of people. Moreover, intensifying global inequality ensures that those who are better able to dominate the economy can define the terms of commercial transactions in their own interests and determine what choices are "realistic." In the era of the coronavirus pandemic and foodbanks, this has been increasingly evident in healthcare and basic nutrition. Current market mechanisms often make it uneconomic to produce for people with the greatest need and weakest spending power. Where crisis is normality, a truly reconstructive vision is necessary to affect the transformation that is so desperately needed.

While prominent eco-activist and social critic George Monbiot highlighted the striking trend towards increased rates of malnutrition since 2014, this deterioration has intensified even further since. The United Nations now estimates that up to 828 million people—9.8% of the world population—were experiencing hunger in 2021.[4] It is important to accentuate the point that current multiple crises are consequences of mis-policies based upon an unsustainable paradigm that predates the so-called "perfect storm" of oft-cited explanatory reasons. Coronavirus, the Russian invasion of Ukraine, conflict in the Middle East, and indeed Brexit, are undoubtedly exacerbating factors, but they are symptoms of ecological stress underlying geopolitical and commercial rivalry, rather than ultimate causes. Within this context, the UK has a small population and is losing influence; yet, with its colonial legacy and as a major instigator of neoliberal policies, its role also remains significant and symbolic. There are two metrics that serve as an indictment that underscores the extent of the UK's specific social and ecological failures. First, it has been cited as "one of, if not the, worst performing nations in the European Union" in terms of food insecurity.[5] Second, the UK is one of the world's most nature-depleted countries.[6] My argument will advocate, therefore, efforts to identify concrete measures and transitional demands underpinned by collective solidarity to change the facts on the ground in England and Wales in a planetary context.

Notes

1   John Cowper Powys, *The Art of Happiness* (London: Bodley Head, 1935), 60.
2   Murray Bookchin, "Radical Agriculture," 3–13 in *Radical Agriculture*, ed. by Richard Merrill (New York: Harper Colophon, 1976), 7.
3   The Food and Agriculture Organization of the United Nations (FAO) claims that just three grains account for more than half of calories consumed: "Just 15 crop plants provide 90 percent of the world's food energy intake, with three – rice, maize and wheat – making up two-thirds of this." "Staple Foods: What do People Eat?," accessed 11 July 2022, https://www.fao.org/3/u8480e/u8480e07.htm. Moreover, just four companies control global wheat production.
4   George Monbiot, *Regenesis: Feeding the World Without Devouring the Planet* ([London]: Allen Lane, 2022), 39. Monbiot has commented sympathetically on Murray Bookchin's theories of social ecology and participatory democracy, "Feeling the Urge to Take Back Control from Power-Mad Governments? Here's an Idea," *The Guardian*, 13 July 2022, https://www.theguardian.com/commentisfree/2022/jul/13/take-back-control-governments; World Health Organization, "UN Report: Global Hunger Numbers Rose to as Many as 828 Million in 2021" (6 July 2022), https://www.who.int/news/item/06-07-2022-un-report--global-hunger-numbers-rose-to-as-many-as-828-million-in-2021.

5   Commons Select Committee Environmental Audit, "Hunger, Food Insecurity and Malnutrition in the UK," citing evidence from the UK Stakeholders for Sustainable Development and the Food Foundation (10 January 2019), accessed 25 December 2022, https://publications.parliament.uk/pa/cm201719/cmselect/cmenvaud/1491/149105.htm. In September 2022, statistical tracking by the Food Foundation found that food insecurity continues to affect 9.7 million adults and 4 million children, accessed 25 December 2022, https://foodfoundation.org.uk/initiatives/food-insecurity-tracking.

6   Biodiversity in the UK: Bloom or Bust? HC 136. First Report of Session 2021–22. Environmental Audit Committee, House of Commons, Jun. 2021, 5, accessed 25 December 2022, https://committees.parliament.uk/publications/6498/documents/70656/default/.

PART I
SOCIAL ECOLOGY AND AGRICULTURE

MURRAY BOOKCHIN'S RADICAL AGRICULTURE

Let us begin at the beginning: Mesopotamia. Watered by the Tigris and Euphrates, Mesopotamia became the cradle of settled agricultural society following the Neolithic Revolution. Here in the Middle and Near East, somewhen around 10,000 BCE, a hazardous venture was undertaken, incrementally shifting from tribal networks subsisting on hunting and gathering to settled societies based upon agriculture. This transition had existential repercussions for most of humanity's social evolution thereafter. Technical processes such as irrigation and the selection and domestication of cereals, legumes, and other plants, as well as animals, redefined the human relationship to the living world and afforded profound social changes. The capacity to store foodstuffs and accumulate wealth enabled the accentuated division of labour and the hierarchical structuring of societies, from which eventually emerged the state.

Anthropologist James C. Scott radically reframes the way that we think about deep history in this regard, drawing upon the latest archaeological evidence relating to this Agrarian Revolution that took place 12,000 years ago, constituting perhaps only 5% of human history, with a lag of some 6000 years to the emergence of the state—a process often assumed to be contemporaneous.¹ Both farming and the state materialised in the near and Middle East, incorporating the so-called Fertile Crescent. It is, therefore, a fitting point of departure for social ecology, a philosophy that attributes the deep roots of the exploitation of and our alienation from the living world to the rise of hierarchical, patriarchal society. Furthermore, much of historic Mesopotamia is coextensive with the predominantly Kurdish region in the present day. Where better, then, to explore the ecological experiments within the paradigm of democratic confederalism and their implications for global food production?

Murray Bookchin, the author from whom this work takes its title, is not widely considered as a writer on farming. As a former foundryman and auto-worker from the Bronx, New York, he would scarcely be expected to be.² His work on cities comes more readily to mind for those with an interest in the pioneer of social ecology. Nevertheless, Bookchin researched the challenges of food production assiduously, and applied his critical mind to agricultural matters long before he became renowned as an eco-philosopher. In his earliest full-length book, *Our Synthetic Environment* (1962), he extended his analysis of the negative effects of chemical fertilisers and pesticides such as DDT, chlordane, and lindane upon human health and the environment. He first expressed this fear in 1952, in an essay entitled "The Problem of Chemicals in Food."³

His published concerns about chemical residues from crops for agricultural workers and consumers therefore predated those in Rachel Carson's famous book, *Silent Spring*, published, like *Our Synthetic Environment*, in 1962.⁴ This coincidence of publication, while unfortunate for Bookchin, was nevertheless a significant step in the emergence of the present-day ecology movement.⁵ With her eloquently written and more attractively titled *Silent Spring*, Carson made a bestseller of what might have seemed an unpromising topic. The evocation of silence proved eerily resonant. She presented a compelling argument with verve, rigorously evidenced with recent research, and had the merit of focus. *Silent Spring* was so influential that it provoked reform, leading to the ban of DDT in the United States in 1972, and the UK in 1984.[6]

Bookchin's effective yet more abstract presentation of the facts was perhaps less impactful than the unsettling idea of a hushed countryside absent of songbirds, but the merits of his works were also of a different order. Ultimately, his wider contextualisation of the systemic issues at stake had even more momentous consequences, since they became a pathway to the development of powerful political ecologies that represent a revolutionary alternative to capitalist industrialism.

From his first works on agriculture, Bookchin sought to understand, expose, and confront the deep causes of inseparable social and ecological crises. His ideas were distilled and refined over 3 decades from his earlier research in "The Problem of Chemicals in Food" (1952) and *Our Synthetic Environment* (1962) to "Radical Agriculture" in 1972 and his fullest expression of social ecology, *The Ecology of Freedom* (1982). At the heart of his criticism is Bookchin's attempt to distinguish between the value of industry and technology (of which agriculture is an expression as part of human culture), but against what he considered to be the mistaken ideology of industrial capitalism. For Bookchin, the undoubted productive efficiency of the capitalist approach has enabled the supposed "mastery" of the natural world and thereby allowed dominant economic classes to harness vast political power. He endeavoured to demonstrate that such an approach is also catastrophically self-destructive, since it cuts off the wellsprings of life on Earth and thereby the sources of human livelihood and well-being.

Bookchin identified several themes relating to food production that have a bearing upon the practical discussion to come.[7]

First, he discusses capitalism's role in disenchanting the natural world in order to commodify it. Cultivating the land necessarily involves managing and directing the growth of other species to suit human ends. However, Bookchin argues, the process of the disenchantment of the earth went further by affecting a fundamental divergence in attitudes during the early modern period.[8] Before, the earth was conceived as an "enchanted world brimming with life, purpose and spirituality";[9] since, the living world has come to be regarded no longer as a home but as an inert repository of "natural resources," in a process Carolyn Merchant extensively documented in *The Death of Nature* (1980).[10] While the rejection of supernaturalism and what Bookchin regarded as the mystification of nature had progressive aspects, the shift fundamentally altered prevailing ideas about the human relationship to the natural world. If the land is no longer respected for its immanent life-force, there are potentially far-reaching consequences for its treatment. It matters profoundly whether the land is conceived of as a soil community or as real estate.

Second, and relatedly, this status of land as an "alienable commodity," rather than as humanity's home, has brought about a philosophical and physical separation between urban society in particular and other living things.[11] For Bookchin, humanity is always a part of nature, even though we have increasingly evolved a particular self-consciousness that renders us "second nature."[12] However, due to a radical division of labour, we have lost control of the processes that contribute to our own sustenance and self-realisation. In this context, urban society has become divorced from a world that is comprehensible and has human-scale, with the consequence that, under industrial capitalism, individuals are increasingly left "faceless and estranged."[13] Inspired by the ideas of E.A. Gutkind, who coined the term "social ecology," Bookchin advocated for a more decentralised human society to address such alienation, with the development of the accompanying structures and ecotechnologies necessary to create more liveable conditions.

Third, a discourse of the mastery and domination of the natural world accompanied the idea of the disenchantment of the earth and its attendant sense of estrangement. Intrinsic to the rupture between human society and the living world was a notion of competitive antagonism, again with consequences for the approach to the land. This development was the logical outcome of a hierarchically structured society based on the strengthening institutions of the state and emerging capitalism. Bookchin argues that

> Not until we come to the modern capitalist era do humanity and nature separate as almost complete foes, and the "mastery" by human over the natural world assumes the form of harsh domination, not merely hierarchical classification.[14]

Such observations were to crystallise into the core principle of social ecology as espoused in *The Ecology of Freedom*: that "the very notion of the domination of nature by man stems from the very real domination of human by human."[15] The gendering of this process is not merely incidental to its time in the early 1980s. For Bookchin, the idea of a society based on domination has entailed a gendered division of labour and the hierarchical norms of patriarchal society—a theme developed further by feminist historians, notably Carolyn Merchant, Maria Mies, Val Plumwood, Vandana Shiva, and Silvia Federici.

A fourth theme in Bookchin's critique of agricultural practices within the paradigm of industrial capitalism is what he considered to be the "disastrous" trend towards simplification. The theme of "diversity and simplicity" was prominent, for example, in "Ecology and Revolutionary Thought" (1965), Bookchin's first major exposition of social ecology.[16] Industrial agriculture scales up production by diminishing crop diversification in favour of a significantly reduced number of—hopefully reliable—varieties of cultivar. Furthermore, complex, naturally evolving ecosystems are replaced with vast fields and plantations of single, chemically maintained crops. Such standardisation reconfigures landscapes from complexity to simplicity. Bookchin was alarmed about the outcomes of this ostensible progress, fearing that it put the process of organic evolution into reverse as "a simplification that occurs on such a global scale that it may well throw back the planet to an evolutionary stage where it could support only simpler forms of life."[17] Present-day social-ecologist critics such as Chaia Heller are echoing such concerns about "risky" monoculture and advocating for the diversification of production using systems of polyculture.[18] It is argued that conserving and enhancing Indigenous and traditional, human-scale forms of farming can help to build resilience into the food-production systems of the future.

Potentially, therefore, over-reliance upon single, often export-oriented, crops is a hazardous strategy. Relatedly, historical lessons such as the Irish Potato Famine, the mass famines in Raj-era India, and other tropical colonial territories, as Mike Davis memorably alleged in *Late Victorian Holocausts* (2001), warn us of the potentially catastrophic consequences of this over-reliance. If a monocultural harvest is poor, systems of fair distribution according to need are disrupted. While Bookchin's ideas shifted over time, he always recognised famine as primarily a social problem that demands solutions founded on social justice. In essays such as "The Population Myth" (1988–1989), he excoriated neo-Malthusians and those within the deep-ecology movement who he regarded as apologists for famine as a form of "natural" population control. Dismissing the notion that famine was a simple outcome of overpopulation, Bookchin suggested a complex of factors, including the allocation and distribution of land and harvests, the efficacy of social forms of population control (including women's empowerment) for smaller families, and shortages due to the excesses of militarism and consumerism. Citing cases such as Sudan with its fertile soils, he attributed severe food shortages to factors such as the colonial dispossession and accumulation of land and labour for profit-driven export crops such as cotton. So, for Bookchin, the "social roots of hunger" have multiple and intertwined causes.[19]

Bookchin's persuasive analysis largely holds firm. Additional stresses such as climate change already threaten to further undermine food security. The practice of nominating communities and regions as designated production zones for specific commodities, exploiting comparative advantage, and placing so-called "hinterlands" at the service of urban populations, raises not just historic questions but pressing issues in the present day. Of course, this slicing-up of land regionally and globally to suit a "rational" division of production and labour is not politically and economically neutral. Outsourcing the extraction of raw materials and production of commodities to the Global South, often coerced by foreign debt, is a longstanding expression of colonial development, and as such, continues to have social as well as ecological consequences. In recent years, for example, there has been significant growth in the import to the UK—as air freight—of mangetout from Kenya and tomatoes from Morocco, while domestic agricultural production is dependent upon phosphorus from Morocco and the Western Sahara (a contested territory). Not only do the export-based systems of such global monocultures seem inequitable and unsustainable means to supply food, the empty salad vegetable shelves in UK supermarkets in 2023 have shown they could also be unreliable.

A final core theme that persuades Bookchin that conventional intensive agriculture is not viable stems from the expansive dynamics of capitalism. His view that "modern capitalism is inherently antiecological" underpins his conviction that post-capitalist alternatives are indispensable. In this respect, radical agriculture, liberatory technology, and ecocommunities were practical elements of Bookchin's overarching alternative to capitalism: social ecology. Capitalism's drive to make profit for the wealthy, regardless of wider social needs and the impact upon the living world, and its commitment to perpetual economic growth is a fundamental flaw in terms of sustainability.[20] Bookchin felt the prevailing emphasis on quantity over quality in food production to be misconceived, since nutritional needs and public health were overriding priorities.[21] Assessment of the impact of toxic chemicals on both workers and consumers in all parts of the supply chain is essential. The notorious 1984 disaster at the Union Carbide Plant in Bhopal, India, and the ongoing rates of acute poisoning and mortality from pesticide use shows that Bookchin's concerns were not unwarranted.[22] Following the approach of what is now termed the precautionary principle, he feared that the impetus to develop new chemical fertilisers and pesticides for profit works against the need to ensure prudent safeguards, advocating a system of rigorous checks before releases of novel, potentially highly toxic, chemicals into the productivity cycle.[23] Such instances, pertaining to chemicals in food, "the issue he knew best," enabled Bookchin to rehearse arguments that were to become the building blocks of his fuller expositions of social ecology to come.[24] He asserted in "Radical Agriculture," for example, that

> Capital's law of life of infinite expansion, of "production for the sake of production" and "consumption for the sake of consumption," turns the domination and exploitation of nature into the "highest good" of social life and human self-realization.[25]

The observation that it is impossible to expand endlessly within a finite space, while a commonplace among political ecologists, is mostly absent from mainstream discourse. Twenty years after *Radical Agriculture*, the notion that capitalism cannot be limited was to get its fullest expression in Bookchin's forthright and often-quoted statement in *Remaking Society*:

> The moral pieties, that are voiced today by many well-meaning environmentalists, are as naive as the moral pieties of multinationals are manipulative. Capitalism can no more be "persuaded" to limit growth than a human being can be "persuaded" to stop breathing. Attempts to "green" capitalism, to make it "ecological," are doomed by the very nature of the system as a system of endless growth.[26]

Bookchin's collision with the principles and practice of agribusiness, therefore, helped him to formulate and refine his broader critique of industrial capitalism. In his analysis, the profit motive distorted a responsible, evidence-based, and compassionate approach to farming. For Bookchin, agriculture was a case study demonstrating the negative effects of capitalism and its ultimate unsustainability.

Damian F. White found the introduction of this systemic idea "perhaps the most striking feature" of Bookchin's earliest essay on the topic, "The Problem of Chemicals in Food."[27] Brian Morris, another sympathetic commentator, noted Bookchin's concern that industrial agriculture had a range of far-reaching negative impacts—for example, that it would lead to widespread soil exhaustion and adversely affect the nitrogen cycle.[28] Characteristic of his style, Bookchin's agricultural writings are a synthesis of pragmatism and idealism, zooming in to look at phenomena with a bearing on human and non-human well-being at the cellular level, then panning out to the macrocosmic. He connected real-world detail and broad structural analysis as continuous with revolutionary re-envisioning. As Peter McCord has argued, this markedly distinguishes Bookchin's approach to the effect of synthetic chemicals upon food production and processing from Rachel Carson's work.[29]

Brian Morris pays tribute to Bookchin's conclusions and propositions relating to synthetic chemicals, convinced that "recent studies of the ecology and politics of industrial agriculture have more than confirmed Murray Bookchin's earlier insights and reflections."[30] His principles concerning agriculture are of a piece with other ideas Bookchin was formulating from the 1960s onwards, complementing his wider body of work to help consolidate social ecology as a practical and realisable programme as well as a set of philosophical theories. For example, he was willing to embrace technologies in agriculture if they lightened the load of the agricultural worker, and never idealised toiling on the land per se as a morally virtuous activity.

In keeping with Bookchin's ideas about liberatory technology, however, it was imperative that the decisions about the employment of such technologies were human-scale and socially oriented, were subject to democratic oversight, respected the agency of the workers who used them, and were ecologically sound. Furthermore, perhaps anticipating aspects of present-day ideas about fully automated luxury communism, Bookchin believed that human ingenuity could help bring about a sustainable post-scarcity society.[31]

To summarise, Bookchin articulated a comprehensive critique of industrial agriculture's interlocking impacts upon social and ecological well-being, grounded in notions of commodification, alienation, domination, simplification, and the profit-driven commitment to economic growth. He deemed that these were expressions of hierarchically structured societies and were intrinsic to capitalism, believing this ideology to be fundamentally anti-ecological due to its commitment to perpetual expansion. Consequently, it would be impossible to reform.

Many post-capitalist writers have since confronted the apparent conflict between the notion of sustainable capitalism and the dynamic of infinite economic growth (even if purportedly "green growth") on a finite planet.[32] Bookchin's response to this problem was solutions-based, emphasising values such as complementarity, solidarity, abundance, and quality of life. Notwithstanding theoretical disagreements, social ecologists tend to prioritise such intangible social goods.

Bookchin also presented cogent ideas on what human-scale, ecologically aware farming could become. He expounded a profoundly holistic view of human well-being, based on prudent environmental health measures, preventative medicine, and psychological insights.[33] This should be unsurprising, given that food constitutes a vital dimension of what makes us human. For us, as for all other living organisms, food is essential for the nutrition and energy required for basic functioning, and for that reason, our well-being relies entirely upon the health of the ecosystems within which we are grounded.

As we shall see, according to Bookchin's humanistic philosophy, we have evolved to become unique biota, at once fully immersed in, yet never identical with, the rest of the living world, due to an experiential cultural existence of which food is an aspect. Agriculture, therefore, is foundational to the synthesis of society and ecology that became social ecology. For social ecologists, ecological issues are, therefore, symptoms of social dysfunction.

Notes

1. James C. Scott, *Against the Grain: A Deep History of the Earliest States* (New Haven, CT: Yale University Press, 2017), 3.
2. Janet Biehl, *Ecology or Catastrophe: The Life of Murray Bookchin* (Oxford: Oxford University Press, 2015), Chapter 2.
3. [Murray Bookchin], writing as "Lewis Herber" "The Problem of Chemicals in Food," *Contemporary Issues* 3, no. 12 (Jun–Aug 1952), 206–41, accessed via Anarchy Archives: http://dwardmac.pitzer.edu/Anarchist_Archives/bookchin/HerberChem.html. Carson's interest in DDT began during the mid-1940s. Bookchin's research is not cited in *Silent Spring*. Again writing as "Lewis Herber," Bookchin also wrote "A Follow-Up on the Problem of Chemicals in Food," *Contemporary Issues* 6, no. 21 (Jan–Feb 1955).
4. Stephen E. Hunt, *Green Romanticism: The Natural World and Human Well-Being, 1775–1900* (VDM Verlag Dr. Müller, 2011).
5. Pérez Cebada and Juan Diego, "An Editorial Flop Revisited: Rethinking the Impact of Murray Bookchin's Our Synthetic Environment on its Golden Anniversary," *Global Environment*, 6, no. 12, (2013), 250–273 (p. 24): https://doi.org/10.3197/ge.2013.061211.
6. Although Carson did not explicitly call for a ban on DDT.
7. Murray Bookchin, "Radical Agriculture," 3–13 in *Radical Agriculture*, ed. by Richard Merrill (New York: Harper Colophon, 1976), 7.
8. A notion adapted from Romantic writer Friedrich Schiller by Max Weber, the first author cited in the acknowledgements for Murray Bookchin, *The Emergence and Dissolution of Hierarchy* (Palo Alto, CA: Cheshire Books, 1982), viii.
9. Bookchin, "Radical Agriculture," 4.
10. ibid., 3.
11. ibid.
12. A fundamental tenant of Bookchin's philosophy of dialectical naturalism, discussed in detail in *The Philosophy of Social Ecology*.
13. Bookchin, "Radical Agriculture," 6.
14. ibid., 4.
15. Bookchin, *Ecology of Freedom*, 1.

16 Murray Bookchin, "Ecology and Revolutionary Thought" (1965), 55–82 in Murray Bookchin, *Post-Scarcity Anarchism* (London: Wildwood House, 1974).
17 Bookchin, "Radical Agriculture," 5.
18 Chaia Heller, *Food, Farming, and Solidarity: French Farmers Challenge Industrial Agriculture and Genetically Modified Crops* (Durham, NC: Duke University Press, 2013), 204.
19 Murray Bookchin, "The Population Myth" I and II, originally published in *Green Perspectives*, no. 8 (July 1988) and no. 15 (April 1989) respectively; available from https://theanarchistlibrary.org/library/murray-bookchin-the-population-myth, accessed 15 March 2023.
20 [Bookchin], writing as "Lewis Herber," "The Problem of Chemicals in Food."
21 ibid.
22 W. Boedeker, M. Watts, P. Clausing et al., "The Global Distribution of Acute Unintentional Pesticide Poisoning: Estimations Based on a Systematic Review," *BMC Public Health* 20, 1875 (2020): https://doi.org/10.1186/s12889-020-09939-0.
23 [Bookchin], writing as "Lewis Herber," "The Problem of Chemicals in Food," *Our Synthetic Environment*, 12.
24 Biehl, *Ecology or Catastrophe*, 82.
25 Bookchin, "Radical Agriculture," 5.
26 Murray Bookchin, *Remaking Society: Pathways to a Green Future* (Boston, MA: South End Press, 1990), 57.
27 Damian F. White, *Bookchin: A Critical Appraisal* (London: Pluto, 2008), 17.
28 Brian Morris, "Murray Bookchin and Radical Agriculture," in *Enlightenment and Ecology: The Legacy of Murray Bookchin in the 21st Century*, ed. Yavor Tarinski (Montréal: Black Rose, 2021), 33.
29 Peter A. McCord, "Divergences on the Left: The Environmentalisms of Rachel Carson and Murray Bookchin," *Left History: An Interdisciplinary Journal of Inquiry and Debate* 13, no. 1 (2008): 14–34, https://doi.org/10.25071/1913-9632.24606.
30 Morris, "Murray Bookchin and Radical Agriculture," 34.

31 Aaron Bastani, *Fully Automated Luxury Communism* (London: Verso, 2019).
32 To give some examples from social ecologists and others, Herman Daly (ed.) *Toward A Steady-State Economy* (1973); Joel Kovel, *The Enemy of Nature: The End of Capitalism or the End of the World?* [2002], updated and expanded ed. (London: Zed Books, 2008); David Schweickart, "Is Sustainable Capitalism an Oxymoron?," *Perspectives on Global Development and Technology*, 8, nos. 2–3 (2009): 559–580: https://doi.org/10.1163/156914909X424033; Paul Mason, *Postcapitalism: A Guide to our Future*, Chap. 9, "The Rational Case for Panic" (London: Penguin, 2016); Emet Değirmenci, "A Critique of The Limits of Growth from a Social Ecology Perspective," in Part 1 of *Social Ecology and the Right to the City: Towards Ecological and Democratic Cities*, ed. by Federico Venturini, Emet Değirmenci, and Inés Morales (Montréal: Black Rose, 2019; Eleanor Finley, "Beyond the Limits of Nature: A Social-Ecological Perspective on Degrowth as a Political Ideology," *Capitalism Nature Socialism* 30, no. 2 (2019): 244–250, https://doi.org/10.1080/10455752.2018.1499122. Their interpretation of the repercussions and their alternative economic models in response to this dilemma vary.
33 Bookchin, *Our Synthetic Environment*, 88.

THE PRINCIPLES OF SOCIAL ECOLOGY

As a version of political ecology, the hybrid term "social ecology" brings together and prioritises human concerns, attributing the ecological crisis to social causes. Social ecologists share the belief that confronting the philosophical devaluing of the living world, and the destructive and exploitative practices that are a consequence of this, are core tasks to be addressed for the sake of both humanity and other species. Thus, social ecology continues to evolve. Just as Bookchin's ideas were dynamic and shifted across the decades, subsequent social ecologists have continued to be inspired by, develop, and at times contest and diverge from his work, adapting social-ecologist thought to twenty-first-century contexts. For sympathiser Federico Venturini, for example, Bookchin's ideas and those of social ecologists more generally, represent both a critique of prevailing political approaches and a "reconstructive and revolutionary vision for an ecological post-scarcity society."[1] The lack of widely shared social imaginaries able to conceive of viable alternatives does much to entrench current hegemonic power structures. It is not my intention to precis or reiterate the extensive literature about social ecology here, but to consider its core principles and their ramifications in relation to the prospects for food production. I set out below ten relevant principles and themes extrapolated from the literature of social ecology as an organising framework. In what follows, these will form the context for diverse themes underpinned by practical case examples.

Challenging dominatory agriculture

Critique of social hierarchy is indispensable to social ecology, holding that societal malaise and the ecological crisis lie in relationships of dominance, both within society and in the subordination of the non-human world. The origins of the latter are explained by an evolutionary turn in deep history, accounting for patriarchy and social oligarchies, predating even the emergence of the state and capitalism. Nevertheless, the magnitude of the present-day ecological crisis is largely attributed to the relatively recent development of expansive capitalism since the early modern period. Dominatory and exploitative structures and practices are reflected in agriculture as in other sectors. Indeed, as we shall see, colonial modes of production relating to food and other consumable commodities, such as intensive plantation agriculture, based on monoculture and high levels of extractivism, were to pattern the factory system of the Industrial Revolution. Thereafter, the human and ecological consequences were profound. Social ecologists' visions of a free, ethically informed society explain their principled opposition to systems of agriculture deemed to be dominatory due to their reliance upon the exploitation of human labour for profit and perpetuation of the degradation of the living world.

Internationalism on the model of democratic confederalism

Social ecologists take a rigorously internationalist and inclusive approach to food justice. War is a leading cause of disruption to food production and distribution. At the time of writing, food shortages are a significant consequence of multiple ongoing wars, including those in Ukraine, Palestine, and Yemen, sectarian and internecine conflict such as those between factions in Sudan and Haiti, and the actions of repressive regimes such as Myanmar and North Korea.

Increasing geopolitical tensions are likely to exacerbate supplies still further, both through outright conflict and by undermining international cooperation. There are important demarcations to make clear regarding internationalism. Social ecology sets itself firmly apart from free-trade globalisation, seen as a form of transnational capitalism that controls production for the benefit of economic and political elites, while maintaining borders that block the free movement of people. Social ecologists also distinguish themselves from nationalistic versions of anti-globalisation. Chaia Heller, for example, speaks of activists' adoption of the term "alter-globalization," rejecting "xenophobic and nationalist right-wing critics of globalization."[2] In keeping with this principle, Heller explains the concept of "food sovereignty" as a gesture of linguistic resistance with a precise definition distinct from nationalist presumptions: "For subaltern actors, sovereignty entails the self-determination of local on-the-ground communities."[3]

Social ecology also opposes versions of state socialism that are seen to repress and exploit minorities and erase cultural diversity in the name of a unitary socialist state. By contrast, social ecologists largely respect and celebrate Arturo Escobar's notion of a "pluriverse" of cultural diversity and local distinctiveness.

In recent years, social ecologists have frequently expressed sympathy with Abdullah Öcalan's formulation of democratic confederalism, adapted from Bookchin's ideas, where "all societal groups can express themselves in local meetings, general conventions and councils." Ultimately, social ecologists seek to harmonise a model of political autonomy through local and regional entities that "liberates, diversifies and democratises," with a World Democratic Confederation to attain "a more secure, peaceful, ecologic, just and productive world."[4]

Access to land and usufruct

To begin with the land, it is necessary to have access to space to cultivate and thrive. Core to Bookchin's vision of social ecology was the concept of usufruct, which he defined as "the freedom of individuals in a community to appropriate resources merely by virtue of the fact that they are using them."[5]

According to this critical distinction from proprietorial ownership, usufruct is seen as the source of a truly transformational relationship with the land. Usufruct refers to right by respectful and sustainable use, envisioning an extension and revitalisation of traditional forms of commoning in respect to the land and natural resources. The economist Elinor Ostrom subsequently did much to substantiate the intellectual justification for voluntary and accountable forms of democratic commoning.[6]

By contrast, we have seen private landlords and multinational corporations intensifying their control of agricultural regions as part of what Fred Magdoff and Brian Tokar call the "international scramble for land."[7] Countervailing trends include collective struggle to defend and reclaim access to the land by networks such as the Brazilian Landless Workers' Movement, and popular moves to extend urban farming and gardening. For prominent spokesperson Jose Bové, the French Confédération Paysanne emerged from campaigns where, he insisted, "we had fought for the paysan right to work the land, not to own it."[8] Elsewhere, scholar-activists in the social-ecology tradition such as Dimitrios Roussopoulos advocate for the development of Community Land Trusts as a strategy to ensure access to urban and rural land as a social good.[9]

Food sovereignty and abundance through a solidarity economy

Another core concept in Bookchin's work is the notion of an irreducible minimum, attributed to the anthropologist Paul Radin. By this principle, assured access to life's essentials "must be extended from the kin group to humanity as a whole."[10] Here once more, social-ecological thinking is not only at odds with the emphases of industrial agriculture's economic system, but is fundamentally antagonistic.

Relatedly, then, social ecologists such as Brian Tokar have been sharply critical of the increasing corporate dominance of food-supply chains and the concentration of economic and political power that this entails. Such concentration has strengthened wealthy consumers' command of land use and food distribution, leading to inefficient distribution and unjust outcomes for the global majority.

The reversal in progress in addressing chronic food shortages during the recent decade has helped to corroborate such criticisms. Social ecologists have been advocating a transition to solidarity economies in response to ongoing food crises, privileging production for social needs and aspiring to an abundance of high-quality, nutritional food for all, counter to export-driven production of consumer commodities for private profit.[11]

Regenerative agroecology

Confronting the systemic causes of the food and ecological crises, social ecology demands better prospects for future generations of humans and other species. It looks to develop regenerative agroecology, adopting cyclical and sustainable ecologically literate economic systems to produce food and other necessary consumables.

Respect for ecological integrity

Unsurprisingly, social ecology is rooted in deep respect for the living world and its ecosystems. First, it celebrates the biosphere for its intrinsic value, permeated in its elegant diversity, dynamism, and complexity. Second, the living world is of profound significance in Bookchin's ontological philosophy, dialectical naturalism, as expounded in *The Ecology of Freedom* and elsewhere.

Social ecology regards humanity as at one with and indivisible from nature, but crucially distinct from non-human species in its propensity for abstract thought, its historical dimension (that is, its capacity to generate accumulative knowledge exponentially by indirect communication across multiple generations of ancestors through symbolic language), and due to its meta-awareness of planetary context. This categorical distinction causes Bookchin to conceive of non-human biota as first nature, and humanity as second nature.

Moreover, Bookchin more speculatively posits a third, future emancipatory potential, termed "free nature."[12] Within this metaphysical domain, humanity realises its own potentiality through developing relationships with the rest of nature that are characterised by complementarity rather than alienation, domination, and conflict. The avoidable loss of natural habitat and biodiversity, leading to anthropogenic mass extinctions, therefore represents an irrational reversal of organic evolution. This human destruction constitutes acts of immense species self-harm and an indictment of capitalist expansionism.

Social ecology's philosophical basis in Bookchin's dialectical naturalism clearly has far-reaching consequences for the treatment of habitats, whether cultivated lands such as farms, parks, and gardens, for self-regulated wilderness (so far as it can be deemed to have survived), or rewilded terrain. Efforts to prevent the Earth's degradation and, moreover, to assist the restoration of ecological integrity are political and ethical imperatives. However, we shall see that the interpretation of the practical consequences of dialectical naturalism remains a matter of debate.

Agroecological knowledges

To better ensure abundant supplies, and to alleviate the ecological crisis, it is vital that knowledge of food production is protected, developed, and shared. Resilient agroecological production relies upon both sensitivity in observing, listening, and (in all ways) sensing local ecosystems, microclimates, and geological factors, as well as our versatility in adapting to them. It is in turn dependent upon strands of traditional wisdom, inclusion in educational curricula, and ongoing research to monitor and experiment with optimum growing conditions.

Liberatory technology

In his influential early essay "Towards a Liberatory Technology" (1965), Bookchin viewed prevailing technologies as expressions of the military-industrial complex. For social ecologists, in agribusiness as in other sectors of the economy, the commissioning of research and development, the implementation and operation of hardware and technologies of bioscience, digital systems, and artificial intelligence through to the logistical technologies of distribution are engineered to serve the interests of dominant political and economic elites. Nonetheless, in an unashamedly utopian turn, Bookchin proposes an emancipatory concept of people-centred, ecologically sustainable technology, under democratic self-management to serve the needs of society, not capital.

Liberatory potential offers intelligent criteria for the ethical and political evaluation of emerging technologies and their social and ecological impacts. Dan Chodorkoff recalls, when assessing whether a technology was authentically "alternative" at the Institute of Social Ecology, "our primary concern was always with the social and ecological matrix in which any technology is embedded."[13] In the agricultural context, for example, factors such as ownership and control would inform decisions about the implementation of a mechanical innovation, as well as whether it can reduce drudgery and toil, be sustainably powered, and boost effectiveness. The potential of vertical gardening and radical materials science are among the possibilities that follow. Whether such can be truly considered to be liberatory technologies involves asking questions regarding the social relations within which they are situated and the outcomes they tend to deliver.

Right livelihoods

When considering basic human needs, it is common to speak first of food and shelter, reflecting food's priority for all. For social ecologists, gathering, cultivating, and otherwise producing high-quality food through fulfilling work, in service of the local communities in which it is embedded, is a core aspiration. The first principle of the Confédération Paysanne, for example, is "Providing production and distributions that allow for the maximum number to work as farmers, earning a viable income," while farming is also considered as a "social project," with meaning and purpose beyond a profession.[14] This requires respect for the resilience and creativity of land work and welcomes maximum social participation in food production and governance. Beyond the consideration of food as a commodity for profit, connecting into its production and processing is conceived as an art and science integral to personal and cultural self-realisation through "becoming existence," both in itself and as a precondition to sustain and nourish all other cultural activity.[15]

Quality of production, of consumption, and of life

The final relevant principle of social ecology that informs attitudes to food production concerns such intangible aspects as the enhancement of the quality of life. While there is an (often warranted) anti-mysticism in Bookchin's secularist writings, we have seen an underlying metaphysical dimension present in his work. Intangible elements such as spirituality and quality of life form part of Chodorkoff's libertarian utopia, which he defines as a "combination of critique and reconstructive program—a holistic vision of the new society that insists on the integration of the various psychological, social, economic, political, and spiritual aspects of society."[16]

We will later discover a form of Japanese agriculture with a strong spiritual impulse, Shumei, in the English countryside, and consider the prospects for a resurgence in convivial eating together, or commensality, as a celebration of the positive social value of food. But first, we will turn to Abdullah Öcalan's characterisation of farming as a "sacred activity," fostering social cohesion and resilience. The example of DAANES is deeply relevant because it is the only territory where social ecology is being consciously applied for political reasons and as part of a struggle for survival.

Notes

1. Federico Venturini, "The Value of Social Ecology in the Struggles to Come," 3–23 in *Ecological Solidarity and Kurdish Freedom Movement*, ed. by Stephen E. Hunt (Lanham, MD: Lexington Books, 2021), 4.
2. Chaia Heller, *Food, Farms, and Solidarity: French Farmers Challenge Industrial Agriculture and Genetically Modified Crops* (Durham, NC: Duke University Press, 2013): https://www.jstor.org/stable/j.ctv111jhsp, 15.
3. Heller, *Food, Farms, and Solidarity*, 266.
4. Quotations from Abdullah Öcalan, *The Political Thought of Abdullah Öcalan* (London: Pluto, 2017), 42, 43, and 45. See the following throughgoing study of the challenges and value of democratic confederalism: Thomas Jeffrey Miley, *Self-Determination Struggles: In Pursuit of the Democratic Confederalist Ideal* (Montréal: Black Rose, 2023).
5. Bookchin, *Ecology of Freedom*, 50.
6. In works such as *Governing the Commons: The Evolution of Institutions for Collective Action* (1990).
7. Fred Magdoff and Brian Tokar, "Agriculture and Food in Crisis: An Overview," 9–30 in *Agriculture and Food in Crisis: Conflict, Resistance, and Renewal*, ed. by Fred Magdoff and Brian Tokar (New York: Monthly Review Press, 2010), 24.
8. Heller, *Food, Farming, and Solidarity*, 147.
9. Joshua Hawley and Dimitrios Roussopoulos (eds.), *Villages in Cities: Community Ownership, Cooperative Housing, and the Milton Parc Story* (Montréal: Black Rose, 2019).
10. Bookchin, *Ecology of Freedom*, 322.

11 For initiatives to further food sovereignty and the solidarity economy across several continents, see Heller on the Confédération Paysanne's "solidaire rationality," in *Food, Farms, and Solidarity*; the integration of solidarity economy in the platform of Cooperation Jackson, Kali Akuno and Ajamu Nagwaya, *Jackson Rising: The Struggle for Economic Democracy and Black Self-Determination in Jackson, Mississippi* ([Cantley, QC]: Daraja Press, 2017); and the importance of solidarity to maintain resilience in the wake of extreme weather-events in Puerto Rico as stressed by Nelson Àlvarez Febles and Georges F. Félix, "Hurricane María, Agroecology, and Climate Change Resiliency," Chap. 9 in *Climate Justice and Community Renewal: Resistance and Grassroots Solutions*, ed. by Brian Tokar and Tamra Gilbertson (Abingdon: Routledge, 2020); Andrew Bennie and Athish Satgoor, "Deepening the Just Transition through Food Sovereignty and the Solidarity Economy," Chap. 14 in *The Climate Crisis: South African and Global Democratic Eco-Socialist Alternatives*, ed. by Vishwas Satgar (Johannesburg: Wits University Press, 2018).

12 According to Bookchin's theory of dialectical naturalism, humanity is able to strive toward "free nature," a more complex higher species realisation based on "a conscious and ethical nature," *The Philosophy of Social Ecology*, 25. John P. Clark suggests Bookchin's idea has its origins in Élisée Reclus's notion that "Humanity is Nature becoming self-conscious" in the late nineteenth-century text *L'Homme et la Terre*, in "Municipal Dreams: A Social Ecological Critique of Bookchin's Politics," 137–190 in *Social Ecology After Bookchin*, ed. by Andrew Light (New York: Guilford Publications, 1998), 183n.8.

13 Dan Chodorkoff, *The Anthropology of Utopia: Essays on Social Ecology and Community Development* (Porsgrunn: New Compass, 2014), 39.

14 Heller's translation in *Food, Farms, and Solidarity*, 99 and 70.

15 I take the qualitative principle of "right livelihood" from E.F. Schumacher's famous essay, "Buddhist Economics," which advocates unalienated and meaningful work that is people-centred and ecologically sensitive as a path to "becoming existence," in *Small is Beautiful: A Study of Economics as if People Mattered* [1973] (London: Abacus, 1974), 44–45.

16 Chodorkoff, *Anthropology of Utopia*, 57.

PART 2
PRINCIPLES OF SOCIAL ECOLOGY IN PRACTICE

THE "SACRED ACTIVITY": SOCIAL ECOLOGY AND FOOD PRODUCTION IN THE KURDISH REGION

From his cell on the island of İmralı,[1] Abdullah Öcalan, the imprisoned figurehead of the Kurdish freedom movement, declared, "The world view for which I stand is close to that of Bookchin."[2]

Öcalan read Bookchin's works in Turkish translation with great attention and urged the movement to do so too.[3] In 2005, on Newroz (the Kurdish new year), he announced a new paradigm of thinking known as "democratic confederalism," embracing social ecology, participatory democracy, and gender equality.[4] Although Bookchin was not the only influence upon the rejection of state socialism and the emergence of the Kurdish ecology movement, his ideas, nevertheless, were impactful and strongly represented.

This is not the place to investigate theories about the inevitability, duration, or efficacy of the state, but the essential argument of social ecologists that multiple social crises and the ecological crisis are of a piece is relevant. Bookchin had argued in "Radical Agriculture," for example, that the need for irrigation systems to cultivate the arid environment "clearly fostered" the centralised character of the near East's ancient empires.[5] While social ecologists can be disputatious regarding their approaches, they hold as axiomatic that the ecological crisis cannot be effectively addressed without confronting the system of oppression and injustice under the institutions of the state, capitalism, and patriarchy that together constitute capitalist modernity. Scott's observation that the process whereby humans "selectively breed, protect and exploit" plants and animals in the process of cultivation and domestication could be applied to the treatment of women, captives, and slaves[6] corroborates the spirit of Bookchin's *The Ecology of Freedom*, a text sometimes challenged for its overly speculative approach to the sweep of prehistory and anthropology.[7] Öcalan, in keeping with and developing Bookchin's view, also made the emergence of hierarchical relations a centrepiece of his philosophy. This especially applies to the imposition of patriarchy. Inspired by Maria Mies's writings too, Öcalan deems that a wrong turn in cultural evolution made women the first colony, with devastating and mutually reinforcing consequences for exploitation in human relations and ecological destruction thereafter.

Already, Mesopotamia has been mentioned as the seedbed of both the first agrarian societies, and the earliest states, and as largely coextensive with the present-day Kurdish region. It is ironic, therefore, that the Kurdish freedom movement has begun to advocate post-state governance in the predominantly Kurdish region that spans Turkey, Syria, Iraq, and Iran, substantially overlying ancient Mesopotamia. It is relevant to look, in particular, at the example of what is still popularly known as Rojava, officially the Autonomous Administration of North and East Syria, because it is unique as a territory where social ecology is influencing the administrative principles.

This administration, largely consisting of settlements and lands liberated from the Islamic State, is antagonistic towards capitalism and the state, and serious about efforts to implement post-state experiments in polycentric governance as an alternative democratic process for the Middle East and beyond. Supporters of the predominately Kurdish but multi-ethnic project of democratic confederalism have taken the opportunity of the Rojava Revolution of 2012 to set up assemblies and committees at the neighbourhood, municipal, and regional level to administer all aspects of civil society, including agriculture. While Bookchin's perspectives were embedded in the Western Enlightenment tradition, the implementation of participatory decision-making in the Kurdish context draws upon a long tradition of anti-colonial struggle. Öcalan has been keen to confront hegemonic thinking and to reverse presuppositions that determine the power relations within Kurdistan and the wider Middle East. He asserts, for example, that "Capitalism is not the economy; on the contrary, it is the most effective tool for undermining the economy."[8] This perspective has profound ramifications for the treatment of the living world and for agriculture.

While Öcalan and other prominent Kurdish revolutionaries such as Sakine Cansiz have been anti-capitalist, however, not any old anti-capitalism will do. Since Öcalan's work is not widely read in English, it is worth briefly pausing to note the grounding of social ecology in his ideas. As part of a narrative specifically against the ideology of industrialism, Öcalan suggests in *The Sociology of Freedom* that "the real crisis of urbanization emerged with the nineteenth-century Industrial Revolution." Somewhat updating the notion of a Fall, Öcalan claims that, before this upheaval, more harmonious coexistence characterised the human relationship with the natural environment. It was as if "a direct dialogue" with other species had been underway with the "common language being agriculture."[9]

Öcalan's understanding of a shift "transforming the symbiotic relationship with nature into one of domination and colonialism" is clearly in keeping with the philosophy of social ecology.[10] While Öcalan inaccurately believes that the "Romantics effectively stopped at literature," his concept of Democratic modernity arising from countercultural "Anti-system forces," which emerged during the French Revolutionary era, signifies that his thinking is infused with the tradition of Romanticism, not in its weak form as sentimentalism, but in its critical and meaningful sense as a set of complex social forces of resistance, both emancipatory and reactionary, with a cultural lineage dating back as far as the eighteenth century.[11]

For Michael Löwy and Robert Sayre, Romanticism is defined as a spectrum of anti-capitalism.[12] Romanticism therefore informs the conceptual framework of social ecology and the way that it understands agriculture.[13] Given the foregoing, it is unsurprising that Kurdish movement activists take the notion of agriculture back to its roots, observing cultivation's role in evolving culture since the neolithic agrarian revolution. Öcalan vests agriculture with supreme significance as a "sacred activity" and as an "inseparable existential aspect of society."[14] It is imperative, then, to take a qualitative as well as quantitative approach to the production of food.

This appeal is far from unique. Countless Indigenous horticulturalists and food reformers have been advancing the principle. For Miyoshi Nakamura, Natural Agriculture farmer and teacher of the Shumei approach, "Just like music or painting, farming is an art whose product touches your soul."[15] For E.F. Schumacher, care for the health of the land is a meta-economic issue that should be considered as an essential end in itself.[16] The Real Farming Trust seeks to promote "a complete rethink, a renaissance, for our food chain" using its college to explore all aspects of agroecology, including science, metaphysics, morality, and ecology to feed the world sustainably.[17] The Slow Food Foundation prioritises quality and taste in the production and consumption of food as in all areas of life.[18] Slow Food have supported Kurdish projects, recognising the critical role of self-provisioning in Rojava, where agroecological techniques are in part compelled by the lack of fertilisers due to embargoes.[19] The production of nutritional food—with a commitment to the diversification of production, cooperatives, and local markets—is at once an essential matter of economic survival, a symbol of liberation, and a bid for cultural resurgence. Öcalan argues that, since food production returns less profit than other sectors such as finance, investment in agriculture is low, despite being a vital human need. Indeed, states that channel finance into subsidising agriculture can risk fiscal difficulties. He predicts that "humanity will, and has even begun to, experience its worst counterrevolution in the agricultural area."[20] In this respect, industrial and financial interests are driving control of the land, and hence concentrating economic and political power into fewer hands. This explains the social-ecological view that the domination of land and food production must be opposed and why these are at the heart of a reconstructive vision for society. Increasingly, moreover, ecological stresses and armed conflict are mutually exacerbating factors in the Middle East and beyond. In this context, drought-resistance techniques and political resistance appear side by side in North and East Syria, where the Kurdish freedom movement is attempting to put radical agriculture into practice.

Insurgent vegetables

The predominantly Kurdish region of North and East Syria has long been a living larder for Syrian agriculture, but recent uncertainties impact food production as all else. With the outbreak of the Civil War in 2011, and the subsequent advance of ISIS, Syria gained world attention, at least initially, as the Middle East's major flashpoint. This intractable conflict developed into a proxy war for regional adversaries and international superpowers, with contested claims as to its root causes.

The region's division into colonial spheres of influence under the now notorious Sykes-Picot Agreement (1916), including the quartering of Kurdistan, left a legacy of animosity in this oil-rich territory. In recent decades, factors relating to agriculture and ecology have also been implicated as both causes and critical outcomes, and have been weaponised in the Syrian tragedy. Ba'athist industrial agricultural policies accelerated the replacement of enduring traditional farming systems, based on the complex integration of crop types using practices and varieties adapted to local climactic and geological conditions.[21] This profound change boosted yields during the late twentieth century, but by the early 2000s the costs in terms of water shortages, soil losses, and wider ecological degradation were becoming apparent. A series of droughts and the impact of displacement of populations from the rural areas exposed the limits of Syria's resilience as an agricultural producer. Whatever the overriding cause of conflict in this complex of factors, the repercussions continue in the present volatility.

Available literature and data show an increase in agricultural production in Syria during the earlier Ba'athist era, with an uptick during the 1970s and 1980s.[22] It became a major producer of cotton, wheat, and barley. While Syria's rate of food self-sufficiency was 78% in 1970, by the early 1990s it had fallen to just 48%.[23] Syria was a net exporter of wheat from 1995–2008, after which time it became a net importer again.[24] These isolated figures suggest two things. First, they evidence the argument advanced by experts such as Raymond Hinnebusch and Marwa Daoudy that the Syrian Arab Republic no longer regarded high levels of domestic self-sufficiency as a priority to meet the objective to guarantee food security. Instead, it increasingly subsidised "strategic crops" for export to gain foreign currency with which to purchase other foodstuffs on the world market, and so ensure that its population's needs were met.[25] Second, they suggest that some disturbing trends were already apparent around the turn of the millennium. As we would expect, agricultural production has been severely disrupted since the outbreak of the Syrian Civil War in 2011. This acute crisis is largely, yet not entirely, explained by more than a decade of war. But the difficulties of Syrian agriculture, it turns out, predate the outbreak of the conflict. A critical factor was a series of poor harvests brought on by droughts and, in the opinion of Daoudy, "unsustainable" practices relating to water and agriculture.[26] The extent to which climate change was a specific causal factor in precipitating the Syrian conflict, or whether emphasis should be placed foremost upon profound stresses within the republic's political structures and policies, is a matter of debate and controversy.[27] In 2023, 12.1 million people are estimated to be facing food insecurity out of Syria's population of 21.7 million.[28] So what have been the consequences of the legacy of Ba'athist industrial agriculture in the major agricultural area under the Autonomous Administration?

During Hafez al-Assad and Bashar al-Assad's regimes, the Ba'ath Party rigorously imposed a system of monoculture upon farming in North and East Syria. Intensive production concentrated on staples and cash crops such as wheat, cotton, olives, and barley to meet the needs of consumers elsewhere in Syria and for export. Kurdish growers regarded such arrangements as a system of colonialism, since value was added by processing in other regions, with few benefits accruing in their communities. The planting of fruit and nut trees was effectively forbidden.[29]

Climate change represents a further significant threat to agriculture in North and East Syria. There is a trend towards increased aridity due to reduced rainfall, this being a primary cause of reduced yields.[30] Water shortages are persistent because of decreasing rainfall and unsustainable long-term water and irrigation policies.[31] And there are also intentional causes, such as the interruption of water supplies due to the impact of the Turkish dam systems causing the diminished flow of the Euphrates and Tigris, and alleged targeting of water stations by ISIS and Turkish forces.[32] As agricultural subsidies began to be reduced and water stresses increased, such restrictions and impacts began to make livelihoods from farming unviable.

Efe Can Gürcan argues that the deterioration in the agricultural sector compelled the mass displacement of rural workers to the cities, resulting in pressures on the infrastructure that brought about conflicts of interests, ultimately leading to the outbreak of civil unrest.[33] It is for good reason, then, that the uprising has been called a "rural and rurban Intifada."[34] It has been estimated that more than half a million people from the predominantly rural North and East moved to Aleppo.[35] It is therefore important not to contextualise the catastrophic chain of events in Syria as the direct consequence of "natural" disasters. They were, rather, the outcome of inappropriate measures within the republic and upstream, and unstable climatic patterns, a combination which had mutually aggravating ramifications.

The former state policies, and what De Châtel terms "rapid economic liberalisation,"[36] undermined the support networks and social resilience that had traditionally been able to cope with aridity and drought. However, while De Châtel offers a legitimate corrective to the idea that climate change was straightforwardly a cause of the 2011 uprisings and subsequent conflict, her analysis, mostly based upon the situation in North and East Syria, and Jazira in particular, overlooks the colonial dimension to the "resource mismanagement" and land distribution in this agricultural area.

The dynamics of so-called "Arab Belt" policies were evident in patterns of ethnic preference and disadvantage, uneven development, and the vulnerable political status of Kurdish farming communities.[37] For Gürcan, the bigger picture further suggests that Syria's national policies were in part driven by global economic and geopolitical pressures to pursue "extractivist" policies.[38] De Châtel attributes blame to the Syrian "government's failure to address a humanitarian and environmental crisis that had been taking shape for more than a decade" (an allegation that could be extended to Turkey and other neighbouring states in the Middle East), a major shortcoming to be understood within the wider geopolitical matrix in which such states operate.[39]

Since the revolution of 2012, intermittent but ongoing economic embargos have been enforced in response to the creation of the Autonomous Administration of North and East Syria.[40] Attempts to raise levels of self-sufficiency through increased domestic production and processing have been underway to safeguard access to food, because cross-border trade is constrained and unreliable. Parallels are sometimes drawn with Cuba's predicament, when Russian support ceased after the collapse of the Soviet Bloc, combined with the continuing US embargo. Similarly, obstruction of chemical fertiliser and pesticide imports has made a form of agroecological production a necessity. It is a reasonable comparison, but Rojava's present challenges are further compounded by ongoing conflict and a far more arid climate.

Armed attacks have been threatening food security in the region; the 2018 invasion of Rojava's canton of Afrin by Turkey and allied armed groups has had severe consequences, resulting in the loss of productive land in this traditionally olive-producing area. Swathes of historic olive groves have been destroyed, and the harvests of those that remain have been seized and transported to Turkey.[41] Military attacks and incursions have continued to cause damage to infrastructure and mean that workers must be taken away from agriculture to meet the demands for self-defence. The 2019 invasion and occupation of the area around Sere Kaniye and Tal Abyad resulted in a further setback due to the seizure of some of the richest agricultural land and the destruction of many agricultural cooperatives.[42] Resources to support fresh agricultural projects are limited in this context.[43] The oil industry and other sources of pollution cause further ecological problems by damaging air quality and the soil.[44]

The withdrawal of the Ba'ath administration from North and East Syria after 2011 brought about a marked shift in approaches to food production, but also multiple challenges. Since, the agricultural transition has been a combination of principle and, due to force of circumstances, pragmatism. Parts of the Kurdish movement have welcomed the reduced reliance on synthetic chemicals as in keeping with the new paradigm's ecological principles. Under DAANES control, agricultural cooperatives are managing much of the communalised land as part of efforts to build a solidarity economy.[45]

This phase is characterised by a shift from monocultural systems to initiatives for crop diversification.[46] In particular, shorter supply chains have been encouraged, with crops such as lentils and other vegetables, spices, and bulgur wheat being harvested for local consumption.[47] The imposition of price controls, minimum wages, and material support for internally displaced persons and those injured and traumatised by the war, all intended to bring about a solidarity economy, are measures that echo Bookchin's aspiration that every member of society should enjoy an irreducible minimum. Michael Pimbert documents, furthermore, the partial adoption of regenerative, re-localising agroecology.[48] In this way, there are attempts to reclaim some of the resilience of the rich, diverse, and complementary forms of traditional agriculture that evolved to suit the area's geographical particularity and microclimates.

That women's cooperatives drive many of these approaches is indicative of the interlocking aspects of the project for democratic confederalism, such as gender equality and the solidarity economy. Closely linked to the communal assemblies, cooperatives have a central role in the programme to create a solidarity economy run on democratic lines.[49] Ulrike Flader and Çetin Gürer note in particular the integration of women's cooperatives into the DAANES municipal system.[50] Azize Aslan writes of the coordinating role of the women's economic committee, AborîyaJIN, in setting up cooperatives and localised markets.[51] In keeping with the Kurdish freedom movement's anti-patriarchal principles, women are fully represented in decision-making committees and assemblies, which have male and female co-chairs and require a proportion of at least 40% of women to be present to be quorate. Separate women's organisations are also convened as part of the Kongra Star federation, as checks and balances to ensure women's political and economic emancipation, and to address historical legacies of disempowerment.

It is acknowledged that there are challenges, contradictions, and compromises in efforts to evolve alternative methods of production and distribution without reproducing the model of exploitative capitalist exchanges. Bookchin became more sceptical of the role of cooperatives, which he feared would need to adopt the same ruthlessly competitive practices as any other enterprises if they are to survive in the capitalist marketplace. John Holloway more recently echoed this sceptical turn as he expressed doubts about

Öcalan's analysis of "money and markets." It is questionable that local markets could thrive in a way that could somehow maintain integrity and autonomy without being integrated into the hegemonic mechanisms of international trade and what Holloway terms capitalist's "totalizing system."[52] Nonetheless, Öcalan's recentring of women as the driving force at the heart of the economy, given women's leading role in the priority sectors of self-provisioning, health, and education, represents a powerful impetus in the struggle to radically transform social production:

> In essence, economy is everything that has to do with nourishment. It may seem peculiar, but I believe that woman is still the creator of economy, despite all attempts to overrun and colonise her. A thorough analysis of the economy will show that woman is the most fundamental force of economy. Indeed, this is clear when we consider her role in the agricultural revolution, and how she has gathered plants for millions of years.[53]

In the present, the agricultural and food cooperatives set up by the Women's Economic Committee and Kongra Star reflect the leading role women continue to have in cultivating and processing food. While the cooperatives are modest ventures in terms of the overall economy, they remain strategically significant since they enable the women involved to have livelihoods with some independence from male family members or private bosses. In this way, the Kurdish cooperatives are a means to affect structural change that complements efforts to empower women by transforming traditional cultural attitudes. Progress in this respect is limited since women mostly also shoulder the additional burden of domestic labour. In practice, agriculture is a front in North-East Syria's multifaceted struggle to survive and promote its alternative vision for the region, since it is inseparable from the battle for social equality, but also for water, economic survival, security against armed attacks, and the struggle for international recognition.

In this respect, Joost Jongerden, a sympathetic commentator, sees civil efforts to build a resilient and flourishing agricultural base, grounded in principles of solidarity, as akin to the resilience of the armed struggle required for the Kurdish fighters to defeat ISIS and for the displaced and traumatised populations of the Autonomous Administration to move ahead with their multi-ethnic democratic revolution.[54] Moreover, agricultural programmes to cultivate monocultures are analogous to the Syrian and Turkish states' imperatives to enforce cultural homogenisation and to suppress minorities as attempts to create and maintain unitary states. For more than a decade and against the odds, the self-administration has been reversing such policies through its attempts to diversify agriculture and to cultivate pluralistic direct democracy.

There are further ways that the politics of food are embedded within the project for democratic confederalism. A presentation that included Meral Çiçek, co-founder of the Kurdish Women's Relations Office (REPAK) in Iraqi Kurdistan, was an opportunity to discuss aspects of communal cooking and food consumption within the Kurdish movement. Çiçek observes that during the 1990s, when the PKK academy was based in Syria, Öcalan challenged traditional roles, insisting that men should do all of the collective cooking since "women have been cooking for 5000 years." Despite such efforts within militant circles, the gendered division of labour persists in present-day Rojava, with little evidence of communal cooking in daily life and women still undertaking most cooking within the private sphere of the family households.

By contrast, collective cooking is firmly embedded in the daily practice at Rojava's hundreds of educational academies. Everyone is expected to take responsibility for food preparation and cooking, which is organised by rota, and meals are consumed together.[55] More broadly, the commitment to the sharing of food inherent in Kurdish and other near and Middle Eastern cultures can be seen as part of the mores that connect established ways of life to the kind of gift economy and ecological solidarity that are the basis of a liberatory society.

THE "SACRED ACTIVITY"

In Syrian Kurdistan, we have seen that there are endeavours to cultivate a mutually enhancing relationship between society and ecologically sustainable agricultural production. Even when ecologically intentioned, human farming practices typically involve simplifying the multiple symbiotic interactions of an organically evolving ecosystem. If the experiments in this area continue, there will inevitably be trade-offs between managed production for human needs and the spontaneous growth of the living world.

Several other predicaments and questions present themselves. The agricultural sector largely remains dependent upon diesel to work mechanical pumps in the context of depleted water supplies, due to deliberately restricted flow and droughts, likely exacerbated by climate change. Animal farming has also faced immense challenges due to water scarcity and the consequent reduction in harvests of rain-fed crops for fodder, unaffordable costs of imported grains, and the lack of veterinary medicines.[56] Some land-workers decide to leave for urban areas, after undertaking strenuous and sometimes demoralising labour, in extreme temperatures and with limited mechanisation.[57] Enduring regular Turkish drone attacks, the Autonomous Administration's security challenges limit the revenue available to pay farmers high prices as an incentive to produce more and further the solidarity economy. How to develop truly liberatory eco-technologies when research and development tends to innovate technologies that express and perpetuate the values of the hegemonic socio-economic systems that implement them? How to relocate and build agroecological knowledges in an area where monocultures of industrial agriculture have long been imposed? The communities within the Autonomous Administration are negotiating such dilemmas in the most intense and urgent circumstances, a foreboding microcosm of challenges that are increasingly being faced across the world. Nevertheless, as it moves into its second decade, DAANES stands out for its audacious efforts to sustain a radical praxis in unpromising soil, for its resistance, and for its resilience.

The insurgent fruit and vegetables of Rojava take their place alongside committed crops found across the political spectrum, including the lentils that nourished Republicans during the Siege of Madrid during the Spanish Civil War (ironically termed "Dr Negrin's resistance pills"), the produce of war-time Britain's victory gardens, the American right-wing "freedom fries" that saw service in the invasion of Iraq, up to the feisty internationalist carrots of Food Not Bombs. Despite setbacks, in North and East Syria efforts to address multiple challenges continue by growing drought-resistant crops and by extensive tree-planting programmes.

The defiant trees of Green Tress

Let us now look at the application of Kurdish ecological theory and practice in an ambitious initiative to address the human and ecological crises that confront them.

The Green Tress Association (*Keziyên Kesk*) is a heartening example of a practical initiative rooted in ecological principles in North and East Syria.[58] Launched in October 2020, this is an ambitious project to plant four million trees, with the aim of increasing vegetation cover from the current situation, which is around 1.5%, to up to 10% of the land. Drought-resistant trees and plants are being selected to cope with the arid environment, many of them chosen for their edible produce, including grapevines, olives, mulberries, figs, peaches, and pomegranates. According to Gulistan Sido, the Vice-President of Green Tress, the aim is to "create a kind of balance between perennial fruit trees and forest trees."[59] These are intended to boost social resilience through improved food sovereignty.

The project also has a strong educational component, with close connections to the University of Rojava at Qamishli, enabling Green Tress to draw upon expertise from the Faculty of Agricultural Engineering and to use tree nurseries on the campus. Volunteers seek to develop their own awareness, enabling them to train others.

They work closely with teachers to green the school environment and "bring knowledge to the new generation."[60]

Green Tress is a democratically constituted society with local groups of around a dozen members with female and male co-chairs, acting as "focal points" within the communities. Appointed individuals have areas of responsibility, such as managing volunteers, external relations, and the media. Committees of delegates coordinate projects across municipalities and communicate within neighbourhood communes to encourage volunteers. In this way, the whole community can be involved.[61] Workdays are sociable events, attracting volunteers from Kongra Star and others in the women's movement, young people, war veterans, and those from the Armenian community.

While Green Tress began in Qamishli, its nursery work is being extended to several further locations: Kobanî, Raqqa, Derik, and Haseke. It is further hoped that the sight and smell of proliferating green profusion could eventually inspire and foster ecological awareness and practice more widely, and there is already some coordination with "environmental stakeholders" in "Syria in general."[62] The choice of name and logo—fresh green leaves sprouting and rooting from a plaited tress of hair—is telling and deeply symbolic, expressing profound cultural strands of meaning. It explicitly references the traditional braids of Yazidi women, and therefore, a Green Tress representative explained, is a reminder of the mothers and daughters that Islamic State captured from the Shingal area for the slave markets of Mosul, Raqqa, and Idlib.[63] She was also mindful of the heritage of work underway in the lands of Mesopotamia, where the Tigris and Euphrates and their tributaries water rich alluvial plains.[64] Furthermore, Green Tress are keenly aware that their struggle for ecological restoration is vulnerable due to its location, surrounded by both Turkey and Assad's Syria—regional colonial states with strategic ambitions hostile to the Autonomous Administration, which are themselves within the purview of dominant global neo-colonial powers.

In common with other parts of Kurdistan, it is impossible, therefore, to consider the prospects for Green Tress outside of the context of military conflict. For the past decade, an impressive social mobilisation of civil society actors such as Green Tress has been underway to address and surmount multiple threats to the survival of DAANES. The control and "weaponisation" of water due to upstream Turkish mega-dams, including those comprising the contentious General Anatolian Project (GAP), directly impacts horticultural projects.

Consequently, Green Tress organisers Zîwer Şêxo and Gulistan Essa cite the lack of water as the primary hazard to the area and for their initiative. They believe there should be greater awareness about "cutting the water from the Kurds," and that the international community must exert pressure and make demands upon the Turkish government to alleviate the problem.[65] Diversion of ground-level waters aggravates reduced precipitation linked to climate change—a further conspicuous vulnerability affecting food production. Relatedly, aridification and loss of tree cover are leading to soil depletion. Widespread pollution, particularly from extraction and combustion related to the oil industry, is an additional factor that contributes to the contamination of groundwater and the loss of agricultural land.[66]

Furthermore, Bashar Al-Assad's government in Damascus prevents the importation of seeds through and from territory under its control into North and East Syria[67] which specifically hinders the agricultural sector and Green Tress. In response to this embargo, Green Tress volunteers gather and propagate their seeds locally. This measure would be necessary in any case due to the high cost of imported varieties and the low exchange value of the Syrian pound. There are benefits too. Home production is in keeping with the "spirit of volunteerism" and wider ethos of autonomy that Green Tress nurtures. Cultivating indigenous species and varieties, moreover, is encouraged because they are more likely to be suited to local soils and climatic conditions.

Nevertheless, the obstacles that confront Green Tress and complementary projects, such as the women's eco-village known as Jinwar and food-growing initiatives in camps for Internally Displaced People, should not be underestimated.[68] Factors including the lack of agricultural machinery, damaged storage and processing infrastructure, and insufficient domestically produced organic fertilisers impede progress. Above all, however, ongoing military incursions and attacks from Turkish armed forces (NATO's second largest army) and allied mercenaries and Jihadists are the gravest threats to the territory and the agroecological experiments that are underway. Green Tress have denounced the intensification of Turkish military attacks upon civilian institutions such as hospitals and schools, as well as infrastructure such as gas and oil, grain silos, and water for the damage they are inflicting upon the wider environment.[69] However, the democratic and ecological experiments in North and East Syria are largely unreported in the UK's mainstream broadcast and newspaper media.[70] It is necessary, therefore, to consider such agroecological initiatives in the context of the absence of mainstream commentary upon the Middle East's predominantly Kurdish areas, and the wider geopolitics within which they are embedded.

Despite the precarious geopolitical predicament in North and East Syria, members of Green Tress maintain good humour and fortitude in their efforts to put principles of social ecology into practice in a rare living revolutionary situation. They report that the Autonomous Administration is recognising that, after the people's protection forces dealing with the security situation, the struggle to enhance the environment and to produce food on the part of initiatives such as Green Tress is a significant priority.[71] After all, progress with these projects has implications for health, education, and the economy. Green Tress have also successfully persuaded the self-administration to set up a separate department dedicated to environmental issues and seek further "synergies," although they concede that attracting funding and labour power remain difficult since the municipalities continue to "have many other things that they think are an emergency, more than ecology."[72]

Unfortunately, if present trends continue, plans for resilience in the face of political and economic instability and ecological degradation are likely to be of increasing urgency for the agricultural futures of growing proportions of the planet's population. In the West, it has often been said, with or without irony, that concern for ecological issues is a luxury that we cannot afford. Yet, the ongoing deterioration of ecosystems as collateral damage for purported "economic growth," of which notorious examples are the rainforests of Brazil and the Democratic Republic of Congo, has jeopardised many lives as a consequence of the resource curse. Moreover, Kurdish critics, such as Sonia Karimi of the Community of Free Women of Eastern Kurdistan, allege the deliberate and strategic implementation of ecocidal policies to make areas uninhabitable, and to control and displace populations deemed dissident, by removing the capacity for agricultural subsistence through means such as the diversion and transfer of water and forest fires.[73] In this situation, ecological resistance is viewed as a matter of cultural survival. Turkey and Iran, states with large Kurdish populations, regularly criminalise and imprison environmental activists.[74] More positively, coordinated interventions such as Green Tress can potentially turn around the economic and ecological circumstances of North and East Syria. If the initiative were to achieve its goal to grow trees and fruit bushes on 10% of the Autonomous Administration's total land, there would be a transformative impact upon the area's resilience.[75]

Green Tress has an outward-looking perspective, aiming to reach out for mutual aid where possible beyond North and East Syria:

> It is a source of pleasure for us to receive the support and expertise from citizens around the world to improve life on our planet; indeed, we are working to hold an international conference that will address the environmental reality of the

region in general. We want to mobilize as an association that will be part of the global ecological movement.

Any person, association, organization has the right to contribute, and we are open to this aspect. We look forward to the help of those who have the capacities, whether scientific or material, to be able to carry out our project. We must build communication bridges with institutions of common interest. We have a need for more machinery, agricultural engineering expertise, and seeds, the cost of which exceeds our financial capacities. All avenues are open to help.[76]

The qualitative purpose is to revitalise the landscape so that degraded areas are converted into abundant oases of horticulture.

Şêxo and Essa concede that the difficulties facing Green Tress are greater than anticipated when it was launched.[77] If successful, the objective to substantially increase vegetation cover would have several ecological benefits, such as helping to prevent erosion and water run-off, sequester carbon dioxide and ease the ferocity of the Syrian summer through cooling and shading, improve air quality, and thereby enhance the microclimate and biodiversity. In turn, it is hoped that this will boost sustainable economic development by improving food sovereignty and securing livelihoods. For Green Tress, the social benefits that follow from this are many, including improved health through better nutrition and a reduction in respiratory diseases, greater inclusion of women and girls, more community participation, and heightened environmental awareness.

Notes

1   Where he has been held in solitary confinement and mostly incommunicado since 1999.

2   Öcalan's lawyers reported that he said this in late 2004, according to Joost Jongerden, "Learning from Defeat: Development and contestation of the "new paradigm" within Kurdistan Workers' Party (PKK)," *Kurdish Studies 7*, no. 1 (2018): 72–92, https://kurdishstudies.net/menu-script/index.php/KS/article/view/163.
3   Janet Biehl, Bookchin's long-term collaborator and biographer tells me that a social ecology group in Istanbul were the "unsung heroes" that undertook English-Turkish translations of Bookchin's major works during the mid-1990s—personal e-mail to the author, 23 October 2023.
4   Abdullah Öcalan, "Declaration of Democratic Confederalism in Kurdistan," (2005): http://www.freemedialibrary.com/index.php/Declaration_of_Democratic_Confederalism_in_Kurdistan (site discontinued). Accessible via Wayback Machine, March 30, 2021. https://web.archive.org/web/20160929163726/; http://www.freemedialibrary.com/index.php/Declaration_of_Democratic_Confederalism_in_Kurdistan.
5   Murray Bookchin, "Radical Agriculture," 3–13 in *Radical Agriculture*, ed. by Richard Merrill (New York: Harper Colophon Books, 1972).
6   Scott, *Against the Grain*, 12.
7   For example, by sympathetic critics White, *Bookchin: A Critical Appraisal*, Chapter 2; Andy Price, *Recovering Bookchin: Social Ecology and the Crises of Our Time* (Porsgrunn: New Compass, 2012), Chapter 5.
8   Abdullah Öcalan, *The Sociology of Freedom: Manifesto of the Democratic Civilization*, Volume III (Oakland, CA: PM Press, 2020), 95.
9   Both quotations from Öcalan, *Sociology of Freedom*, 113.
10 Öcalan, *Sociology of Freedom*, 278.
11 ibid., 268 and 284.
12 Löwy and Sayre's Romantic typology is a broad spectrum. It ranges from reactionary, feudal, and even fascistic worldviews, but includes cultural forms, such as science fiction and mystical creeds too. There are also avowedly revolutionary forms, exemplified by Percy Bysshe Shelley and William Blake's ideas. Romantic anti-capitalism embraces calls for a "re-enchantment" of the earth and *Naturphilosophie* on the part of the

democratic, internationalist, republican and revolutionary elements among the German Romantics in the era of high Romanticism through to the 1960s counterculture and the modern ecology movement. Michael Löwy and Robert Sayre, *Romanticism Against the Tide of Modernity*, trans. by Catherine Porter (Durham, NC: Duke University Press, 2001); see also *Revolutionary Romanticism*, ed. by Max Blechman (San Francisco, CA: City Lights Books, 1999). The contested nature of Romanticisms—due to their varied relationships towards rationality and subjectivity, individualism (even sympathisers can find the cult of personality and "Apoism" relating to Öcalan problematic) and community—and their impact upon democratic modernity (alongside indigenous influences such as Alevism and decolonialism) is beyond the scope of the present discussion.

13 Bookchin's attitudes to Romanticism were nuanced and fluid. He spoke positively, for example, of the Romantic movement's advocacy of a "symbiotic" and harmonious relationship with the natural world, rather than an "antagonistic" one modelled on "patriarchal domination," in *The Ecology of Freedom*, 227. Later concerned about the deep ecology and new age movements' uncritical acceptance of notions of the "oneness of nature," he admonished that "It requires only a minor ideological shift from the ideas of the nineteenth-century Romantic movement and William Blake's mystical anarchism to arrive at Richard Wagner's mystical nationalism," in *The Philosophy of Social Ecology: Essays on Dialectical Naturalism*, 2nd ed. (Montréal: Black Rose Books, 1996), 56. While there is a significant distinction between Blake's inclusive internationalism and proto-fascism, the warning is well made.

14 Öcalan, *Sociology of Freedom*, 99.

15 Yatesbury Natural Agriculture Farm homepage: https://shumei.uk/yatesbury/, accessed 24 April 2022.

16 E.F. Schumacher, "The Use of the Land," [1969], 172–181 in *This I Believe and Other Essays* (Dartington: Resurgence, 1998).

17 Ian Rappel, "[Real] Farming: It's only human," Real Farming Trust website: https://realfarming.org/news-features/real-farming-its-only-human/, accessed 29 May 2024.

18 Slow Food, "Good, Clean and Fair: the Slow Food Manifesto for Quality," (2015): https://www.slowfood.com/wp-content/uploads/2015/07/Manifesto_Quality_ENG.pdf, accessed 1 August 2022.
19 Slow Food, "Kobane: An Eco-challenge for Humanity," Slow Food website (1 December 2016): https://www.slowfood.com/kobane-an-eco-challenge-for-humanity/, accessed 1 August 2022; Ercan Ayboğa, "Mesopotamian Ecology Movement at Terra Madre Salone del Gusto," Slow Food (1 December 2016): https://www.youtube.com/watch?v=wFqzIWyVLnM, accessed 1 August 2022.
20 Öcalan, *Sociology of Freedom*, 99.
21 Michel P. Pimbert, "Regenerating Kurdish Ecologies through Food Sovereignty, Agroecology, and Economies of Care," 115–132 in *Ecological Solidarity and Kurdish Freedom Movement*, ed. by Stephen E. Hunt (Lanham, MD: Lexington Books, 2021).
22 Linda Matar, "Degraded Capital Formation: The Achilles' Heel of Syria's Agriculture," 105–117 in *Crisis and Conflict in Agriculture*, ed. by Rami Zurayk, Eckart Woertz, and Rachel Bahn (Wallingford: CABI, 2018), 109.
23 Marwa Daoudy, *The Origins of the Syrian Conflict: Climate Change and Human Security* (Cambridge: Cambridge University Press, 2020), 120.
24 Francesca De Châtel, 527 in "The Role of Drought and Climate Change in the Syrian Uprising: Untangling the Triggers of the Revolution," *Middle Eastern Studies* 50, no. 4 (2014), 521–535: https://doi.org/10.1080/00263206.2013.850076; Matar, "Degraded Capital Formation," 108.
25 Raymond Hinnebusch, "The Ba'th's Agrarian Revolution (1963–2000)," in *Agriculture and Reform in Syria*, ed. by Raymond Hinnebusch, Atieh El Hindi, Munzer Khaddam, and Myriam Ababsa, St Andrews Papers on Contemporary Syria (Fife: University of St Andrews Centre for Syrian Studies, 2011), 11; Daoudy, *Origins of the Syrian Conflict*, 120.
26 Daoudy, *Origins of the Syrian Conflict*, 103.
27 De Châtel, "Role of Drought and Climate Change in the Syrian Uprising"; Jan Selby, Omar S. Dahi, Christine Fröhlich, and Mike Hulme, "Climate Change and the Syrian Civil War Revisited," *Political Geography* 60 (September 2017): 232–44: https://doi.org/10.1016/j.

polgeo.2017.05.007; Peter H. Gleick, "Climate, Water, and Conflict: Commentary on Selby et al., 2017," *Political Geography* 60 (2017): 248–50; Simon Dalby, "Climate Change and Environmental Conflicts," 42–53 in *Routledge Handbook of Environmental Conflict and Peacebuilding*, ed. by Ashok Swain and Joakim Öjendal (Abingdon: Routledge, 2018); Mark R. Read, "Climate and the Syrian Civil War," 167–76 in *The Environment-Conflict Nexus: Climate Change and the Emergent National Security Landscape*, ed. by Francis Galgano, Advances in Military Geosciences (Cham, Switzerland: Springer 2019); Konstantin Ash and Nick Obradovich, "Climate Stress, Internal Migration, and Syrian Civil War Onset." *Journal of Conflict Resolution*, 64, no. 1 (2020): 3–31. https://doi.org/10.1177/0022002719864140; Daoudy, *Origins of the Syrian Conflict*.

28 Food and Agricultural Organization of the United Nations, "Syrian Arab Republic," https://www.fao.org/emergencies/where-we-work/SYR/en, accessed 19 July 2023.

29 Michael Knapp, Anja Flach, and Ercan Ayboğa, *Revolution in Rojava: Democratic Autonomy and Women's Liberation in Syrian Kurdistan* (London: Pluto, 2016), 192.

30 Rahaf Youssef, "Syrians' Strategic Resources Wheat, Cotton Face Challenges," *North Press Agency* website (3 November 2022): https://npasyria.com/en/86726/.

31 Gürcan cites the "multi-season drought" of 2006–2011 as the "worst case in modern Syria's history," Efe Can Gürcan, "Extractivism, Neoliberalism, and the Environment: Revisiting the Syrian Conflict from an Ecological Justice Perspective," *Capitalism Nature Socialism* 30, no. 3, (2019): https://doi.org/10.1080/10455752.2018.1516794.

32 Wladimir van Wilgenburg, "Turkish-backed Group Cuts Water Supply to Northeastern Syria for Fourth Time," *Kurdistan 24* website, (30 March 2020): https://www.kurdistan24.net/en/news/e2a45738-8bad-41a1-a5f9-b65c7ad62e43. Disruption to clean-water supplies is likely a causal factor in the cholera outbreak that the area suffered in 2022.

33 Gürcan, "Extractivism, Neoliberalism, and the Environment."

34 De Châtel, "Role of Drought and Climate Change in the Syrian Uprising," 521, citing A. Bank and E. Mohns, "Die Syrische Revolte:

Protestdynamik, Regimerepression und Internationalisierung," *Arabellions. Zur Vielfalt von Protest und Revolte im Nahen Osten und Nordafrika*, eds Annette Jünemann and Anja Zorob (Wiesbaden: VS Springer, 2013), 85–106.

35   Knapp, Flach, and Ayboğa, *Revolution in Rojava*, 194. Sheikh Maqsoud is Aleppo's predominantly Kurdish district.

36   De Châtel, "Role of Drought and Climate Change in the Syrian Uprising," 532.

37   The political and economic disenfranchisement of Kurds due to the Arab Belt policy is noted, however, in Daoudy, *Origins of the Syrian Conflict*, 135–37.

38   Gürcan, "Extractivism, Neoliberalism, and the Environment," 104.

39   De Châtel, "The Role of Drought and Climate Change in the Syrian Uprising," 532.

40   Sometimes the Kurdish areas have been exempted from embargoes on horticultural produce imposed on other areas of the Syria Arab Republic, according to Food and Agriculture Organization of the United Nations, "Special Report: FAO/WFP Crop and Food Security Assessment Mission to the Syrian Arab Republic" (5 September 2019), 22: https://www.fao.org/3/ca5934en/CA5934EN.pdf.

41   Because Turkish Agriculture Minister Bekir Pakdemirli, declared "We do not want revenues to fall into PKK hands [...] We want the revenues from Afrin [...] to come to us. This region is under our hegemony," as cited in a BBC report, according to [Unnamed correspondent] "Turkey's Operation Olive Branch Forces in Syria Accused of Plundering [...] Olives," *Intellinews - MENA Today* (February 1, 2019) accessed 8 August 2022, [via Nexis database]; *North Press Agency*, "Turkish-backed SNA factions cut down 250 trees in Syria's Afrin," (9 August 2022): https://npasyria.com/en/81682/.

42   Rojava Information Center, "Explainer: Cooperatives in North and East Syria – developing a new economy," Rojava Information Center website (8 November 2020): https://rojavainformationcenter.com/2020/11/explainer-cooperatives-in-north-and-east-syria-developing-a-new-economy/, accessed 9 August 2022.

43 Rojava Information Center, "Beyond Rojava: North and East Syria's Arab Regions," (June 2021): https://rojavainformationcenter.com/storage/2021/06/RIC-Dossier-Arab-regions.pdf, accessed 10 August 2022, 26–27.
44 Bel Trew, "'It Used to be Green, Now it is Hell': How Oil is Poisoning Northern Syria," *The Independent* (8 November 2021): https://www.independent.co.uk/news/world/middle-east/syria-oil-pollution-isis-civil-war-b1953587.html.
45 Knapp, Flach, and Ayboğa, *Revolution in Rojava*, 199; Pimbert, "Regenerating Kurdish Ecologies," 119.
46 Unpublished research report by T. Barbagli, K. Blauw, J.S. Orpayanda, K.D. Paoli, S. Steinmetz, and K. Teuling, "Revitializing Agriculture in Kobani: Drawing Scenarios for Policy Makers." Wageningen: Academic Consultancy Training Wageningen University and Research (2018), 7, cited in Joost Jongerden, "Autonomy as a Third Mode of Ordering: Agriculture and the Kurdish movement in Rojava and North and East Syria," *Journal of Agrarian Change*, 6 (2021): https://doi.org/10.1111/joac.12449.
47 Jongerden, "Autonomy as a Third Mode of Ordering," 6.
48 Pimbert, "Regenerating Kurdish Ecologies," 119.
49 The Co-operation in Mesopotamia website (https://mesopotamia.coop/) and Twitter account (https://twitter.com/coopmesopotamia) provide regular updates on Rojava's agricultural co-operatives in English.
50 Ulrike Flader and Çetin Gürer, "Building Alternative Communities Within the State: the Kurdish Movement, Local Municipalities and Democratic Autonomy," 177–191 in *Funding, Power and Community Development*, eds Niamh McCrea and Fergal Finnegan (Bristol: Bristol University Press/Policy Press, 2019), 184.
51 Azize Aslan, "Women's Subjectivity and the Ecological and Communal Economy," 149–162 in *Ecological Solidarity and Kurdish Freedom Movement*, ed. Stephen E. Hunt (Lanham, MD: Lexington Books, 2021), 154.
52 John Holloway, foreword to Öcalan, *Sociology of Freedom*, xv.
53 Abdullah Öcalan, *The Political Thought of Abdullah Öcalan* (London: Pluto, 2017), 86. Drawing upon FAO data, Indian food activist Vandana

Shiva emphasises women's continuing role as primary producers of food in Chapter 8 of *Who Really Feeds the World?* (London: Zed, 2015); this is corroborated in a 2023 report that cites more recent data that women "represent 50% of the formal food production force in the world," being the larger part of the workforce in small-scale food production in much of the Global South: Azul Cordo, María Paz Tibiletti, and Damaris Ruiz, "Women Feed the World: Land for the Women Who Work It" (We Effect and LatFem, 2023), 9: https://assets.fsnforum.fao.org/public/contributions/2023/we-effect_women-feed-the-world.pdf.

54 Jongerden, "Autonomy as a Third Mode of Ordering," 2.

55 Meral Çiçek in response to question from the author, "Ecocide and Kurdish Women's Movement," Open Protest Network video on the Peace in Kurdistan website (9 October 2022): https://www.peaceinkurdistancampaign.com/video-pik-ecology-event-on-ecocide-and-kurdish-womens-movement/.

56 ReliefWeb [UN United Nations Office for the Coordination of Humanitarian Affairs (OCHA)], Food Security and Livelihoods Working Group in Northeast Syria, "Northeast Syria Flash Report: Deterioration of the Livestock Feed and Fodder Market" (March 2022): https://reliefweb.int/report/syrian-arab-republic/northeast-syria-flash-report-deterioration-livestock-feed-and-fodder.

57 For example, the women and their families in the following account: Yiyao Yang, "How a Turkish-Induced Water Crisis is Affecting Female Farmers in Northeast Syria," *The New Arab* (8 November 2022): https://www.newarab.com/features/how-turkish-led-crisis-affecting-syrian-female-farmers.

58 I first wrote about Green Tress in "Tresses vertes et arbres rebelles: la lutte écologique kurde dans l'administration autonome de nord-est de la Syrie," 121–142 in *Luttes écologiques et sociales dans le monde: Allier le vert et le rouge*, ed. by Michael Löwy and Daniel Tanuro (Paris: Editions Textuel, 2021).

59 Translated from the French document "Tresses Vertes," supplied by Gulistan Sido to Stephen E. Hunt (personal e-mail, 18 July 2021).

60 Zîwer Şêxo in DAANES, online interview with author through translator Gulistan Essa (4 July 2023).

61 ibid.
62 Green Tress document (February 2022) shared by Zîwer Şêxo (personal correspondence).
63 Green Tress work in Raqqa and it is particularly targeted for their projects due to the trauma the city experienced when under ISIS control, Zîwer Şêxo in DAANES, online interview with author through translator Gulistan Essa (4 July 2023).
64 "Jihan" Green Tress representative, Peace in Kurdistan Ecology Network online webinar "Kurdistan: Ecocide and Forced Demographic Change," (8 May 2022): https://www.peaceinkurdistancampaign.com/video-pik-social-ecology-network-on-kurdistan-ecocide-and-forced-demographic-change/.
65 Zîwer Şêxo in DAANES, online interview with author through translator Gulistan Essa (4 July 2023).
66 Green Tress draw attention to the high incidence of lung cancers in DAANES, due to 12 years of war and the impact of pollution on the people: Zîwer Şêxo in DAANES, online interview with author through translator Gulistan Essa (4 July 2023).
67 "Jihan" Green Tress representative, Peace in Kurdistan Ecology Network online webinar "Kurdistan: Ecocide and Forced Demographic Change" (8 May 2022): https://www.peaceinkurdistancampaign.com/video-pik-social-ecology-network-on-kurdistan-ecocide-and-forced-demographic-change/.
68 See Fabiana Cioni and Domenico Patassini, "Free Life Together: Jinwar, the Women's Eco-Village," 133–147 in *Ecological Solidarity and Kurdish Freedom Movement*, ed. Stephen E. Hunt (Lanham, MD: Lexington Books, 2021); Firaz Dağ, "'How we Built Jinwar' – The Free Woman's Village in Rojava," *Nûçe Ciwan* (9 April 2022): https://www.nuceciwan103.xyz/en/2022/04/09/how-we-built-jinwar-the-free-womans-village-in-rojava/.
69 Green Tress, "Environmental risks as a result of the Turkish army targeting the infrastructure in Rojava" (e-mail to followers, 2 December 2022). There has been a further intensification of Turkish attacks upon DAANES since October 2023.

70 While this may sound like a bold claim, it can be verified by checking, for example, the Nexis database (accessed in August 2023), a comprehensive electronic repository of English-language news sources and the BBC website.
71 "Jihan" Green Tress representative, Peace in Kurdistan Ecology Network online webinar, 8 May 2022. To use land for this purpose, the project has the backing of Ferhed Hemo—Co-Chair of the Rojava Committee North-Eastern Syria according to a Green Tress document (February 2022) shared by Zîwer Şêxo (personal correspondence).
72 Zîwer Şêxo in DAANES, online interview with author through translator Gulistan Essa (4 July 2023).
73 Sonia Karimi, Peace in Kurdistan Ecology Network online webinar "Kurdistan: Ecocide and Forced Demographic Change," 8 May 2022: https://www.peaceinkurdistancampaign.com/video-pik-social-ecology-network-on-kurdistan-ecocide-and-forced-demographic-change/.
74 See Ekin Kurtiç, "Criminalizing Environmental Activism in Turkey," *Middle East Brief*, no. 147 (March 2022): https://www.brandeis.edu/crown/publications/middle-east-briefs/pdfs/101-200/meb147.pdf [accessed 10 August 2022]; and reports of Hengaw Organisation for Human Rights: https://hengaw.net/en.
75 Green Tress document (February 2022) shared by Ziwer Şexo (personal correspondence).
76 Translated from the French document "Tresses Vertes," supplied by Gulistan Sido to Stephen E. Hunt (personal e-mail, 18 July 2021).
77 Zîwer Şêxo in DAANES, online interview with author through translator Gulistan Essa (4 July 2023).

DOMINATORY AGRICULTURE: FROM SLAVE PLANTATIONS TO FACTORY FARMING

Plantations

The turn towards decolonisation in recent decades has partly consisted of the exploration and exposure of the exploitative antecedents of industrial agriculture. From the origins of monocultures in slave and colonial plantations to factory farming, there are many instances of what I shall term dominatory agriculture. This is expressed, for example, in the intimate connections, both metaphorical and actual, that have been made between industrial agriculture—with its development of plantations, synthetic chemicals, and battery farming—and institutionalised slavery, war, and colonialism. I shall look at the emergence of plantations in the Canary Islands and consider their fraught history in relation to India, before briefly noting the explosive development of chemical fertilisers and factory farming, with reference to the case of the poultry industry.

While Capitalocene and Plantationocene—the latter being Donna Haraway's coinage—are unwieldy terms, such names express two important contentions.[1] First, that the current ecological crisis is not, as the more common concept of the Anthropocene suggests, simply a result of the evolution of human society, but of specific types of production that developed in the early modern period.[2] Second, the notion of the Plantationocene contends that the emergence of a particular, although variably implemented, mode of plantation cultivation is a fundamental characteristic of industrial agriculture's rise as a prototype for factory production, and thereby foundational to wider industrialism.

Modern plantations are outcomes of conquest and land seizure, representing a globalised model imposed upon Indigenous populations and local practices. The claim that the Plantationocene era determines human development and life on Earth, therefore, rests on three closely linked premises.[3] First, that the boom in plantation economies and the upscaling of slavery was a part of a single process, ongoing in colonial and neo-colonial relationships. Second, that this process tends to erase geographical, ecological, and cultural differences with a uniform template. Third, this process is dependent on the kind of ecological simplification and narrowing of crop types that Bookchin feared would stall the incremental impulse towards complexity that is the impetus for organic evolution. Insofar as it rests upon a supposition that the ecological crisis has a socio-economic origin, the notion of the Plantationocene is compatible with the ideas of social ecology, which hold that exploitative practices are the logical outcomes of a mindset of domination integral to hierarchal structures of social organisation and thought.[4]

The origin of industrial agriculture was not the matter of a moment, but of a decisive transition towards the integration of the production of food and other commodities within a capitalist global market, eventually based upon financial derivatives. A leading contention is that the modern model, based on the intensive cultivation of monocultures for large-scale export, can be traced back to the establishment of sugar plantations by Portuguese and Spanish colonial settlers on Madeira and the Canary Islands during the 1400s.[5] This systematic, investment-driven cultivation of sugar cane connects older forms of production undertaken by Christians and Arabs across the Middle East and Mediterranean with the exploitation of slave labour, and to the exportation of the plantation system to Brazil and across the Americas and West Indies from the sixteenth century onwards.

Natural history writer Richard Mabey records that the model of slave production of luxury exports on Madeira became a "template" for the slave plantations of the West Indies and so-called "New World":

> All the components were in place early on: the seizing and rationalization of land, the destruction of natural habitats and indigenous cultures, the establishment of crop monocultures, the employment of a cowed labour force.[6]

The appearance of the large-scale plantation economy was therefore far from auspicious for improving the lot of the workers who were undertaking such production. Indeed, in reference to the Guanches, the Canary Islanders who made up a large proportion of the people first enslaved on the islands, Richard Grove records, "both forests and indigenous people were decimated."[7] While their fate is controversial—with Stefan Halikowski Smith, for example, pointing out that there is evidence of genetic continuity from Guanche ancestors through to the present day—an apparent genocide took place insofar as they were wiped out as a functioning ethnic group with a distinct culture.[8] Furthermore, there was a far-reaching reconfiguration of the islands' ecology to make way for the plantations. Even as direct slavery ended in the nineteenth century, coercive labour practices and land-grabbing continued not as unfortunate side-effects, but as central to the process of scaling up industrial capitalism throughout the European empires.

India's colonial food traumas

Such prototypes in plantation cultivation and enclosure during the early modern era were to have far-reaching and sharply contested consequences, being indispensable to the emergence of what the political sociologist Immanuel Wallerstein was to characterise as a world system of commodity exchange.[9]

Alongside the evolution of the plantation, the other package of features that came to be consolidated into the world food system included dispossession and enclosure for land privatisation, a shift to a wage-based economy, and a colonial matrix of commodity importation and exportation. In Britain, where they were first imposed, such developments are associated with the widespread dismantlement of the open-field system and often forced clearances from the fifteenth century onwards. As the British Empire became the pre-eminent global power during the nineteenth century, India, with its vast plantations, was at its heart.

In *Late Victorian Holocausts,* Mike Davis argues that, for producers of cash commodities, integration of agriculture into the "London-centred world economy," far from ensuring food security, was a contributory factor effecting mass starvation in India, and beyond, in times of climatic stress or price fluctuations.[10] According to Richard Grove's groundbreaking account, *Green Imperialism,* also dealing in part with the colonial-era catastrophes in India, a monolithic characterisation of the colonial mindset would be a mistake. Grove traces the "emergence of colonial environmental sensibilities," based on a combination of Indigenous knowledges and empirical observation and science.[11] This is evidenced by debates demonstrating conflicting perspectives regarding free trade as against more interventionist approaches to forest conservation among contemporary independent, reformist, and often radical, thinkers and professionals within the subcontinent and other regions under colonial administration, who feared for the consequences of extensive deforestation and were critical of the dominant policies of the East India Company.[12]

According to Davis's extensively evidenced and compellingly argued thesis, at a time of repeated El Niño occurrences, several factors led to a staggering number of deaths, with combined and accumulated estimates of famine mortality in India, China, and Brazil ranging from 31.7–61.3 million people.[13] For Davis, causes of the horrific famines in colonial India included the loss of subsistence farming and reduced local granaries due to the transition towards cash cropping and export-oriented production, facilitated by the development of infrastructure such as rail networks and the Suez Canal, which diverted supplies away from the areas of most urgent need; the violently coercive imposition of taxation; deforestation; and an intensive programme of enclosure of common lands.[14] *Late Victorian Holocausts* argues that a utilitarian mindset, in which harsh Malthusian attitudes were bolstered by Social Darwinist ideas, drove such policies, thereby undermining resilience and fatally exacerbating famine and mass starvation. While this is sharply contested territory, and Davis has several critics, the evidential basis of his case has not been persuasively challenged, and he substantially reframed and refocused debates about the Indian famines under the East Indian Company and the British Raj.

Today, India remains on the frontline of debates about industrial agriculture and its alternatives. Its intensive inputs of capital, water, and fossil fuels, and development of huge plantations of cash crops, mega-dam projects, and the rapidly expanding factory-farming sector are coming under renewed scrutiny. In the post-Colonial era, the Green Revolution boosted the outputs of selected staple crops, and is believed to have relieved world hunger at a time of rapidly increasing population growth, thwarting fears of a repeat of mass famines in India from the latter half of the twentieth century onwards.[15] Other factors helped to reduce food insecurity, such as relative peace, aid programmes, and modest cooperation in efforts to tackle global poverty on the part of international organisations in the aftermath of the Cold War.

However, incremental progress is now in jeopardy and even being reversed, since these factors are no longer ensured in the context of global financial volatility, geopolitical instability, and ecological crises. In the present day, the challenge to feed India's population is again formidable. It has a deteriorating position in the Global Hunger Index, where it is ranked as 107th out of the 121 countries listed, with 16.3% of the population calculated to be undernourished, and prospects for food insecurity rated as "serious," while national and United Nations data indicate that India overtook China as the world's most populous country in 2023.[16]

Priya Rampal, of the Observer Research Foundation, identifies many causes that she claims obstruct India's food security, including soil salinisation and depletion due to excessive use of fertilisers, impacts from climate change and other ecological crises, economic and logistical barriers to food distribution, and WTO pressure against subsidies for the agricultural sector to ensure food security.[17] Prominent critics, such as Indian food activist Vandana Shiva and novelist Arundati Roy, have also called attention to ongoing social injustice and ecological destruction.

Recently, India has seen the largest and most high-profile backlash against neoliberal agricultural reforms. Concerns that the Farm Acts would subject India's millions of farmers to the power of global corporations and the sink-or-swim vacillations of market forces account for the intensity of the resistance against the Modi administration's "reforms" in favour of market liberalisation in 2021. Prominent among the agricultural social movements successfully resisting the changes has been the Indian Coordination Committee of Farmers' Movements, allied with La Via Campesina, of whom more shortly.

India also boasts the world's largest agroecological programme, in Andra Pradesh, a state which is in the process of converting six million farmers to agroecological methods by 2030.[18] A study of the results, based on 10% of farmers who have already converted their production, shows positive outcomes so far.[19] Elsewhere,

Sikkim is the first state to convert all agricultural production to organic methods and Kerala is aspirational to do the same.[20] Varied motivations for such transitions include the desire to free farmers from debt dependency, concerns about residues from synthetic chemicals upon human health, soil improvement, and the production of organic status crops that typically command higher prices. Unlike the immediate imposition of organic agriculture, which provoked a political backlash in Sri Lanka, such changes are being introduced incrementally. Finally, observers have also noted a trend away from the colonial legacy of plantation estates, albeit modest in scale and economically vulnerable. Where this has occurred, and smallholders and workers' cooperatives have acquired land, there tends to be more varied production to spread the risk from reliance on single crops in a volatile market.[21]

Embattled fields

As we have seen, synthetic chemicals have been a focus of concern about the impact of industrial agriculture. Historians have linked geopolitical struggles for hegemony and forms of dominatory agriculture. Marion Dixon identifies superphosphate fertiliser as a "strategic natural resource" among the extractive commodities for which increasing demand drove the impetus for imperial expansion and the "international division of labour," benefiting the core nations in the world system rather than the colonised suppliers on the periphery, such as France's north African colonies.[22]

The origins of the chemical compounds that form the basis for twentieth-century industrial agriculture are inextricable from modern warfare. The highly controversial chemist Fritz Haber scaled up the process for synthesising ammonia, thus boosting world food production through fertilisers, but also unleashing the chlorine gas and explosives that killed thousands during the First World War.[23] There was a direct transfer of technical expertise and production from military to agricultural purposes as part of efforts to find new markets in the interwar period.[24] Nitrogen-based explosives had properties that were developed into chemical fertilisers, and the tear gas chloropicrin was adapted as an insecticide used in farming.[25] In interwar America, the war on insect pests increasingly took the form of aerial bombing campaigns, as industrial quantities of arsenic, copper, and other insecticides were dropped in a context that was more than analogous to a martial programme.[26] While such experimental work could be positively framed as "swords-into-plowshares" initiatives, historian Timothy Johnson concludes that the outcomes were less benign, benefiting the corporations that attracted large subsidies far more than American farmers, and mostly serving the long-term interests of the chemical industry.[27] After linking a new generation of agricultural chemicals to the chemical warfare developments of the Second World War, Rachel Carson noted that the relationship could also work the other way. Nazi-era German scientist Gerhard Schrader's synthesis of new organophosphate insecticides turned out to have direct application to the development of nerve agents, such as tabun and sarin.[28]

The cages of free enterprise and the rise of chicken power

From the mid-twentieth century onwards, the factory farming of animals has become another indispensable feature of industrial agriculture. The case of the humble battery chicken shows where several aspects of dominatory agriculture intersect. Controversies relating to the intensive indoor production of chickens, pigs, and other animals, have not only centred around welfare issues but also contrasting attitudes towards freedom and independence, and to productivity, profitability, and affordability. It turns out that the emergence of intensive poultry rearing in the UK is directly of a piece with the end of the so-called post-war consensus regarding the welfare state, and the drift of mainstream Conservatism towards hard-right libertarian economics.[29]

Factory farming was first popularised and scaled up during the early 1930s, when know-how books such as Milton Arndt's *Battery Brooding* (1931) and *A New Road to Independence: Poultry Raising the Arndt New Era Way; Definite Plans are Set Forth Showing How to Use the Complete System of Rearing Poultry for Profit* (1933) were published for American readers and would-be entrepreneurs. While the title of "Road" is something of a cliché, it is a coincidental foreshadowing of Friedrich Hayek's *Road to Serfdom* (1944), and the subtitle tellingly indicates a venture for freedom through capitalism.

In England, the introduction of battery chicken farms followed a conversation between businessman Antony Fisher and one of Hayek's acquaintances, F.A. Harper, an agricultural economist, free-market libertarian, and fellow member of the Mont Pelerin Society. Several commentators have observed that the fortunes of intensive poultry farming and a particular vision of free-market economics are interlinked, since Fisher was inspired to set up the first UK think-tank, the Institute for Economic Affairs (IEA), following a meeting with Hayek.[30] Ironically, since the spectacle of birds imprisoned in small cages has long been a symbol of liberty lost, it was to represent free enterprise for Fisher. Backyard self-sufficiency and get-rich-quick-from-poultry schemes have traditionally attracted small-scale producers who have seen them as a means of independent employment and an alternative to wage slavery.

Eton-educated Fisher, however, had several advantages and he was able to draw upon his contacts and capital to think big, exploiting the new battery-system technologies as Britain came out of post-war austerity. The already wealthy Fisher became a multi-millionaire when his Buxted Chicken Company generated huge profits from battery chicken production. His brave new chickens enabled him to fund the right-wing libertarian IEA, which he founded in 1955. For Kojo Koram, the IEA became highly influential when it attracted the likes of Ralph Harris and rising Conservative MP Enoch Powell (who remained Fisher's life-long friend), and consequently did much to coalesce the New Right in the UK. According to his biographer Gerald Frost, Fisher was to become "Britain's, and probably Europe's, biggest chicken farmer."[31] Furthermore, he was a character of hidden consequence. In Conservative politician Oliver Letwin's words, "Without Fisher, no IEA; without the IEA and its clones, no Thatcher and quite possibly no Reagan; without Reagan, no Star Wars; without Star Wars, no economic collapse of the Soviet Union. Quite a chain of consequences for a chicken farmer."[32]

From a social and ecological point of view, however, factory farming was soon to become a leading example of dominatory agriculture. With the publication of *Animal Machines* in 1964, Ruth Harrison exposed issues concerning the conditions of factory-farmed animals in a way comparable to Rachel Carson's revelations about the impact of synthetic chemicals in *Silent Spring*. Even proponents of battery systems now adduce their case largely in terms of welfare as well as cost. Poultry workers' welfare has less often attracted attention, even though the sector has become notorious for exploitation and poor working conditions, particularly of migrant workers. However, Oxfam America have been undertaking a long-running campaign to expose and improve conditions for the workforce in the United States especially, due to the size of the industry and the extreme conditions that have prevailed.[33] Nearly a century after the emergence of poultry farms in the 1930s, they continue to be identified as sources of pollutants of water courses as well as air and soil.[34]

Despite its vast scale, factory farming is largely invisible and marginal to urban consumers. When (and if) considered, it is assumed to deliver an affordable source of protein and consumer choice. But the hidden costs of externalities—such as poor working conditions, animal suffering, and public and environmental health concerns—are often marginal to public discourse too. Yet it is the preeminent form of agribusiness, based on the use of monopolistic vertical integration to dominate the food sector, to the detriment of other smaller food producers making available more varied diets. It is no exaggeration to say that this command of the food chain is based on the profound reengineering of life on Earth since the global takeover of domesticated chickens as by far the planet's most populous bird.[35] As a prevailing mode of dominatory agriculture, factory farming literally and symbolically represents the way that the growth of neoliberalism has been manifest in the collapse in the distinction between the economic power of corporations and the authority of the state, based on consolidation of control of key areas of the economy where the capital-intensive food industry, agrochemicals, and the pharmaceutical sector (supplying anti-biotics and growth hormones) intersect and are mutually dependent.

In summary, since its origins, industrial agriculture has taken a dominatory form that exemplifies the exploitative paradigm social ecologists have blamed for negative social and ecological consequences, and that they would argue, moreover, is an inevitable expression of a hierarchically structured society. Historians will need to deal with the counterfactual questions as to whether alternative development pathways could have been followed, but we shall shortly turn to movements for agricultural resistance in the present and future. In the sections that follow, we will look at alternatives to dominatory agriculture through discussions of issues related to social-ecology principles, using case examples from the international and domestic context.

Notes

1 Sociologist Jason Moore popularised the term Capitalocene. For the term Plantationocene's origins see Donna Haraway, Noboru Ishikawa, Scott F. Gilbert, Kenneth Olwig, Anna L. Tsing and Nils Bubandt, "Anthropologists Are Talking – About the Anthropocene," *Ethnos* 81, no. 3 (2016), 535–564: https://doi.org/10.1080/001418 44.2015.1105838.

2   While the term *Anthropocene* is in common use, it was not officially adopted by the International Commission on Stratigraphy in March 2024, as had been anticipated.
3   See "Reflections on the Plantationocene: A Conversation with Donna Haraway and Anna Tsing," moderated by Gregg Mitman (18 June 2019), ed. by Addie Hopes and Laura Perry, *Edge Effects Magazine*: https://edgeeffects.net/wp-content/uploads/2019/06/PlantationoceneReflections_Haraway_Tsing.pdf, accessed 3 November 2022.
4   Brian Tokar cites evidence of slave-like conditions on sugarcane fields "with long working hours for little pay, restricted diets and frequent deaths from exhaustion," in the present century: "Biofuels and the Global Food Crisis," 121–138 in *Agriculture and Food in Crisis*, ed. by Fred Magdoff and Brian Tokar, 129.
5   Sidney M. Greenfield, "Madeira and the Beginning of New World Sugar Cane Cultivation and Plantation Slavery: A Study in Institutional Building," *Annals of the New York Academy of Sciences* 292, no. 1, (1977), 537: https://doi.org/10.1111/j.1749-6632.1977.tb47771.x; Richard H. Grove, *Green Imperialism: Colonial Expansion, Tropical Island Edens and the Origins of Environmentalism, 1600–1860*, Studies in Environment and History (Cambridge: Cambridge University Press, 1995), 31; Vibeke Bjornlund, Henning Bjornlund, and Andre F. Van Rooyen, "Why Agricultural Production in Sub-Saharan Africa Remains Low Compared to the Rest of the World – A Historical Perspective," *International Journal of Water Resources Development* 36, sup. 1, S20–S53 (2020), 325: https://doi.org/10.1080/07900627.2020.1739512.
6   Richard Mabey, *Fencing Paradise: Reflections on the Myths of Eden* (London: Eden Project/Transworld, 2005), 120–121.
7   Grove, *Green Imperialism*, 29.
8   Stefan Halikowski Smith, "The Mid-Atlantic Islands: A Theatre of Early Modern Ecocide?," *IRSH* 55, Supplement (2010), 51–77: https://www.jstor.org/stable/26405418, [accessed via Jstor database].
9   Both Wallerstein and Ferdinand Braudel, who informed his thinking on commodity exchange, have been key influences upon Abdullah Öcalan's criticism of capitalist modernity.

10 Mike Davis, *Late Victorian Holocausts: El Nino Famines and the Making of the Third World* [2001] (London: Verso, 2002), 9.
11 Grove, *Green Imperialism*, 474.
12 ibid., 481.
13 Davis, *Late Victorian Holocausts*, 7. A figure not inclusive of many other deaths suffered globally.
14 ibid., 111.
15 Raj Patel examines the colonial context and legacy of the Green Revolution in *Stuffed and Starved: From Farm to Fork: The Hidden Battle for the World Food System*, 2nd rev. ed. (London: Portobello, 2012), Chapter 6.
16 Currently, the population of India is estimated as 1435.23 million and China as 1425.49 million, according to Statista, "Twenty Countries with the Largest Population in 2024," (22 May 2024), https://www.statista.com/, accessed 30 May 2024.
17 Priya Rampa, "A Roadmap for Sustainable Food Security," Observer Research Foundation (26 April 2021): https://www.orfonline.org/expert-speak/roadmap-sustainable-food-security/. The Observer Research Foundation is an Indian think-tank.
18 Global Academy of Agriculture and Food Security (University of Edinburgh), "Lessons from India on Scaling Up Natural Farming," *Bloom News* website (15 November 2021): https://www.ed.ac.uk/global-agriculture-food-security/research/projects/bloom/bloom-news/lessons-from-india-on-scaling-up-natural-farming.
19 Global Alliance For The Future Of Food, *Executive Summary: Assessing Natural Farming Through a Wider Lens* (25 April 2023): https://futureoffood.org/wp-content/uploads/2023/06/ga_natfarmingexecsummary_05.pdf.
20 Pooja Yadav, "Explained: How Sikkim Became World's First Organic State," *India Times* website (16 June 2022): https://www.indiatimes.com/explainers/news/how-sikkim-became-worlds-first-organic-state-572280.html.
21 K.J. Joseph, "Towards a Sustainable System of Innovation: The Case of Plantation Sector in Kerala," Centre for Development Studies NRPPD discussion paper (2013): http://14.139.171.199:8080/xmlui/

handle/123456789/550; Miriam Wenner, "Towards an Alternative Indian Tea Economy: Examples of Producer Cooperatives from Darjeeling," *Economic and Political Weekly* 55, no. 45 (7 November 2020): https://www.epw.in/journal/2020/45/special-articles/towards-alternative-indian-tea-economy.html.

22   Marion W. Dixon, "Chemical fertilizer in Transformations in World Agriculture and the State System, 1870 to Interwar Period," *Journal of Agrarian Change* 18 (2018), 768–786: https://doi.org/10.1111/joac.12259.

23   The far-reaching ramifications included the suicide of his wife, Clara Immerwar in protest at the horrors his actions inflicted. Collin Smith, Alfred K. Hill, and Laura Torrente-Murciano argue that Haber's role was "decisive in setting the current geo-political borders," due to the immense impact of such armaments in global conflict, also making possible the Zyklon B used in Hitler's death camps, and positively green hydrogen, "Current and Future Role of Haber–Bosch Ammonia in a Carbon-free Energy Landscape," (Analysis) *Energy and Environmental Science* 13 (2020), 331–344. Although Haber received the Nobel Prize for Chemistry for the breakthrough, he was not the originator of the process according to Alan Dronsfield, "Who Really Discovered the Haber Process?," Royal Society of Chemistry website (1 May 2007): https://edu.rsc.org/feature/who-really-discovered-the-haber-process/2020277.article, accessed 18 December 2022.

24   Albert Howard, *An Agricultural Testament* (London: Oxford University Press, 1940), 32, as cited by Vandana Shiva, *Staying Alive: Women, Ecology, and Development* (London: Zed, 1989), 143.

25   J.H. Perkins, *Insects, Experts and the Insecticide Crisis* (New York: Plenum, 1982), 5, as cited by Shiva, *Staying Alive*, 156.

26   James E. McWilliams, "'Let us Spray': Mosquitoes, War, and Chemicals," Chapter 5 in *American Pests: The Losing War on Insects from Colonial Times to DDT* (New York: Columbia University Press, 2008).

27   Timothy Johnson, "Nitrogen Nation: The Legacy of World War I and the Politics of Chemical Agriculture in the United States, 1916–1933," *Agricultural History* 90, no. 2 (Spring 2016), 226: https://doi.org/10.3098/ah.2016.090.2.209.

28 Rachel Carson, *Silent Spring* [1962] (London: Penguin, 1999), 31 and 42. Both nerve gases were dropped to devastating effect during the 1980s in the Iran–Iraq War and the 1988 Halabja Massacre (inflicted by Saddam Hussein's forces against the population of a Kurdish city), while the Syrian Arab Republic's air force has released sarin during the Syrian Civil War. Dilshad Jaff, "The Use of Chemical Weapons: Unhealed Scars from Contemporary Mass Atrocities," *Medicine, Conflict and Survival,* 37:3, 184–186 (2021): https://doi.org/10.1080/13623699.2021.1961351.

29 It is important to note that social ecologists have also highlighted connections between another form of dominatory thinking—fascist and far-right traditionalist tendencies—and the origins of organic farming, as exalted by Food and Agriculture Minister Richard Walther Darré and Alwin Seifert during the Nazi Third Reich, and Soil Association founders such as Lady Eve Balfour, Jorian Jenks, and Rolf Gardiner in England: Janet Biehl and Peter Staudenmaier, *Ecofascism: Lessons from the German Experience* (Edinburgh: AK Press, 1995), 19–23; Gershuny, *Organic Revolutionary,* 18–20.

30 Adam Curtis, "The Curse of TINA," The Medium and the Message BBC Blog (13 September 2011): https://www.bbc.co.uk/blogs/adamcurtis/2011/09/the_curse_of_tina.html, accessed 13 December 2022; Kojo Koram, *Uncommon Wealth: Britain and the Aftermath of Empire* (London: John Murray, 2022), 100–101.

31 Gerald Frost, *Antony Fisher: Champion of Liberty* [Profile Books, 2002], condensed for publication by David Moller (Institute of Economic Affairs, 2008), 13, available from https://iea.org.uk/publications/research/antony-fisher-champion-of-liberty. Fisher later lost his fortune following an ill-fated venture into turtle farming.

32 Quoted by Frost, "Anthony Fisher: Champion of Liberty," Institute of Economic Affairs website: https://iea.org.uk/publications/research/antony-fisher-champion-of-liberty, accessed 28 February 2023.

33 Oxfam America, "Lives on the Line: The Human Cost of Cheap Chicken," Oxfam America website (26 October 2015): https://www.oxfamamerica.org/explore/research-publications/lives-on-the-line/; Oxfam America, "No Relief: Denial of Bathroom Breaks in the Poultry Industry,"

Oxfam America website (9 May 2016): https://www.oxfamamerica.org/explore/research-publications/no-relief/, the campaign is ongoing at the time of writing. The British poultry industry has also attracted the wrong kind of attention due to multiple cases of mistreatment of its workforce according to the findings of the Equality and Human Rights Commission report, "Meat and Poultry Processing Inquiry Review Report of the Findings and Recommendations" (November 2012): https://www.equalityhumanrights.com/sites/default/files/meat_and_poultry_processing_review_report_0.pdf. Efforts have been made to improve the sector's reputation since the Gangmaster's Licensing Authority successfully sued an employer of chicken catchers it called "the worst UK gangmaster ever," Gangmasters Licencing Authority, "DJ Houghton Ltd – 'Worst UK Gangmaster Ever,'" Gangmasters and Labour Abuse Authority website (5 March 2014): https://www.gla.gov.uk/whats-new/press-release-archive/5314-dj-houghton-ltd-worst-uk-gangmaster-ever/, accessed 15 December 2022.

34 G. Gržinić, A. Piotrowicz-Cieślak, A. Klimkowicz-Pawlas, R.L. Górny, A. Ławniczek-Wałczyk, L. Piechowicz, E. Olkowska, M. Potrykus, M. Tankiewicz, M. Krupka, G. Siebielec, L. Wolska, "Intensive Poultry Farming: A Review of the Impact on the Environment and Human Health, *Science of the Total Environment* 858, pt. 3 (1 February 2023): https://doi.org/10.1016/j.scitotenv.2022.160014; World Wildlife Fund, "Land of Plenty: A Nature-Positive Pathway to Decarbonise UK Agriculture and Land Use" (February 2022), 22: https://www.wwf.org.uk/sites/default/files/2022-02/WWF_land_of_plenty.pdf. Given their market dominance, it is perhaps unsurprising that, when they were operational, Buxted Poultry, and its rival Bernard Matthews, the turkey producer, were singled out as offenders, "Farms 'Destroy Rivers'; River Pollution; Insight," *Sunday Times* (5 March 1989) [accessed via Nexis database, 17 December 2022]. The 2 Sisters Group, a subsidiary of food industry conglomerate Boparan Holdings, subsequently bought out both Buxted and Bernard Matthews.

35 C.E. Bennett, R. Thomas, M. Williams, et al., "The Broiler Chicken as a Signal of a Human Reconfigured Biosphere," *Royal Society Open Science* 5, no. 12 (December 2018): https://doi.org/10.1098/rsos.180325.

INTERNATIONALISM ON THE MODEL OF DEMOCRATIC CONFEDERALISM

La Via Campesina

La Via Campesina (LVC) was founded in 1993 from a network of small agricultural producers aligned with the global justice movement. It soon emerged as a giant within the coalition that mobilised in the celebrated and combative demonstrations against the WTO in Seattle in 1999, and since as a leading presence in the World Social Forum. Even though LVC claims that it "represents about 200 million small-scale food producers" in 81 countries, the organisation is not well-known in the UK.[1]

This perhaps reflects the relatively low priority the media gives to issues concerning food production and to voices from the Global South. LVC's size, duration, and effectiveness makes it the best real-world example of a mass movement of food activists participating in direct democracy at the local, regional, and international level. It is argued that LVC's horizontal and inclusive organisational structures and processes illustrate how the idealistic theory and aspirations of a movement closely compatible with social ecology can be realised and scaled across in a practical way. Indeed, prominent members of the Institute for Social Ecology, such as Chaia Heller and Brian Tokar, have written favourably about LVC.[2]

LVC's critique of the current dominant agribusiness model is combined with practices that seek to present versions of potential future farming based on agroecology and democratic commons. This prefiguration takes the form of what Sophie von Redecker and Christian Herzig call "positive commonality," by developing a "unifying strength" in the face of multiple issues and challenges.[3] LVC's organisational unity among millions of peasants and small-scale food producers across the planet further complements social ecology's emphasis on "unity in diversity."

LVC has been evolving an effective form of poly-governance through its non-hierarchical structure and processes. This is compatible with assemblies and councils found in a historic tradition espoused by admirers of direct democracy, such as Murray Bookchin and Hannah Arendt. It is also in keeping with the forms of participatory decision-making and accountability that communalist movements such as the Kurdish freedom movement are presently attempting to implement.

As a form of counterpower to the centralised non-democratic realm prevailing in the free market model, LVC members seek to attain what Michael Menser terms "maximal democracy" by fully incorporating individual food workers' agency, and thereby their interests, in collective deliberation.[4] Menser describes LVC's organisational structures as "associative horizontality" and "transnational regionalism," meaning that there is a commitment to inclusivity and equality at the grassroots level, alongside an impetus to effectively coordinate individual groups and cooperatives internationally. It is explained that this takes the form of local and national assemblies, which send delegates to assemblies in seven world regions. These regional gatherings in turn send delegates to international conferences.[5]

LVC is ultimately constituted according to a confederal-type model in which two representatives (one woman and one man) from each region go forward to make up a fourteen-member International Coordinating Commission.[6] Every 4 to 5 years, this is supplemented by an International Conference for decisions affecting the running of the organisation.

Another hallmark of a social-ecology approach is that the LVC's International Operational Secretariat, tasked with implementing organisational decisions, is non-policymaking.[7] Such processes attempt to transcend the alienating power games of limited "representational democracy," which social ecologists dismiss as "statecraft." Behind the abstractions of horizontality and poly-governance lie lively debates.

LVC forums are intended to breathe life into a raw and authentic realm of politics in its positive sense of empowering decision-making about things that matter. They are about the production, distribution, and allocation of food and drink that are essential to sustain social well-being. There are countless energising exchanges expressing passions and grievances concerning specific regional issues or overarching themes such as food sovereignty, biotechnologies, the role of rural women workers, or access to seeds. Councils and assemblies are not merely historical relics but could be empowering models for a more equitable and just future.

Despite its collaborative approach and efforts to build consensus, however, such a populous and complex international organisational project entails, of course, conflicting perspectives. For example, critics have identified tensions between proponents of liberal human rights discourse and revolutionary aspirations for more fulsome class liberation.[8] Class segmentation inevitably leads to contrasting or competing interests, with workers growing for a combination of self-provisioning through family and community subsistence, producing food for home markets and export markets, and cash-cropping for large landowners and corporations.[9]

Typically, peasants make available food that is produced and consumed outside of the market context, while also participating in capitalist market relations. They can be at once owners of the means of production and dependent upon wages to make a living. There are also potential differences between Western perspectives and those from the Global South. Such divisions cause some commentators, such as Thomas Henderson, to be sceptical of the LVC's progress in achieving "unity in diversity."[10] Nonetheless, the guiding ethos of affinity for empowerment against the needs of capitalist modernity generates a will to build trust and make common cause across network actors and regions.

There has also been criticism regarding the fair representation of women within LVC. Annette Aurélie Desmarais noted that gender parity was not initially a visible priority, and that gender issues only began to be addressed "in a concerted and systematic fashion" from 1996 onwards, with the formation of a Women's Commission and Women's Assembly.[11] This situation has since been transformed, to the extent that, as Desmarais writes in a co-authored 2022 article,

> While LVC is still debating the meaning and practice of peasant and popular feminism, it is clear that for the movement, feminism is a broad political strategy of structural transformation to eradicate gender inequality, all forms of violence, and patriarchal systems that harm both people and nature.[12]

Now, of the fourteen delegates in the International Coordinating Commission, women must make up half as a matter of principle and in recognition of women's proportionally larger role in small-scale agricultural production globally.[13]

Despite significant progress, Desmarais's initial concerns about the inclusion of women may yet be well founded. This stems from shortcomings in women's full participation in some of the national farming organisations affiliated to LVC.[14] Henry Veltmeyer notes that traditional peasant communities are diverse, and sometimes feature patriarchal norms and practices, thus presenting a tension if these are looked to as a basis for wider aspirations for democracy and inclusion.[15] However, as an international organisation, LVC has been taking a dynamic role in prioritising gender parity.[16] This is both a principle of social justice and a recognition that it is necessary to mobilise the full strength and energy of independent food producers—of which the majority are women—if LVC is to be successful in furthering key aims, such as defending and redistributing land to feed a growing world population with nutritious food in an ecologically sustainable way.

Other elements of LVC's structure add to its cohesion and underpin its democratic ethos. LVC is not about subscribing to a membership package and consuming a service; affiliation nurtures creative participation to advance practical, cultural, and political aspects of food production. To this end, inclusion is given substance by drawing from the affinity of diverse groups through ongoing programmes of research and education.

In recent years, a digital peasantry has emerged that mediates between the soil and cyberspace. Ingeborg Gaarde observes the role of information and communication technologies in boosting the capacity for direct participation, knowledge sharing, linguistic translation, and other aspects of cross-cultural exchange.[17] Gaarde also notes that LVC has implemented carefully selected and diversified funding strategies to protect the network's autonomy.[18]

Organisational integrity is further protected by measures to prevent nepotism and corruption. In contrast to hierarchically managed rivals in multinational corporations and state institutions, LVC is process-oriented, consensus-seeking, and values high levels of organisational transparency and accountability in respect to its representatives.[19] Some of the logistical drawbacks of elaborate decision-making processes are acknowledged, since the quest for mutual understanding is often time-consuming. Yet it can also be motivational.

The necessary connections between means and ends also invites comparison between the contrasting approaches to fast-food efficiency and the qualitative aspirations of Slow Food, a kindred spirit of LVC. Social value is placed on higher-quality decision-making as an ongoing seasonal process that rests upon a little more deliberation.

Democratic empowerment through direct participation, therefore, aims to elicit multiple voices, engage social obligation, nurture fulfilment, and address alienation. It is, moreover, an end in itself. In this way, the structures and processes of LVC as an international network of small-scale food producers would seem to complement the paradigms of social ecology and democratic confederalism. For social ecologists, a basic principle has been that power must be democratically controlled and dispersed, rather than wished away, to avoid the problem of the tyranny of structurelessness.

That power should be distributed and accountable was foundational for Bookchin's libertarian municipalism, later developed into the concept of communalism. Since the role of LVC has been, in Terisa Turner's words, to "champion food sovereignty, gender equality and global grassroots solidarity," it closely complements the three pillars of democratic confederalism.[20] In this respect, the LVC's co-representation and implementation of a Women's Assembly mirrors the structures of the Kurdish freedom movement with its inclusive, decentralist, communalist principles. LVC is, therefore, a significant real-world example of a network of international agricultural producers scaled across to contribute to the broader alter-globalisation movement through its presence at the World Social Forum.

We will now look at the MST in Brazil, a major national network following principles of agroecology within LVC. As we shall see, the regional composition and gender equality of representatives strives to ensure that the concerns of all participating food activists are fairly and proportionally weighted.

Notes

1. According to its own figures: La Via Campesina, *La Via Campesina: The Global Voice of Peasants!* (Bagnolet, France: La Via Campesina, 2021), 2: https://viacampesina.org/en/wp-content/uploads/sites/2/2021/12/LVC-EN-Brochure-2021-03F.pdf.
2. Chaia Heller's focus is upon LVC member Confédération Paysanne in *Food, Farms, and Solidarity* (2013); Brian Tokar, "Toward Food Sovereignty in Vermont and Northern New England," Institute for Social Ecology website [2009]: https://social-ecology.org/wp/2009/05/toward-food-sovereignty-in-vermont-and-northern-new-england/, accessed 4 March 2023.
3. Sophie von Redecker and Christian Herzig, "The Peasant Way of a More than Radical Democracy: The Case of La Via Campesina," *Journal of Business Ethics* (2020), 660–664: https://doi.org/10.1007/s10551-019-04402-6.
4. Michael Menser, 2008. "Transnational Participatory Democracy in Action: The Case of La Via Campesina." *Journal of Social Philosophy* 39, no. 1 (Spring), 20: https://doi.org/10.1111/j.1467-9833.2007.00409.x.
5. Menser, "Transnational Participatory Democracy in Action," 30.
6. Menser, "Transnational Participatory Democracy in Action," 30.
7. Ingeborg Gaarde, *Peasants Negotiating a Global Policy Space: La Via Campesina in the Committee on World Food Security*, Routledge studies in food, society and the environment (London: Routledge, 2017), 35.
8. Priska Daphi, Felix Anderl, and Nicole Deitelhoff, "Bridges or Divides?: Conflicts and Synergies of Coalition Building Across Countries and Sectors in the Global Justice Movement, *Social Movement Studies* 21, nos. 1–2 (2022),16: https://doi.org/10.1080/14742837.2019.1676223.
9. Thomas Paul Henderson. "The Class Dynamics of Food Sovereignty in Mexico and Ecuador," *Journal of Agrarian Change* 18, no. 1 (January 2018), 5: https://doi.org/10.1111/joac.12156.
10. Henderson, "Class Dynamics of Food Sovereignty in Mexico and Ecuador," 19.
11. Annette Aurélie Desmarais, "The Via Campesina: Peasant Women on the Frontiers of Food Sovereignty," *Canadian Woman Studies* 23, no. 1

(Fall 2003/Winter 2004), 140–145: https://cws.journals.yorku.ca/index.php/cws/article/view/6372.

12 Jessie MacInnis, Nettie Wiebe, Annette Aurélie Desmarais and Maywa Montenegro de Wit, "'This Feminism is Transformative, Rebellious and Autonomous': Inside Struggles to Shape the CFS Voluntary Guidelines on Gender Equality and Women's Empowerment," *Agroecology and Sustainable Food Systems* 46, no. 7, (2022), 955–956: https://doi.org/10.1080/21683565.2022.2091717.

13 Menser, "Transnational Participatory Democracy in Action," 31; Gaarde, *Peasants Negotiating a Global Policy Space*, 35.

14 Desmarais, "The Via Campesina"; Henderson, "Class Dynamics of Food Sovereignty in Mexico and Ecuador, 18.

15 Henry Veltmeyer, "Moving Towards Another World: Pitfalls and Possibilities," *The Essential Guide to Critical Development Studies*, eds Henry Veltmeyer and Paul Bowles, 2nd ed. Routledge critical development studies (London: Routledge, 2021), 295.

16 La Via Campesina, "Women in La Via Campesina," LVC website: https://viacampesina.org/en/women-la-via-campesina/, accessed 17 July 2022.

17 Gaarde, *Peasants Negotiating a Global Policy Space*, 36–37.

18 Gaarde, *Peasants Negotiating a Global Policy Space*, 37.

19 Gaarde, *Peasants Negotiating a Global Policy Space*, 33.

20 Inside cover of Annette Aurélie Desmarais, *La Vía Campesina: Globalization and the Power of Peasants* (London: Pluto, 2007).

ACCESS TO LAND AND USUFRUCT

MST and agrarian reform

The high concentration of land ownership and extreme inequality accounts for the urgency for agrarian reform in Brazil. Today, the MST (*Movimento dos Trabalhadores Rurais Sem Terra*, or Landless Workers' Movement) is at the heart of the struggle for land redistribution. Yet the social movement faces a daunting historical legacy and persistent attacks from vested interests hostile to its aspirations.

Recent statistics reveal that Brazil continues to be one of Latin America's most unequal countries. For example, the standard measurement for economic inequality, the Gini coefficient, is estimated at between 0.73 and 0.86 in terms of land distribution in 2017.[1] As we have seen, Brazil became one of the first modern plantation economies after the colonial model, developed on Madeira and the Canary Islands, was exported and scaled up from the early sixteenth century.[2] With this colonial past, deep structural inequality has been perpetuated across the intervening centuries, continuing through the years of the 1964–1985 military dictatorship, and recently recapitulated during the administration of Jair Bolsonaro.[3]

In recent years, neoliberal policies have widened the wealth gap further by concentrating land ownership and multiplying the cultivation of coffee, soya beans, sugar cane, maize, beef, and poultry, and other cash commodities for export, as well as biofuel production. Brazil has become a leading producer of food commodities and seen global investment portfolios attracted to expand into what has been called the "'new' agricultural frontier regions."[4] In sensitive Amazonian areas, such as in Pará state, evictions of Indigenous peoples and landless rural workers are an indispensable, not incidental, part of this process.[5]

Such a legacy represents a pressing challenge for Lula da Silva's second government. While seeking to advance social policies to address poverty, with Marina Silva as Environment Minister, the government have also launched an Action Plan to protect Indigenous communities and stop deforestation in the Amazon by 2030.[6] Whether such measures will be compromised in the face of a powerful backlash from an opposition-dominated Congress heavily representing the interests of agribusiness, and by the government's own large-scale infrastructure projects, remains to be seen.[7] In May 2023, the Brazilian Congress has also launched a Parliamentary Commission of Inquiry into the MST. The MST believe that the intention is to criminalise their 40-year-old popular movement.[8]

Such a move demonstrates the MST's power in contesting the oligarchical hold of large landowners in many parts of Brazil. Since its foundation in 1985, the MST has grown into one of Brazil's biggest and most successful social movements.[9] It is also a founder and the largest affiliated organisation within the international peasant and agricultural workers' network, La Via Campesina. Through the MST, rural workers have successfully established settlements and taken control of agricultural production in many areas. In this way, the organised mass movement put forward a counternarrative and achieved sufficient counterpower enabling it to survive the Bolsonaro government's ideological hostility.

While the Brazilian constitution makes provision for the redistribution of land deemed to be unproductive, challenges to dominant land ownership are highly contentious. Despite such legal concessions, land is rarely won without confrontation with both private landowners and state authorities. To establish claims on land, MST members set up encampments and undertake occupations, which, if successful, may evolve into longer-running settlements. In keeping with MST principles, families work land settlements with secure tenure under usufruct arrangements, while ultimately remaining in public ownership.[10]

The MST is committed to agroecology and has robust conservation policies concerning ecologically sensitive areas, including a policy of "zero deforestation" in the Amazon and Cerrado.[11] Other aspects of the MST's platform make it compatible with the principles of social ecology, and it has connections to the Network for the Alternative Quest, a major gathering of Kurdish freedom supporters in Europe, with which it shares a common programme—for example, in the ambition to "democratize the land."[12] The MST enjoys devolved democratic decision-making processes and structures and a collective leadership. Women have a strong voice; each MST encampment coordination committee must have a man and a woman as co-chairs and send one of each as co-representatives to any higher forums to which it is connected.[13] A radical educational programme is also delivered through more than 1200 schools across the settlements.[14]

Inevitably, in an era of ascendent neoliberal values, such a social-oriented and politically conscious organisation faces both external threats and internal pressures. Outright conflicts over land escalated during the Bolsonaro era.[15] Marlon Sanches and Eluza Gomes stressed that one of Bolsonaro's main goals was the "dismantling" of the MST education system on the agricultural settlements.[16]

In addition to state hostility, global forces and differing priorities represent further challenges to the MST's declared objectives. Food production on the settlements typically combines the cultivation of commercial crops for sale on the market, with some subsistence growing to support families and the immediate community. Continuing dependence upon commercial sales makes the cooperatives subject to the ruthless competition of the capitalist economy and vulnerable to the vacillations of market forces. The cooperatives' collective power ensures some advantages, such as sharing machinery and economies of scale. Furthermore, setting up communal kitchens and linking to schools and health centres creates symbiotic relationships for mutual aid and solidarity, with some stability between suppliers and consumers.[17] Nevertheless, the imperative to secure steady profits in competition with subsidised agribusiness creates tensions with the MST's principles of political and economic autonomy.[18] Wendy Wolford's fieldwork suggests a further mismatch between the political ideals of the MST's platform and influential thinkers, and the more pragmatic motivations of grassroots members, who may not, for example, share a commitment to the programme for land reform or methods of agroecology.[19]

Nonetheless, the MST continues to be a powerful force for profound transformation within Brazil and an inspiration as Latin America's largest mobilisation for resistance against land grabbing by large landowners and multinational corporations. By successfully achieving land rights, the MST has been able to secure livelihoods and productive work for thousands of otherwise destitute and marginalised rural workers. Commentators have pointed out that, in contributing to socially necessary agricultural work, the movement has boosted the well-being and esteem of food producers. Collective action through the occupations has given rural workers renewed agency in their lives, enabling them to realise and express a sense of fulfilment, dignity, and citizenship.[20]

Kleingärten

Europe lacks organised movements for collective land access on a comparable scale, but popular urban growing merits attention for its social impact and productivity.[21] There is increasing evidence that most demand for vegetables could be met by cultivating spaces within urban conurbations.

Patchworks of Kleingärten (literally "little gardens") are a familiar sight when travelling by train across central Europe, especially in Germany, but also Austria, Poland, Switzerland, the Czech Republic, and beyond. In Germany, the most common variety, Schrebergärten, are distinguished from English allotments by their summerhouses, whereas at best only a toolshed is permitted in England; they are also of a more generous size, which is typically around 300 m².[22] The mass provision of the eponymous Schrebergärten is particularly associated with the influence of Daniel Gottlob Moritz Schreber (1808–1861) in the nineteenth century. It is estimated that there are a million Schrebergärten in Germany, with five million gardeners.[23] Since the sea is a far-distant prospect for many in central Europe, the Schrebergärten function as mini resorts, retreats to recuperate—inland equivalents, perhaps, of the plotland chalets and bungalows appearing, historically, in clusters along the English coast.

The phenomenon of the Schrebergärten has a particular, and debated, cultural resonance since it has been associated with a socially conservative mindset. German plotholders have been widely mocked as *Laubenpieper* (bower pipits), for obeying directories of local and national rules and restrictions that micromanage the space, for kitsch taste, and for their conformism and individualism.[24] Nonetheless, the backstories behind these diverse forms of urban gardening tell of contested origins and ideological eclecticism. The plotholders, with their managed profusion of greenery, are sometimes a source of suspicion as a troublesome bastion of "awkwardness" from the point of view of the authorities that host them.[25] In recent years, ecologically motivated social activists have adopted more collective forms of urban gardening. The Kleingärten are fascinating examples of popular access to land under democratic governance, contributing to local food plenty.

Assessed according to social-ecological criteria, access to Kleingärten makes an appreciable contribution to fresh food availability and, overall, seems to have a positive impact on sustainability and social justice. These factors are determined by the garden type and the ever-changing circumstances of their neighbourhood locations. However, a cultivated site's duration will be subject to fluctuations in land value, the degree of demand from local people, ecological and climatic conditions, and political attitudes. We learn from human geographers such as Henri Lefebvre and David Harvey that all places have become contested spaces. In this respect, the historic and contemporary impact of Kleingärten has been contradictory. The Schrebergärten have been a mechanism of social control, implemented during the process of industrialisation to reproduce feudal social relations between landowners and rural workers in the urban environment, and intended to thwart growing liberal and socialist ideas by buying off dissent.[26] In this context, Daria Lynch concluded that while the gardens offered respite from the harsh realities of work and poor housing, this was coupled with a rigorous regime imposed on the allotments to discipline working-class bodies, and that they represented "theatres of control of the forces of capitalism and bourgeois values."[27]

Such scepticism as to the role of Schrebergärten is undoubtedly well founded when linked to the spirit of Bismarck's welfare provision, a reform package intended to undermine revolutionary aspirations. However, such an oppressionist account of tenants as victims of control tends to underplay workers' agency, and to overlook segmentation and conflicting perceptions within classes. If the provision of Kleingärten was intended to buy off support for the Social Democrats, it was often unsuccessful, since, as Micheline Nilsen finds, the associations that ran them were frequently left-leaning. Involvement in allotment administration more generally functioned as a "forum for political education."[28] By contrast to their conservative role, therefore, a satirical piece, written in 1914, plays on bourgeois property owners' alarm about the gardening movement, fearing the green plots were a front for red plotters:

[Social Democrats] begin with the Schrebergärten and with shacks, and then they want gardens with villas, and in a few years they will want palaces and we shall become servants and serve them. Whoever is for true freedom, must fight against them. However, not simply we men of politics but also friends of nature should defend ourselves. If there were ever garden cities everywhere, what would that mean, gentlemen? What would we see in these gardens?: red roofs and red window crossbars, in front red carnations and roses, red poppies at the gable, red cabbage in the vegetable garden and in the trees they would suffer only red robins.[29]

The emergence of a new generation of urban gardens in Germany, outside of the constraints of the German Allotment Garden Federation, again connects the Kleingärten to a potential role in advancing social change. There has been a rapid growth in collectively managed and worked community garden projects in recent years, usually created due to ecological motivations. However, while these intentionally have democratic processes embedded in their governance, the traditional Schrebergärten enjoy greater popular participation since they are vastly more numerous.[30]

Encroaching gentrification also threatens the future of community assets, including all kinds of green spaces. The irony is familiar. The reclamation of underused buildings and wasteland for cultural projects creates more desirable neighbourhoods, which in turn draw in construction schemes that develop and erase the features that made them attractive in the first place, ultimately displacing low-income tenants. Human geographer Marit Rosol traces an emancipatory tradition, in part also inspired by the dynamic community gardens movement in New York and other American cities from the early 1970s onwards.[31] While recognising that "even the most well-meaning projects can become engines of gentrification," Rosol takes the argument further in her insightful analysis of Kleingärten, identifying some intensified elaborations of this process. She observes, alongside several other commentators, that, uncannily, forms of voluntary community governance, such as those undertaken by urban gardeners, may have an unsettling resemblance to the neoliberal governance that they typically oppose.

To avoid such "traps and limits," Rosol calls for research into the specific contexts and effects of urban gardening; and for urban gardeners, as practitioners and activists, to be critically aware. Given the radically unequal legacy of decades of neoliberalism, it is clearly wise to be cautious about voluntary projects that subsidise unjust allocations of the commonwealth with free labour on land of precarious claim. If power without responsibility is unconscionable, responsibility without power is also problematic. In any case, as the food crisis worsens, it will be increasingly necessary to make productive use of urban or "peri-urban" land for local self-provisioning.[32] Such will be grounds to assert political claims for immediate human needs above empty office buildings and wasted land, without waiting for a benign and sympathetic central administration to intervene positively. In this sense, it is wise to activate urban gardening as a collective form of commoning that transcends the atomisation of communities into clusters of individuals.

It is also necessary to consider the yields produced on the Schrebergärten. Systematic records of yields do not appear to exist, and in general, yield data for urban growing spaces and relating to nutritional needs is limited.[33] It would, therefore, be helpful to make some estimates.

Kleingärten are fine examples of people's growing spaces, and it's always a great pleasure to visit our friend Karen Tiedtke's chalet garden in Berlin's Weissensee district. Karen has shared the following:

> I don't think statistics on yields for Kleingärten officially exist, but you could work out an average. Plots are usually around 300 m² with a hut measuring max 30 m². Rules stipulate that at least one third of the area be used for growing fruit and veg, and that at least one tenth must be vegetable plots. Most

people will have fruit trees, berries, rhubarb, etc. and then a plot for growing annuals. Optimum use of space allows for quite good yields, I've noticed.[34]

The comments from another contact in Germany also suggest the lack of regular data and the variability of output:

> We intend to gather data on our yield, but due to a major change in the market garden team, we couldn't collect numbers that are representative. Hopefully, this or the next year will provide better numbers for our statistics. From 2022, I only got some numbers for pumpkin (2 kg/m²) & potatoes. Some top varieties of potato produced up to 2 kg per plant. A top potato variety (Lunarossa)[35] in 2021 had an outcome of 6 kg/m² while other, less well-adjusted varieties stayed below 1 kg/m².[36]

In the absence of official statistics, to arrive at a rough estimate for the average production per person per annum for urban areas in Germany, I pieced together the following data:

1,000,000 Schrebergärten in Germany.[37]

225 m² as the average area of plot under cultivation.[38]
1.8 kg/m², estimated weight of fruit, vegetables, and potatoes produced.[39]

Thus, approximate total yield of all German Schrebergärten:
1,000,000 × 225 m² × 1.8 kg = 405,000,000 kg

The population of Germany is approximately 84 million.[40]
Of these, around 65,000,000 people live in urban areas (that is, approximately 78% of the total population).[41]
405,000,000 kg (total yield) ÷ 65,000,000 (total urban population) = 6.23 kg

In Germany, Schrebergärten produce 6.23 kg fruit, vegetables, and potatoes per person living in urban areas per annum.

Each individual Schrebergärten produces on average:
225 m² × 1.8 kg = 405 kg per annum.
405 kg ÷ 3 people = 135 kg per person per annum.

According to my speculative calculations, based on estimated data available, Schrebergärten could supply 6.23 kg per person for all urban residents. This represents only a modest proportion of the diet of Germany's three million urban dwellers—just under 5% of recommended intake. However, each individual Schrebergärten substantially meets the needs of those with access to them. Current National Health Service advice follows the World Health Organisation's guidance that adults should consume at least five 80 g portions of fruit and vegetables—that is, approximately around 400 g per person per day—obviously with variation for factors such as the crops cultivated, body mass, and age.[42] If the available data is reasonably accurate, and my calculations are correct, it suggests that a 300 m² Schrebergärten could provide fruit, vegetables, and potatoes for three people per year, at an allocation of 135 kg per person, which would be just below the above requirements for around 146 kg per annum.[43]

An optimistic study by Lael Walsh et al. suggests that *potential* production for UK urban areas could be as high as 170–280 kg per person, exceeding the National Health Service recommendations.[44] Australian permaculture expert Kat Lavers reports producing an impressive 428 kg herbs, vegetables, fruit, and eggs from her 280 m² plot, of which 100 m² is used for growing food.[45] By contrast, for all its fanfare, the *Reaping Rewards* report on a London-wide initiative could report only an average of 492 g per m²—a yield of only 110 kg per person per growing season.[46] These widely differing figures should clearly be treated with caution due to many negative and positive variables—for example, crop types, labour and material inputs, amount of waste, and the risk that some plots may be lost to development. However, it could be that my figure is an underestimate, because there may be many more Kleingärten that are not members of the national Schrebergärten association, or there could be scope to extend these and community gardens.

There is also potential to expand the use of domestic gardens, vertical horticulture, and city farms to increase production in urban areas. Furthermore, a recent study by Simone et al. concludes that Berlin could largely meet the demand for vegetables if non-traditional spaces, such as rooftops and cemeteries, were to be cultivated. They suggest that up to a quarter of current car parking spaces may become available, freeing up land currently reserved for private vehicles and supporting infrastructure, if ambitious policies to "prioritize eco-mobility" are successful.[47]

Undertaking research based on the UK, Miriam Dobson et al. have also proposed that identifying and restoring underused land to create more accessible growing spaces is possible and could make a valuable contribution to fruit and vegetable provision in Europe's urban centres.[48] Not only would this be a heartening prospect to augment home-grown food production, but it would also bring about an uplift in well-being associated with living in greener surroundings. But urban residents must have access to growing spaces.

Access to growing spaces

If we wish to grow more food and improve its allocation, it is necessary to extend access to land in a democratic way. Struggles even to ramble, picnic, camp, and swim in the countryside have been hard fought, but only to the point where public access applies to a mere 8% of land in England and Wales.[49] We have a long journey to achieve commoning for use of the land to which people are excluded, and to enjoy usufruct rights to put it to better purpose. At the same time, we need to reduce under-utilised land to boost production and space for rewilding in the context of an increasing population, projected to reach 71 million by 2045.[50] The challenges are considerable to produce more plentiful quality food, of more variety, both in the countryside and urban areas.

Unfortunately, access to allotments as a key form of food provisioning in urban areas has declined by an estimated 65% from its mid-twentieth-century peak to 2016, with the most food-deprived areas taking the biggest hit.[51] Here in Bristol, long waiting lists for municipal allotments have led to a trend towards privatised provision, costing £20 per month and a £50 joining fee for a 36 m^2 plot. While the extension of growing space is to be welcomed, disappointingly, such private initiatives risk limiting affordability rather than promoting access for all during a cost-of-living crisis. More inclusively, a council allotment of up to 74 m^2 costs £30 per year (or £15 per annum with low-income discount) with a £15 application fee.[52] Extending urban food production is challenging when commercial and municipal infrastructure, housing, public buildings, shops and community assets, private and public transport, other greenspaces such as parks, recreational grounds, and even nature reserves compete for land. In addition to the significant demand for such purposes, other factors that impact upon making use of growing spaces are insecure tenure, contamination of available sites, that many people are time poor or may lack knowledge about horticulture, or that material essentials such as tools and seeds are expensive or inaccessible.

There are solutions, however. Dobson et al. make the case that even in the crowded modern city, there is scope and potential for the widespread restoration of growing spaces. Such potential has been demonstrated, for example, by London's Capital Growth project, which saw the creation of 2012 new growing spaces as a legacy of the Olympic Games in the year 2012.[53] Less officially, householders, and perhaps longer-term tenants, may also be able to take up concrete and otherwise clear space in domestic gardens to grow more food, with additional benefits such as reduced flood risks and increased biodiversity, enjoying an immediate impact without having to await permission or policy changes. Others, informally exercising their "right to the city," exploit and expand gaps within and beyond the capitalist economy by, for example, clandestine guerrilla gardening or occupying vacant urban sites.

The Mountford Growing Community is a modestly scaled but inspiring project that demonstrates how cultivating an urban space and nurturing a sense of belonging can be mutually supportive sets of activities. Coordinator Rose Gibbs was prompted to set up the community garden in inner-city east London in 2016.[54] The aims were to cooperate with neighbours to "work together and gain greater autonomy over our immediate environment," and to "foster greater social cohesion in resistance to the prevalent racist hostility" (at the time of the divisive Brexit referendum). Rose summarised the key motivating factors as follows:

> To foster and nurture a greater sense of belonging within the estate, to mitigate language barriers through shared activity of gardening where physical tasks predominate, to grow foods and plants that residents use in their cuisines, to green our estate so that it reflects the desires of the residents, to create a shared space that feels more like home.

It was initially necessary for the Mountford gardeners to request that the local Council refrain from strimming and removing plants residents had cultivated to improve their estate, and to seek to reclaim a disused car park.[55] Eventually, and more positively, the Tenants' and Residents' Group were able to cooperate with the council and secured modest support from the Greater London Authority and Friends of the Earth to supplement their fundraising activities.

In addition to the residents' maintenance work, schoolchildren contribute to the project through a twice-weekly "garden classroom" facilitated by Rose. Pensioners have more time to contribute regularly:

My Kurdish neighbour Guzede is the most prolific gardener—she has grown trees from seed and transformed the space outside her home. She makes quantities of dolma and lots of delicious food. Many of my Turkish and Kurdish neighbours grow vines for dolma, making various preserved foods—crystalised aubergine and walnut.

Since gardening can progress as a non-verbal activity, it has been found to have been perfect for enabling members of the multicultural community to work together in a way that transcends barriers of language. This social diversity is reflected in impressive botanical diversity, combining heirloom English orchard fruit with overseas plant varieties. A collaborative cookbook, published to share culinary know-how and raise funds, celebrates these heritages.[56] Such initiatives show how unproductive, ecologically depleted spaces can be transformed into spaces yielding not only colourful and tasty plants but also valuable social harvests.

Such individual and interstitial projects can make welcome contributions to horticulture. It is essential, however, that ambitious social programmes to promote participatory democracy and municipal control in both urban and rural areas are undertaken to scale across to a thoroughgoing transformation of the relationship between local populations and the land as a primary means of production of food and other social necessities. Localist solutions are potentially far more powerful when they are coordinated with a conscious pathway for change through community and regional initiatives, connected into a mutually supportive confederation. In this way, counterpower can be built through an alliance of complementary organisations of a kind envisioned by Symbiosis, an American network much influenced by social-ecological ideas.[57] Similarly, in the UK and Ireland, the Transition Towns network was founded in 2006 to promote local actions relating to food and energy to address climate change. It has since developed from constellations of community activism starring such green-thinking centres such as Kinsale, Totnes, Stroud, and Lewes, towards

ACCESS TO LAND AND USUFRUCT

bridging local initiatives with the wider European municipalist movement.[58]

Freeing up land for growing spaces also causes us to reflect upon rival demands upon land that are partly outside the current discussion's remit, although matters of social organisation such as housing and transport are intimately connected. Existing housing development programmes all too often fail to address deficits where supply is most acute, while encroaching upon green field sites with the loss of productive land or wildlife habitats that this entails. The challenge here is to seek sensitive social incentives to provide homes for all that are not top-down, but enable smarter use of existing housing stock, bringing back to fuller life buildings that are derelict, unoccupied over the long term, second homes that are for the most part vacant, and even significantly under-used, yet sizable, single-occupancy dwellings.

Cultivating domestic gardens and other outdoor spaces currently under concrete, tarmac, or decking might not only contribute to urban and peri-urban food production, but also have additional benefits such as acting as mini carbon sinks and lessening flood risks by reducing surface water. This is, admittedly, often not seen as an attractive prospect for the time-poor, and for those who value hardstanding space as a premium for off-road car parking. More widely, and relatedly, private cars' demand for land in the urban environment is substantial. This is relevant nationally and internationally, since urban policy consultant Stefan Gössling observes that "the private car is the most space-intense transport mode," and that there are now likely in excess of a billion on the world's roads, with recent trends towards larger models.[59] In addition to enhanced public transport, solutions compatible with social ecology could include designing new vehicles for longevity, converting existing petrol vehicles to electric or green hydrogen, and placing them within community carpooling schemes, to proactively reduce numbers and liberate public space. Privatised and largely fossil-fuelled modes of transport are tightly locked into present systems, and clearly raise a complex of contentious issues such as personal interests and security, individual freedom versus social priorities, and hypermobility. Efforts to produce more food in built-up areas, therefore, are entangled with concerns relating to dominant housing and transport priorities, which, although beyond the present conversation, are immediately adjacent to it, due to the magnitude of demand that they represent. While long-term social resilience is enabled by, and depends upon, green spaces for food production and forms of outdoor recreation, availability and access to growing spaces must be asserted in the face of powerful rival claims.

Notes

1. Figures from Brazilian sources cited in Karina Kato and Fabrina Furtado, with Orlando Aleixo Junior and Jessica Siviero, *Global Financial Funds, Land Grabs, and the (Re)Production of Inequalities: A Contribution from Brazil*, The Land Inequality Initiative Case Study (Rome: International Land Coalition, 2020), 9. According to the Gini methodology, coefficient 0 represents complete equality and figures nearer to 1 representing least equality.
2. Leandro Vergara-Camus, "The Experience of the Landless Workers Movement and the Lula Government," *INTERthesis* 2, no. 1 (2005), 3–4: https://doaj.org/article/7c2fac8943e0419aa0529f6664ad6e33; Wendy Wolford, "This Land Is Ours Now: Spatial Imaginaries and the Struggle for Land in Brazil," *Annals of the Association of American Geographers* 94, no. 2 (2004), 411: https://doi.org/10.1111/j.1467-8306.2004.09402015.x.
3. Brazilian sociologist Daniel Bin's account of the centrality of widespread land dispossession to dictatorship policies notes that a leading military "idealist" had yearned to push the exploitation and development of natural resources to the extent that they "inundate the Amazon forest with civilization": "Agricultural Dispossessions During the 1964–1985 Brazilian Dictatorship," *Political Geography* 84 (2021): https://doi.org/10.1016/j.polgeo.2020.102307.

4   John Wilkinson, "The Globalization of Agribusiness and Developing World Food Systems," 155–169 in *Agriculture and Food in Crisis: Conflict, Resistance, and Renewal*, eds Fred Magdoff and Brian Tokar (New York: Monthly Review Press, 2010), 160–163; Kato and Furtado, Global Financial Funds, Land Grabs, and the (Re)Production of Inequalities, 11.
5   Claudia Horn, "In Northern Brazil, Landless Families Resist to Persist," *NACLA Report on the Americas* 53, no. 4 (2021), 344–348, https://doi.org/10.1080/10714839.2021.2000760.
6   Al Jazeera on the Action Plan for the Prevention and Control of Deforestation in the Amazon, "Brazil's President Lula Unveils Plan to End Deforestation by 2030," Al Jazeera website (6 June 2023): https://www.aljazeera.com/news/2023/6/6/brazils-president-lula-unveils-plan-to-end-deforestation-by-2030.
7   Al Jazeera, "Brazil's Congress weakens environmental, Indigenous ministries," Al Jazeera website (1 June 2023): https://www.aljazeera.com/news/2023/6/1/brazils-congress-weakens-environmental-indigenous-ministries.
8   MST, "Installation of the CPI is another chapter in the offensive against MST," MST website (18 May 2023): https://mst.org.br/2023/05/18/installation-of-the-cpi-is-another-chapter-in-the-offensive-against-mst/.
9   Commentators usually cite the membership of the MST as approximately 1.5 million people, for example, B.M. Fernandes, "Territories of Hope: A Human Geography of Agrarian Politics in Brazil. *Environment and Planning E: Nature and Space* 6(3) (2022): https://doi.org/10.1177/25148486221135303.
10 Anthony Pahnke, "Institutionalizing Economies of Opposition: Explaining and Evaluating the Success of the MST's Cooperatives and Agroecological Repeasantization," *Journal of Peasant Studies* 42, no. 6 (2015),1096, https://doi.org/10.1080/03066150.2014.991720; Vergara-Camus, "Experience of the Landless Workers Movement," 17–18; María Elena Martinez-Torres and Federico Daia Firmiano, "Rural-urban Alliances for Community Development through Land Reform from Below," 153–170 in *Class, Inequality and Community Development*, ed. by Mae Shaw and Majorie Mayo (Bristol: Policy Press, 2016), 165n1.

11 Friends of the MST website, "II – Propose a New Program for Brazilian Agriculture," section of "Platform of Via Campesina for Agriculture," (26 May 2010): https://www.mstbrazil.org/content/platform-campesina-agriculture-0, accessed 17 June 2022.
12 Cassia Figueiredo Bechara (representative of the MST National Board of Direction), "Session VI: Democratic Modernity: Perspectives Ahead, Network for an Alternative Quest, Challenging Capitalist Modernity III," *Uncovering Democratic Modernity—Resistance, Rebellion and Building the New* (2017), 223: https://rojava.info/wp-content/uploads/2021/01/NetworkAQ-Challenging-Capitalist-Modernity-III.pdf.
13 Vergara-Camus, "Experience of the Landless Workers Movement," 11–12; Horn, "In Northern Brazil," 347.
14 George Meszaros, "Taking the Land into their Hands: The Landless Workers' Movement and the Brazilian State," *Journal of Law and Society*, 27, no. 4 (December 2000), 529: https://doi.org/10.1111/1467-6478.00166.
15 Horn, "In Northern Brazil," 346.
16 Marlon Sanches and Eluza Gomes, "The Role of Adult Education and Learning in the Landless Workers' Movement (MST) in Resisting the Impacts of the Election of the New President of Brazil, Jair Bolsonaro: A Case Study," 359–366 in *Proceedings of the 38th CASAE Annual Conference*, 1–4 June 2019, University of British Columbia, ed. John P. Egan (Ottawa: Canadian Association for the Study of Adult Education, 2019), 359.
17 Rosset, "Fixing our Global Food System," 197.
18 Vergara-Camus, "Experience of the Landless Workers Movement," 16–17.
19 Wendy Wolford, "Edible Ideology? Survival Strategies in Brazilian Land-Reform Settlements," *Geographical Review*, 86, no. 3 (July 1996), 460: https://api.semanticscholar.org/CorpusID:143379913; Wolford, "This Land Is Ours Now," 409–424.
20 Wolford, "This Land Is Ours Now," 415; Vergara-Camus, "Experience of the Landless Workers Movement," 8–11.

21 Although the French Confédération Paysanne, also a member of LVC, has affinities.
22 For an outline of the chief categories of urban gardening in Germany, see Darya Hirsch, Christian Meyer, Johannes Klement, Martin Hamer, and Wiltrud Terlau, "Urban AgriCulture and Food Systems Dynamics: Urban Gardening and Urban Farming of the Bonn-Rhein-Sieg Region, Germany," *Proceedings in System Dynamics and Innovation in Food Networks* (2016), 409: https://doi.org/10.18461/pfsd.2016.1646, accessed 24 July 2022; more than a hundred "variables" such as governance, ownership, tenure, and access are identified in N. Rogge, U. Frey, C. Strassner, I. Theesfeld, "Categorizing Urban Commons – Collective Action in Urban Gardens," 1st IASC Thematic Conference on Urban Commons (6–7 November 2015): https://dlc.dlib.indiana.edu/dlc/handle/10535/9963, Accessed 27 July 2022. Jan Turowski cites 200–400 m² in "The Schreber Garden: The Green Oasis for City Dwellers," *Cabinet Magazine*, Issue 6 Horticulture (Spring 2002): https://www.cabinetmagazine.org/issues/6/turowski.php. It is cited as 350 yd², according to Michael Leapman, "Take me to your Schrebergarten," in PHS, "The Times Diary," *The Times* (18 October 1976), 14: link.gale.com/apps/doc/CS235241298/TTDA?u=uwesteng&sid=bookmark-TTDA&xid=6daaf7e9 [accessed via *The Times Digital Archive*].
23 According to the *Bundesverband Deutscher Gartenfreunde* (German Allotment Garden Federation), cited by Maria Inês Cabral, "Urban Gardening in Leipzig and Lisbon," *Short Term Scientific Mission report* (2014), 5: https://www.researchgate.net/publication/269334351_Urban_Gardening_in_Leipzig_and_Lisbon, Accessed 23 July 2022.
24 Evelyn Gustedt, "Reflexions on Urban Gardening in Germany. *Challenges in Sustainability* 4, no. 1 (2016) 66: https://doi.org/10.12924/cis2016.04010063.
25 See Turowski, "The Schreber Garden."
26 Noted, for example, among the "unstated goals" of the German Red Cross Workers' Gardens in Micheline Nilsen, *The Working Man's Green Space: Allotment Gardens in England, France, and Germany 1870–1919* (Charlottesville: University of Virginia Press, 2014), 45.

27 Daria Lynch, "*Schrebergärten* in Imperial Germany: Bourgeois Anxieties and the Spatial Politics of an Agrarian Urban Landscape," http://writing.rochester.edu/celebrating/2019/Daria_Lynch.pdf.
28 Nilsen, *Working Man's Green Space*, 17.
29 [Hannes Müllerfeld], "Nieder mit der Gartenstadt!" *Gartenstadt* 8, no. 3 (March 1914): 57, cited by Teresa Harris, *The German Garden City Movement: Architecture, Politics and Urban Transformation, 1902–1931*, unpublished PhD thesis Columbia University (2012), 109–110: https://core.ac.uk/download/pdf/161439728.pdf [accessed 24 July 2022].
30 Rogge et al., "Categorizing Urban Commons," cite 337 urban gardens and 1.24 million allotments, 7; Evelyn Gustedt suggests a ratio of ~1:2, 218 in "Reflexions on Urban Gardening in Germany," *Challenges in Sustainability*, 4 (2016), 68: https://doi.org/10.12924/cis2016.04010063.
31 Marit Rosol, "Politics of Urban Gardening," 134–145 in eds Kevin Ward, Andrew E.G. Jonas, Bryon Miller, and David Wilson, *The Routledge Handbook on Spaces of Urban Politics* (London: Routledge, 2018), 135. In more recent years, Detroit has become a hotbed of grassroots urban growing initiatives.
32 Landworkers' Alliance, "Fringe Farming," [2023] LWA website: https://staging.landworkersalliance.org.uk/fringe-farming/, accessed 2 August 2023.
33 A helpful attempt is Darren R. Grafius, Jill L. Edmondson, Briony A. Norton, Rachel Clark, Meghann Mears, Jonathan R. Leake, Ron Corstanje, Jim A. Harris, and Philip H. Warren, "Estimating Food Production in an Urban Landscape," *Scientific Reports* 10, no. 1 (20 March 2020), 5141: https://doi.org/10.1038/s41598-020-62126-4.
34 Karen Tiedtke, Schrebergärten tenant in Berlin, personal correspondence with author, 9 August 2022.
35 The Lunarossa is a high-yield red-skinned potato variety: Danespo, "Lunarossa," https://www.danespo.com/english/varieties/varieties/all-varieties/lunarossa, accessed 23 July 2023.
36 Matthias, *Waldgartenprojekt / FoodForest Pilot Berlin*, personal correspondence with author, 8 January 2023.
37 *Bundesverband Deutscher Gartenfreunde* (German Allotment Garden Federation), cited by Cabral, "Urban Gardening in Leipzig and Lisbon," 5.

38   That is 300 m², less 10% for chalet (according to Tiedtke's estimate), and less 15% to account for space taken up by other uses such as flowers, lawn, and paths. These dimensions are slightly larger than a standard tennis court for singles.

39   A calculation relating to yield data from a citizen science initiative in Leicester, in the absence of an aggregate figure for equivalent plots in Germany. Jill L. Edmondson, Dylan Z. Childs, Miriam C. Dobson, Kevin J. Gaston, Philip H. Warren, and Jonathan R. Leake, "Feeding a City – Leicester as a Case Study of the Importance of Allotments for Horticultural Production in the UK," *Science of The Total Environment* 705 (2020): https://doi.org/10.1016/j.scitotenv.2019.135930.

40   Worldometer, "Germany population," (17 January 2023), based on Worldometer elaboration of the latest United Nations data: https://www.worldometers.info/world-population/germany-population/, accessed 17 January 2023.

41   Statista, "Germany: Urbanization from 2011 to 2021," (1 June 2023): https://www.statista.com/statistics/455825/urbanization-in-germany/, accessed 17 August 2023.

42   NHS Digital, "Health Survey England Additional Analyses, Ethnicity and Health, 2011-2019 Experimental statistics," (30 June 2022): https://digital.nhs.uk/data-and-information/publications/statistical/health-survey-england-additional-analyses/ethnicity-and-health-2011-2019-experimental-statistics/fruit-and-vegetable-consumption; based on guidance from World Health Organization, "Healthy Diet," (29 April 2020): https://www.who.int/news-room/fact-sheets/detail/healthy-diet.

43   Only slightly below the World Health Organization's recommended consumption of 400 g per day, adding up to 145 kg per person per year in FAO, "Fruit and Vegetables: Essential for Healthy Lives," (2021): https://www.fao.org/3/cb2395en/online/src/html/fruit-and-vegetables.html, accessed 17 January 2023.

44   Lael E. Walsh, Bethan R Mead, Charlotte A. Hardman, Daniel Evans, Lingxuan Liu, Natalia Falagán, Sofia Kourmpetli, and Jess Davies, "Potential of Urban Green Spaces for Supporting Horticultural Production: A National Scale Analysis," *Environmental Research Letters* 17, no. 1 (2022) DOI: 10.1088/1748-9326/ac4730.

45 Happen Films, "Inspiring Woman Growing a Huge Amount of Food in Her City Permaculture Garden," YouTube video (23 February 2019): https://www.youtube.com/watch?v=Y9ZukMyejLk.
46 More positively, this is all on newly created growing spaces, set up as part of the Capital Growth initiative in the run up to the 2012 Olympic Games. There were wide discrepancies due to the diverse growing spaces with a variance of 338 g to 1.9 kg, and pilot sites achieving as much as 3.1 kg. Sustain, *Reaping Rewards: Can Communities Grow a Million Meals for London?* (July 2015): https://www.slideshare.net/JenniferParker9/reapingrewards.
47 Marion De Simone, Prajal Pradhan, Jürgen P. Kropp, and Diego Rybski, "A Large Share of Berlin's Vegetable Consumption can be Produced Within the City," *Sustainable Cities and Society* 91 (2023), 2: https://doi.org/10.1016/j.scs.2022.104362.
48 Miriam C. Dobson, Jill L. Edmondson, and Philip H. Warren, "Urban Food Cultivation in the United Kingdom: Quantifying Loss of Allotment Land and Identifying Potential for Restoration," *Landscape and Urban Planning* 199 (2020): https://doi.org/10.1016/j.landurbplan.2020.103803. My own city of Bristol currently has five-year waiting lists for municipal allotments.
49 Under the Countryside and Rights of Way Act 2000, according to Nick Hayes, *The Book of Trespass: Crossing the Lines that Divide Us* (London: Bloomsbury, 2021), 88–89.
50 Office for National Statistics, *National Population Projections: 2020-based Interim* (12 January 2022): https://www.ons.gov.uk/peoplepopulationandcommunity/populationandmigration/populationprojections/bulletins/nationalpopulationprojections/2020basedinterim.
51 Dobson et al., "Urban Food Cultivation in the United Kingdom."
52 A 2023–24 consultation by Bristol City Council proposing to implement substantial above-inflation price increases and intensive regulation has proved hugely controversial.
53 Sustain, *Reaping Rewards*.
54 The information and quotations in the following come from personal e-mail exchanges between Rose Gibbs and the author in 2022–2023.

55 A perfect example of a strategy for marginal urban communities to access land advocated by Terry Leahy, *The Politics of Permaculture*, FireWorks series (London: Pluto, 2021), 184.

56 Mountford Growing Community website: https://mountfordgrowingcommunity.org/, accessed 17 July 2023.

57 Symbiosis Research Collective, "How Radical Municipalism Can Go Beyond the Local," *The Ecologist* (8 June 2018): https://theecologist.org/2018/jun/08/how-radical-municipalism-can-go-beyond-local.

58 Municipalities in Transition homepage: https://municipalitiesintransition.org/, accessed 20 January 2023.

59 Stefan Gössling, "Why Cities Need to Take Road Space from Cars – And How This Could Be Done," *Journal of Urban Design* 25, no. 4 (2020), 443–444: https://doi.org/10.1080/13574809.2020.1727318.

FOOD SOVEREIGNTY AND ABUNDANCE THROUGH A SOLIDARITY ECONOMY

Food sovereignty in the United Kingdom

"Can Britain feed itself?" is an essential question. Simon Fairlie presents one of the most engaging and valuable attempts to address this issue in *The Land* magazine. Inspired by Kenneth Mellanby's 1975 book *Can Britain Feed Itself?*, Fairlie's rough calculations lead him reassuringly to conclude that the answer is still yes, and could remain so, even with a substantially larger population than present.[1] Yet this single question leads to multiple supplementary questions, such as those relating to land use, inputs, types of production, nutritional balance, patterns of consumption, and many other factors.

Let us first consider the UK's mixed circumstances regarding food. It is still a relatively wealthy nation (the fifth wealthiest by national net wealth, but lower by other economic measurements) and so supposedly easily able to feed its population.[2] But food issues are complex, and malnutrition has increased in recent years.

Malnutrition has three principal, partially overlapping, causes: underlying health conditions that affect the absorption of nutrients, a lack of access to healthy food due to income and logistical factors, and the consumption of inappropriate diet. To exaggerate the point, we could, of course, quickly meet our quantitative calorific needs with chips and doughnuts, but no one would seriously claim that such a diet would meet our nutritional needs. The impact of the global fast-food diet has become controversial, yet even more prevalent, since critics such as Eric Schlosser and Morgan Spurlock highlighted its contribution to malnutrition at the start of the millennium.[3] An adequate diet demands, of course, not just sufficient calorific intake but a balanced nutritional regimen incorporating the main food types: carbohydrates, proteins, fats, fibre, water, and micronutrients (vitamins, and minerals). The lack of micronutrients such as iron, vitamin A and iodine is the most common cause of malnutrition, while the planet does not currently produce enough fruit and vegetables to meet global demands for these critical food types.[4]

Affordability and class are major considerations in ensuring that people have access to a healthily balanced diet and are sufficiently informed to understand basic nutrition. Failures in wealth distribution are reflected in deficiencies in the distribution of, and ability to prepare, good quality food.[5] The appearance and widespread growth of food banks since the 2008 Financial Crisis is a visible indicator of the difficulties now facing many vulnerable households.[6] Tim Benton and Helen Harwatt note the challenges in supplying agreed international standards of healthy food to the global population using sustainable horticulture, given that an assessment based simply on calorific needs may be inadequate to supply the nutritionally balanced diet required to support human health.[7]

Britain uses approximately 70% of its land area for food production, while importing at least half of its food. It is not likely or even desirable that Britain will produce all its food domestically, especially tropical fruits. Nevertheless, there is a significant gap between complete self-sufficiency and 50% self-sufficiency, and, bluntly, it is not good enough to depend upon an ecologically unsustainable land footprint and neo-colonial trade relations to meet the population's needs.

The agricultural land of England, Wales, and lowland Scotland is roughly divided between the areas suitable for arable farming, largely in the south and east, mixed farming in central regions, and pasture lands in Wales and the West Country.[8] The pasture lands are currently mostly used for grazing ruminants and account for a quarter or more of UK land use.[9] Ruminant digestion ("enteric fermentation") is estimated to represent around 53% of the UK's greenhouse gas emissions.[10] Maintaining Britain's farm animals also requires additional imported grains and other fodder. It is understandable, then, that food and land reformers have paid pasture lands critical attention. However, even among those that wish to improve Britain's sustainability, the potential conversion of land use meets with several obstacles and there is controversy about alternative options. Advocates of a shift towards a more plant-based diet also acknowledge the cultural impediments that such a transition entails.[11] Furthermore, the meat and dairy industries represent strong vested interests, for the most part being advanced by the imposing National Farmers' Union, to maintain the status quo.

The substantially increased home production of more temperate fruit would seem to be a win-win strategy. We have already seen Green Tress's ambitious plans for tree-planting for ecological benefits and as food crops in Syrian Kurdistan. Unfortunately, it seems that British society's cultural fascination with food as entertainment for television and dining out does not extend, for the most part, to issues about the conditions and circumstances of its production and distribution. Yet, interest and pleasure in fruit trees may be turned to account once more.

As part of benign municipalist projects of the interwar period, council housing developed along garden-suburbs lines was accompanied by apple, pear, plum, and cherry saplings in the generous-sized gardens. While mulberry trees tend to be relics of earlier plantings, rare standards such as quinces and medlars are attracting fresh, if niche, interest. In Bristol, we planted many fruit trees when the Transition Town movement first sprouted in the late noughties. Perhaps we were guilty of that short-term "projectitis" that Tim Lang identifies, as local groups folded in favour of the following years' eco-trends.[12] Nevertheless, many urban trees were grown, as well as community orchards that continue to host wassailing, apple days, and other popular events.[13] Such spaces are an opportunity for the preservation of heritage trees, of which there are 270 varieties held at the nationally important East of England Fruit Collection in Norfolk.[14] The diversity can be enhanced further with free-range chickens, if a means can be found to protect them from foxes. In both urban and rural areas, however, access to growing spaces faces obstacles when higher-value uses and developments compete for land.

Diversification of production

There is no single, certain solution to food sovereignty, so here I am exploring and suggesting several routes. I have already called for the need to produce an increased quantity of food domestically, but also hinted that greater diversity would be welcome, encouraging something of a horticultural folk revival, through experimentation with traditional, often disappearing, varieties.

The greatest accomplishment and strength of life on Earth is its diversity and complexity. Ultimately, this applies to human food supplies too. As we have seen, Bookchin expressed hopes for developing highly diversified farming and railed against the perils of monotony and uniformity of production. In 1962, he warned that "Simplification of the landscape, followed by a diminution in the variety of fauna, creates highly favorable conditions for an infestation."[15] In the same year, Rachel Carson also objected to the dangerous trend towards the increasing removal of complexity from the living world:

> Nature has introduced great variety into the landscape, but man has displayed a passion for simplifying it. Thus he undoes the built-in checks and balances by which nature holds the various species within bounds.[16]

Since, despite wider recognition of this problem, the trend towards uniform monocultures and the narrowing of diversity has continued apace.[17] In *Eating to Extinction*, food journalist Dan Saladino regrets the loss of food diversity, noting that just nine plant species make up a large proportion of the global diet, while, historically, humans have eaten 6000 plant species. Echoing the concerns of Bookchin and Carson at the advent of the present-day ecology movement, Saladino deplores how "where nature creates diversity, the food system crushes it."[18]

In response to this loss of plenitude, the World Vegetable Center, based in Taiwan, has been promoting research on crop diversification for health and ecological benefits since 1971.[19] The emergence of ambitious seed bank projects—with the largest being the Millennium Seed Bank (a project of the Royal Botanic Garden, Kew, seeking to repurpose its colonial endowment) and the Svalbard Global Seed Vault—also addresses the problem.[20] Such genetic repositories offer a practical insurance policy to safeguard genetic diversity for future generations. However, there are no perfect solutions. Centralised facilities require expensive construction and securitisation measures to protect them against extreme circumstances, such as extreme weather events and conflicts.[21] Since seeds degrade over time, seed collections must have sufficient representative quantities of seeds of adequate quality and be routinely monitored, with many requiring repeat germination and collection to maintain their viability.[22]

While the urgent work of collection is making rapid progress, the majority of the world's plant diversity is yet to be collected. Since the seeds are preserved *ex-situ*, detached from their natural context, their situation is anomalous. This great bounty exists in a kind of exile from the ecological niche within which species evolved and thrive. If that niche is obliterated, where a unique soil type and microclimate are needed, the prospects for the species can be doubtful, even if siblings are cradled in a seed bank. For this reason, it is vital that such *ex-situ* preservation is complemented by strategies for *in-situ* conservation, looking after wild and domestic plant varieties in place, where necessary completing the circle of restoration.[23] This is done brilliantly and ambitiously in the UK through the Millennium Seed Bank Project, which, while based in Sussex, also connects distributed networks of seed banks around the world. The Global Seed Vault—an *ex-situ* seed bank in Svalbard, Norway—has already started to prove its value. Women refugees from the Syrian War have benefited from the withdrawal of some local plant varieties, originally deposited from Aleppo, germinating them in a farming restoration project in Lebanon.[24]

One of the most appetising initiatives to protect the living heritage of threatened species and varieties is the Slow Food Foundation's Ark of Taste. This is a project to create a "red list" of endangered regional foods.[25] The Ark of Taste lists more than 6000 foods, while an additional 600 products have been nominated for assessment.[26] Of the foods already aboard the Ark of Taste, 190 are from the regions of the United Kingdom. Read aloud, their names sound like a delicious incantation. In addition to such local specialties as Yorkshire forced rhubarb, the Dorset Blue Vinny and Kentish cobnuts, another 12 foods await evaluation to establish whether they meet the acceptance criteria for inclusion. Many culinary types considered "at risk" are varieties of orchard fruit and meat from rare breeds. From the Ark of Taste's menu, I would like to choose two varieties of largely lost and forgotten vegetables, now rediscovered, that are representative of my native West Country, namely martock beans and Wessex einkorn, and, also, feature a brief case example of the Bath asparagus.

First, I am selecting the martock bean for its resilience, since it is believed to be a landrace variety, one of the oldest recorded, and, also, was often dried so that it could sustain labourers with a source of protein through the harsh winter months.[27] As a legume, the plant would have had a valuable nitrogen-fixing role. While no longer grown commercially, martock beans are still available. Gardening enthusiasts who cultivate such living varieties help to preserve genetic diversity *in situ* and contribute to variety in diet. Such varieties also generate interest in food and horticulture through their contribution to cultural history.

Such arguments also apply to ancient grains, with renewed interest leading to small-scale efforts to revive their cultivation, and the complementary growth in artisanal baking, increasing in recent years. This reflects energetic campaigns underway, as dedicated growers have been cooperating to conserve surviving varieties through the Gaia Foundation's Seed Sovereignty programme, the James Hutton Institute's Living Field Project, and alliances of farmers and small businesses, such as the Cotswold Grain Partnership. Grains cultivated across the centuries—such as spelt, emmer, bere barley, and black oats—are being harvested and eaten in greater quantities in celebration of rediscovered agricultural heritage, while there are also experiments in growing overseas nutritional folk crops, such as quinoa and amaranth, in England.[28]

For the alternative agronomists behind such work, there is recognition of the importance of conserving biodiversity in respect of varieties as well as species. Among these venerable ancestors of modern wheat is einkorn. "Wessex einkorn" makes it into the United Kingdom section of the Ark of Taste because it is presently being cultivated on West Country farms, including Doves Farm, near Hungerford; and Lawn Farm, near Pewsey. Michael Marriage, Chair at Doves Farm, tells me they are growing a variety of einkorn from Germany that produces "800–1000 kg per acre," which is sold as flour.[29] Currently grown einkorn varieties are adapted varieties of a species believed to predate the Neolithic agricultural revolution, and to have been among the first cultivated and selectively bred in Mesopotamia. Archaeological evidence proves that, anciently, einkorn and emmer would have been grown in the region, since traces of the grains have been identified at Windmill Hill in Wiltshire.[30] The reasons to grow einkorn in the present day—despite its comparatively low yields, relative to modern wheat varieties—are, however, not merely nostalgic. While the world will not be fed on einkorn, the productive discrepancy is narrowed when other properties are taken into consideration. Einkorn is a survivor, having evolved across millennia to be disease-resistant. Furthermore, there is evidence that it has superior nutritional value when compared to more conventionally grown wheats, with greater micronutrient properties, substantially more protein, and, for the gluten intolerant, very low gluten content.[31] Smaller quantities of einkorn can be blended with other flours to enhance their overall nutritional value. There is a robust case, therefore, that ancient grain varieties such as einkorn not only have an impressive historic pedigree but significant culinary value for the future. Their survival and rediscovery can contribute to safeguarding genetic diversity and food security.

My final West Country speciality, the Bath asparagus, perhaps has a weaker claim to contribute to future nutritional needs. Nevertheless, it has a place in culinary history beyond its autotelic value, and shows the cultural worth of edible plants in establishing local distinctiveness and instilling a positive sense of place. Also known as spiked star of Bethlehem (Latin, *Ornithogalum pyrenaicum*) in England, Bath asparagus only flourishes around Bristol, Bath, parts of Wiltshire, and adjacent counties. Even here, the perennial, related to the bluebell, has been in decline. Increasing local scarcity prompted the Avon Wildlife Trust to set up a citizen science initiative for local people to survey the plant's frequency, and to launch the Bath Asparagus Project during the 1990s.

It is speculated that the Bath asparagus arrived with the Romans.[32] Once believed to have been grown commercially in the West Country, historic opinions differ as to its palatability as a food source. The Rev. John Collinson's account from 1791 was disparaging:

> The young shoots of it are eaten by the common people as asparagus, which it much resembles, but it is not very wholsome; for if eaten plentifully, it occasions nausea and oppression of the breath.[33]

A century later, the assessment of W.G. Wheatcroft was more neutral:

> *Ornithogalum pyrenaicum, L.*, grows so plentifully in woods and thickets near the city, that it may fairly be said to be extremely common. The young flower spikes of this plant, made up into small bundles, are sold in our market in the spring as "Bath Asparagus." It is a tender and eatable vegetable, but the writer has been unable to discover any great resemblance in flavour to the highly and deservedly esteemed plant, the name of which has been bestowed upon it by some Bathonians in the past and present. There may be room for differences in opinion in this as in other matters of taste.[34]

And the verdict of an unnamed commentator in the *Food Journal*, writing in 1873, was positive, concluding that

> Experiments made in the culinary direction have elicited the declaration that of all the substitutes for asparagus yet tried, this is the best.[35]

Once sold in local markets, the gastronomic story of Bath asparagus is not only a historical curiosity and does not quite end there. Oral histories record that it was eaten regularly up to the Second World War.[36] In recent years, given the enthusiasm for foraging for wild foodstuffs, there have been reports of the Bath asparagus appearing on the menus of West Country pubs and restaurants as local gourmet chefs have discovered the plant anew.[37]

Plants such as the Bath asparagus have an idiosyncratic charm, and if grown from seed or foraged with care, they make for culinary adventures. My own interest in sampling the hedgerow emporia of wild plants was kindled by such 1970s foraging classics as Richard Mabey's *Food for Free* (1972) and Bernard Schofield's *Urban Dweller's Country Almanac* (1978).[38] This DIY ethic continues in present-day foraging and organised seed-swapping events.[39] Widening the palate by tasting the almost infinite edible miscellany of wild harvests makes for a different kind of abundance with genuine variety, rather than the global standard diet with its perpetual rebranding of a narrowing range of processed foodstuffs. Furthermore, according to Tim Spector and his research team's large primary research studies, there are considerable health benefits from eating a wide-ranging and diverse diet with a weekly consumption of thirty different plant types to boost the chances of maintaining a "healthy gut microbiome."[40] While it would likely make a negligible impact upon self-sufficiency, an extension of consumption of traditional home varieties and wild plants could make a modest contribution to building resilience against diseases and extending the diversity of diets.

Commercial seed production, however, is big business. There are considerable legislative threats to the cultivation of heritage varieties and wild species, due to a regulatory framework that increasingly looks to constrain their propagation and exchange. While ostensibly this aims to ensure the quality and authenticity of horticultural seed, the sale and even swapping of varieties not registered on the National List (managed by the National Institute of Agricultural Botany) has become a semi-legal activity. While the prevailing legislation, the Plant Variations and Seeds Act of 1964, placed restrictions on what could be commercially grown, embedded concessions were deemed to offer small businesses and amateur gardeners some liberty to grow and circulate varieties not on the National List on a small scale, without risk of prosecution.

Controversially, though, subsequent legislative efforts have sought to place thoroughgoing legal obstacles to the small-scale cultivation of non-listed varieties.[41]

In 2014, the European Commission proposed the contentious "Plant Reproductive Material Law," which the European Parliament rejected.[42] More recently, the post-Brexit "Provisional UK Common Framework on Plant Varieties and Seeds" (2022) appears again to prioritise the intellectual property rights of the major seed companies, according them tight proprietorial control over all seed production, distribution, and cultivation.[43] Critics are again scrutinising the detail to see whether the measures potentially jeopardise the conservation and exchange of folk varieties grown for non-commercial purposes.

Controversies have ensued over whether such measures as restricted lists are necessary for quality assurance and to incentivise advances in plant breeding, or an unwarranted encroachment onto the horticultural commons, leading to a diminished gene pool of older varieties and threatening the existence of heirloom plant types. The new proposals may reignite the argument, since previous similar measures have met with stiff national and international resistance from an alliance of seed-sovereignty activists, amateur growers, LVC, and wider civil society organisations. Such critics fear that restricted lists of highly capitalised patented varieties will result in even tighter control of the market on the part of monopolistic multinational corporations, using scarcity of supply to reduce access, inflate prices, and further undermine the autonomy of traditional farmers and small-scale growers. There will be a watching brief on developments to ensure safeguards to protect access and the free exchange of varieties for amateur and small-scale producers, for whom costly annual registration fees would be prohibitive, are maintained.

The "National Food Strategy" cites some astounding figures relating to the narrowing of the availability of diverse foodstuffs, ironically in a free-market context whereby freedom of choice for the consumer is frequently and loudly proclaimed: "Currently, while

300,000 species of plant have edible parts, just 20 species account for 90% of the world's food, and three – wheat, maize and rice – supply more than half."[44] Conserving diversity remains the best strategy for having species and varieties that can adapt to changing climatic and geographical circumstances. Polyculture also hosts a greater range of insects and other invertebrates, and so encourages biodiversity. Attention to the extension of cultivated varieties and the preservation of wild species, therefore, matters for food security, enhances cultural diversity, and has important ecological benefits.

Notes

1   The UK population is projected to rise to around 69.2 million by the mid-2030s. See Office for National Statistics, National Population Projections: 2020-based Interim (12 January 2022): https://www.ons.gov.uk/peoplepopulationandcommunity/populationandmigration/populationprojections/bulletins/nationalpopulationprojections/2020basedinterim, accessed 6 September 2022.
2   World Population Review, "Richest Countries in the World," https://worldpopulationreview.com/country-rankings/richest-countries-in-the-world, [accessed 9 January 2023].
3   Eric Schlosser raised the profile of the issue in his hard-hitting *Fast Food Nation* (2001), while Morgan Spurlock memorably sought to expose the deficiencies and dangers of an exclusive McDonald's diet in the 2004 documentary *Supersize Me*.
4   World Health Organization, "Malnutrition," (9 June 2021): https://www.who.int/news-room/fact-sheets/detail/malnutrition; Sophie Hawkesworth, Alan D. Dangour, Deborah Johnston, Karen Lock, Nigel Poole, Jonathan Rushton, Ricardo Uauy, and Jeff Waage, "Feeding the World Healthily: The Challenge of Measuring the Effects of Agriculture on Health," *Philosophical Transactions of the Royal Society of London. Series B, Biological Sciences* 365, no. 1554 (2010), 3083–97: https://www.ncbi.nlm.nih.gov/pmc/articles/PMC2935110/; Daniel Mason-D'Croz, Jessica R. Bogard, Timothy B. Sulser, Nicola Cenacchi, Shahnila Dunston, Mario Herrero, Keith Wiebe, "Gaps Between Fruit

and Vegetable Production, Demand, and Recommended Consumption at Global and National Levels: An Integrated Modelling Study," *The Lancet Planetary Health* 3, no. 7 (July 2019): https://doi.org/10.1016/ S2542-5196(19)30095-6.

5   The contemporary UK has one of the worst ratios of income inequality in Europe, with the gap between the wealthiest and poorest households significantly wider than in the 1960s. In 2019–2020, the most recent year for which the figure has been calculated, it had a Gini coefficient of 39% after housing costs—data from Brigid Francis-Devine, "Income Inequality in the UK," *House of Commons Library* (30 November 2021): https://researchbriefings.files.parliament.uk/documents/CBP-7484/ CBP-7484.pdf.

6   In 2022, at least 2572 were recorded in the United Kingdom, according to Susannah Irvine, Aleksandra Gorb, and Brigid Francis-Devine, "Food Banks in the UK," *House of Commons Library* (14 July 2022), 4: https://researchbriefings.files.parliament.uk/documents/CBP-8585/ CBP-8585.pdf.

7   Tim G. Benton and Helen Harwatt, "Sustainable Agriculture and Food Systems: Comparing Contrasting and Contested Versions," Chatham House research paper for Environment and Society Programme (May 2022): https://www.chathamhouse.org/2022/05/sustainable-agriculture-and-food-systems, 32.

8   Alasdair Rae, "A Land Cover Atlas of the United Kingdom (Document)," The University of Sheffield. Journal contribution (2017), 5: https://doi.org/10.15131/shef.data.5266495.v1.

9   Rae suggests pastures make up just under 29% of the UK in "Land Cover Atlas of the United Kingdom," 5; The Trading Economics website cites 24.71% based on World Bank data for 2020: Trading Economics, "United Kingdom - Arable Land (% Of Land Area)" (July 2023): https://tradingeconomics.com/united-kingdom/arable-land-percent-of-land-area-wb-data.html, accessed 21 July 2023. This represents a small reduction from 24.96% figure for 2018, accessed on the same webpage 19 September 2022. The Utilised Agricultural Area for the UK decreased by 2.2% between 2021 and 2022, Department for Environment, Food and Rural Affairs; Department of Agriculture,

Environment and Rural Affairs (Northern Ireland); Welsh Government, Knowledge and Analytical Services; and The Scottish Government, Rural and Environment Science and Analytical Services, Agriculture in the UK 2022 (2023), 9: https://assets.publishing.service.gov.uk/government/uploads/system/uploads/attachment_data/file/1170953/auk-2022-13jul23i.pdf.

10 Climate Change Committee, "The Sixth Carbon Budget: Agriculture and Land Use, Land Use Change and Forestry," (2020), 6: https://www.theccc.org.uk/wp-content/uploads/2020/12/Sector-summary-Agriculture-land-use-land-use-change-forestry.pdf.

11 Centre for Alternative Technology, Zero-Carbon Britain, 43; Sajeev Mohankumar, Rebecca Martin, Christopher Waite, and Michael Norman, "Is the UK Ready for Plant-based Diets? Report produced for the Global Food Security Programme" (December 2020), available from www.foodsecurity.ac.uk/publications.

12 Tim Lang, *Feeding Britain: Our Food Problems and How to Fix Them* (London: Pelican, 2020), 23.

13 See Angela King and Sue Clifford, *Community Orchards Handbook*, rev. ed. (Shaftesbury: Green Books / Common Ground, 2011).

14 East of England Apples and Orchard Project website: https://www.applesandorchards.org.uk/about/the-east-of-england-fruit-collection/, accessed 9 January 2023.

15 Bookchin, *Our Synthetic Environment*, Chap. 2.

16 Rachel Carson, "Silent Spring – 1," *New Yorker* (16 June 1962): https://www.newyorker.com/magazine/1962/06/16/silent-spring-part-1.

17 For example, in World Wildlife Fund, "Land of Plenty," 9 and 20.

18 Dan Saladino, *Eating to Extinction: The World's Rarest Foods and Why We Need to Save Them* (London: Jonathan Cape, 2021), 144.

19 World Vegetable Center website: https://avrdc.org/, accessed 4 August 2023.

20 Xan Sarah Chacko, "Digging up Colonial Roots: The Less-Known Origins of the Millennium Seed Bank Partnership," *Catalyst: Feminism, Theory, Technoscience* 5, pt. 2 (2019): https://doi.org/10.28968/cftt.v5i2.31947. Rather than making botanical reparations for past extractive

policies, there is a risk that the corporate sponsorship of such invaluable collections may restrict the wider benefits for feeding the world.

21   A seed bank of world significance, the National Gene Bank of Plants of Ukraine survived, yet sustained damage, when it was shelled during a Russian military attack on Kharkiv in May 2022. The collection remains at risk for as long as the conflict continues. Michael Le Page, "Priceless Samples from Ukraine's Seed Bank Destroyed in Russian Attack," *New Scientist* (25 May 2022) [accessed via Nexis database, 11 October 2022].

22   This is a particular challenge for rare species, since it is recommended that fifty individual seed samples should be retained from fifty different sites. See A.H.D. Brown and A.R. Marshall, "A Basic Sampling Strategy: Theory and Practice," 75–91 in *Collecting Plant Genetic Diversity: Technical Guidelines*, eds Luigi Guarino, V. Ramanatha Rao, and Robert Reid (Cambridge: Cambridge University Press, 1995), 79: http://hdl.handle.net/102.100.100/232956?index=1.

23   Sara F. Oldfield argues that both *in-situ* and *ex-situ* measures are necessary, in "Botanic Gardens and the Conservation of Tree Species," *Trends in Plant Science* 14, no. 11 (2009), 581–583: https://doi.org/10.1016/j.tplants.2009.08.013.

24   A horticultural journey captured in *Wild Relatives* (2018), a documentary directed by Jumana Manna. Lutfia Rabbani Foundation, "Wild Relatives: A Discussion with Director Jumana Manna," Rabbani Talks series YouTube (14 June 2022): https://www.youtube.com/watch?v=SRzgsNmeCRo.

25   Saladino, *Eating to Extinction*, 10.

26   Slow Food Foundation for Biodiversity, "Ark of Taste," https://www.fondazioneslowfood.com/en/what-we-do/the-ark-of-taste/, accessed 15 August 2023.

27   Will Aslett, "(Vicia Faba 'Martock')," Martock Local History Group website: http://www.martockhistory.co.uk/research/bean.php [no date, accessed 21 January 2023].

28   Ollie Cem, "Growing Ancient Grains in the City: Growhampton," University of Roehampton website (22 January 2020): https://blog.roehampton.ac.uk/2020/01/22/growing-ancient-grains-in-the-city-growhampton/; Ione Maria Rojas, "The Smallest Giver of Life," in *With*

the Land: Reflections on Land Work and Ten Years of the Landworkers' Alliance ([s.l.] Landworkers' Alliance, 2023), 20–23.

29 Michael Marriage, personal e-mail to the author, 25 September 2023.

30 "A Research Framework for the Stonehenge, Avebury and Associated Sites World Heritage Site: Avebury Resource Assessment," compiled and edited by Matt Leivers and Andrew B. Powell, *Wessex Archaeology Monograph* 38 (2016), 31: http://www.stonehengeandaveburywhs.org/assets/Avebury-Resource-Assessment-part1-1.pdf. In 2015, there was a surprise discovery of einkorn DNA in the Solent, off the coast of the Isle of Wight, leaving archaeologists to ponder whether it was being imported from an area that falls within what is modern-day Italy, or whether it was being grown in southern England as early as c. 6000 BCE. See David Keys, "The Remarkable Archaeological Underwater Discovery that Could Open Up a New Chapter in the Study of European and British Prehistory; Scientific Tests Suggest that a Major Aspect of the Neolithic Agricultural Revolution may have reached Britain 2000 Years Earlier than Previously Thought," *The Independent* (21 February 2015) [accessed via Nexis database].

31 Fabiana Antognoni, Roberto Mandrioli, Alessandra Bordoni, Mattia Di Nunzio, Blanca Viadel, Elisa Gallego, María Paz Villalba, Lidia Tomás-Cobos, Danielle Laure Taneyo Saa, and Andrea Gianotti, "Integrated Evaluation of the Potential Health Benefits of Einkorn-Based Breads," *Nutrients* 9, no. 11: 1232 (2017): https://doi.org/10.3390/nu9111232.

32 Foregoing details from [P. Hackman?], [Avon] Wildlife Trust, "Bath Asparagus Project" [1995], Bath Records Office, archival record B582.13.

33 Rev. John Collinson, *The History of Somersetshire*, in three volumes (Bath: Crutwell, 1791), I, xx [accessed via Google Books].

34 W.G. Wheatcroft, *The Botany of the Bath District* (1888), 5 [accessed via Google Books].

35 *The Food Journal* (1 September 1873), 415 [accessed via Google Books].

36 D.J. Hill and B. Price, 363–364 in "Ornithogalum pyrenaicum L.," Journal of Ecology 88, no. 2 (April 2000), 354–365 [accessed via Jstor database].

37   For example, Anon., "Going Wild," *The Wiltshire Times* (14 March 2007): https://www.wiltshiretimes.co.uk/news/1258179.going-wild/, and several subsequent foraging blogs.

38   For the record, my copy of *Food for Free* was bought for me later in the 1970s, and I was not an urban dweller. The latter publication was an offshoot of Bernard Schofield and Andy Pittaway's charmingly bucolic underground magazine, *Country Bizarre*.

39   Here in Bristol, the annual seed swap is an important forum for sharing and germinating ideas as well as seeds, a gathering that has attracted food justice activists, permaculturists, and anyone interested in growing and eating, for more than 20 years: https://www.bristolseedswap.com/, accessed 15 August 2023. A much more recent and modest initiative is the innovative seed library hosted by Bishopston public library: https://bristolseedlibrary.wixsite.com/grow, accessed 15 August 2023.

40   Tim Spector, "Nutrition's Dark Matter: The New Science of Eating," *BBC Food Programme*, radio programme presented and produced by Dan Saladino (4 December 2022): https://www.bbc.co.uk/sounds/play/m001fvnx.

41   Ed Hamer's critical analysis gave a clear summary of the issues at stake, "Seeds of Resistance," *The Land*, 15 (Winter 2013–2014): https://www.thelandmagazine.org.uk/articles/seeds-resistance.

42   Janos Ader, "Commission Bows to Calls for Flexibility on CAP Delegated Acts," *Farming Life* (28 March 2014) [accessed via Nexis database, 25 January 2023].

43   Department for Environment, Food and Rural Affairs, Policy Paper: Plant Varieties and Seeds: Provisional Common Framework. How the UK Government and Devolved Governments Propose to Work Together in Policy Areas Covering Plant Varieties and Seeds (3 February 2022): https://www.gov.uk/government/publications/plant-varieties-and-seeds-provisional-common-framework; Practical Law Agriculture and Rural Land, "Provisional UK Common Framework on Plant Varieties and Seeds," [accessed via Practical Law database, 25 January 2023].

44   John Warren, *The Nature of Crops: How We Came to Eat the Plants We Do* (Wallingford, Oxon: CAB International, 2015), 2.

REGENERATIVE AGROECOLOGY

Permaculture

Permaculture is truly where the political meets the personal. Bill Mollison and David Holmgren first published the twelve principles of permaculture, their strategies for "soil regenerative" agriculture, in 1978. These drew upon traditional agroecological knowledges, the increasing interest in ecosystems ecology during the 1970s, and empirical research. They aimed to work holistically with nature to promote low-impact cultivation through careful observation of local ecological, geological, and climatic conditions.

Permaculturists aspire to ensure plentiful yields to feed an increasing world population, while reducing the negative ecological impact of food production and conserving—and ideally, restoring—biodiversity. As Essex permaculturist Graham Burnett stressed in a workshop I attended, "regenerative is always preferable to sustainable."[1] To optimise production, sound design is required to create differentiated and resilient systems. As both a philosophy and practice, permaculture shares common ground with social ecology, as Mollison's following appeal suggests:

The tragic reality is that very few sustainable systems are designed or applied by those who hold power, and the reason for this is obvious and simple: to let people arrange their own food, energy, and shelter is to lose economic and political control over them. We should cease to look to power structures, hierarchical systems, or governments to help us, and devise ways to help ourselves.[2]

It is to be expected, then, that several educators and activists connected to the Institute of Social Ecology have links to the permaculture movement, including Grace Gershuny, Eric Toensmeier, Beverly Naidus, Ana Ruiz Diaz, and Rafter Ferguson. While it does not set out a pathway for a transfer to democratic land ownership, or always even aspire to such an end, this is a common desire. Robert Hart, for example, the permaculturist who did much to popularise the idea of the forest garden in England, expressed admiration for "the decentralised, democratic, self-sufficient rural community."[3]

There are further synergies between concepts of permaculture, aiming to nurture complex growing systems sprouting from thriving polycultures of compatible species, and social structures of poly-governance, based on diversity. Permaculturist Terry Leahy has recently called for a self-critical practice that transcends the "charismatic foundationalism" of its white male instigators, by proactively embedding inclusive and decolonising practice. Such an approach foregrounds questions relating to access to land and the control of the means of production, with Leahy favouring common land ownership and a gifting economy, while providing an excellent analysis of the challenging economics of permaculture within a capitalist context.[4]

Above all, permaculture is not an abstract political programme but a solutions-focused and pragmatic effort to produce plentiful nutritious food through ecologically aware means. For Mike Feingold of Bristol Permaculture Group, there are three elements, namely ethical, attitudinal or philosophical, and design principles:

You start with yourself and take self-responsibility. You can change what you do in life. You might not be able to change Sunak's concepts or whether Trump will get back into power, those big systems. I can't change that. But what I can change is what *I* do. So, it's about taking lots of little steps to try and improve things. It's about working with nature and not fighting it.[5]

What working with nature means in practice is a matter of trial and observation, variability according to local circumstances, and sometimes contention. A significant difference in philosophy and practice relates to the inclusion of mammals and birds within design systems for sustainable growing.

Simon Fairlie draws a critical distinction between contrasting, if not necessarily mutually exclusive, versions of permaculture. Stock-free models of permaculture are mostly vegan and concerned with horticulture and silviculture. Graham Burnett identifies with the "veganic fork" in this divergence. Another symbiotic version is based on the incorporation of domesticated animals, making use of mixed-land types Fairlie memorably evokes as mosaics of light and shade for its combination of pastoral land and forests.[6] Taking inspiration from agroforestry pioneers such as Joseph Russell Smith and Toyohiko Kagawa, Robert Hart decisively moved away from the rearing and slaughtering of mammals and birds, due to what he considered "economic and humanitarian arguments," when he adapted and developed the idea of an edible forest garden in Shropshire.[7] Iain Tolhurst and Jenny Hall's pioneering experiments of "stockfree-organic" methods for sustainable horticulture are also explicitly vegan, and have had successful outcomes. Monbiot claims that Tolhurst has impressively enhanced his soil's fertility and "raised his yields until they hit the lower bound of what intensive growers achieve with artificial fertilizers on good land."[8]

It is essential to monitor whether quantitative and qualitative aspirations for food growing are being met effectively. Such mixed approaches and debates strengthen the case for further development and experimentation to advance permaculture. Permaculturists have long proposed, for instance, growing more perennial crops, due to their lower inputs of labour and fertilisers over time. Social ecologists Eric Toensmeier, Rafter Ferguson, and Mamta Mehra consider the benefits of perennial vegetables for human nutrition and biodiversity with respect to 613 cultivated varieties, noting that currently only 7–8% of agricultural land is given over to their production.[9] The production of fruit and nuts through forest gardening has been the primary consideration, alongside such established favourites as rhubarb, asparagus, and kale. In recent years, more attention has been given to the challenge of developing high-yield perennial grains. The Land Institute, a non-profit research organisation based in the United States, has been developing perennial grains since the 1970s. Monbiot regards such experiments as one of the most encouraging prospects for transitioning to a more sustainable agricultural system. There are several potential advantages—for example, reduced tillage, less inputs of fertiliser, and reduction in strenuous labour. The development of perennial grains through selective breeding of crops such as Kernza (intermediate wheatgrass) is likely to be an area of increasing interest.[10] The Experimental Farm Network is also already exploring the cultivation of perennial sorghum.[11]

More evaluation of the potential to scale across permaculture as a form of agroecology is called for. Whether sustainable growing is labelled permaculture or terms with other emphases are used, shifts towards more diversified and complex production, with careful observation, documentation, and comparison of the results is essential. This involves identifying and acknowledging weaknesses as well as approaches with potential for improvement. Above all, evaluating what works and what doesn't work in the private, community, and commercial sectors by connecting the proliferation of experimental initiatives through knowledge sharing could help to address the significant deficit between the funding and means available to the sustainable growers and the vast resources at the command of agribusiness enterprises. As we shall see, citizen science is a promising means to cultivate just such an intellectual commons for the better development and promotion of sustainable production.

The dark alchemy of human manure

A further proposal is for the better repurposing of human faeces and urine in food growing, energy production, and other uses. Stripped of the euphemisms and puns, there is much wisdom and goodness in the literature regarding human manure.[12] Because of the ubiquity and vast quantities of human bodily fluids and solids that are unfailingly produced, a scaling across of improvements in processing systems can have exponential regenerative benefits—if they enable management as a resource rather than as waste. Practically, solutions fall into two categories and are context dependent. These are use of human waste as an agricultural fertiliser, our main interest here, and conversion into an energy source—for example, through anaerobic digestion.[13] A transition to closed-loop systems for the recycling of human waste is essential to attain an ecologically coherent, circular economy. Yet the quest to perfect this transmutation has proven elusive.

Near to where I am writing, Sir Richard Harington invented the flush water closet at Kelston Manor. The sewage system Joseph Bazalgette implemented during the nineteenth century transformed public health, undoubtedly preventing thousands of premature deaths from waterborne diseases such as cholera and typhoid. Today, water closets remain a comfortable, hygienic, even stylish solution to waste management. However, freely accessible public toilets have become an endangered species and sewage systems are reportedly under severe stress. The ecological consequences of a disjointed system are unsatisfactory at every stage, from logistical disposal problems, to environmental pollution, to the failure to reintegrate the process so that waste becomes a resource.[14]

If we get the design right, enhanced systems for the collection and reuse of human waste could deliver multiple benefits:

- A sustainable source of fertiliser for horticulture, substituting energy-intensive manufactured or mined sources of nitrogen, potassium, and imported phosphorus.
- Disease prevention and improved public-health outcomes through better sanitation.
- Reduced sewage pollution in maritime, estuarine, and inland bodies of water and waterways.
- Better conservation of drinking water, which is typically wasted in flush systems.
- Improved public safety, especially for global majority women and girls.
- Valuable uses for sludge deemed to be too risky for use as fertiliser, such as electricity, biogas, and biochar through anaerobic digestion.

It is necessary, however, to consider the challenges and obstacles to advances in this area. The disposal or recycling of human waste is a contentious and emotive issue. There has been justified public hostility against perceived attempts to deregulate effective sewage management, thereby relieving privatised water companies of investment costs to reduce pollution. While landfilling and incineration are unsatisfactory, there have been serious concerns that current landspreading practices for sewage sludge are risky, given the presence of hazardous toxic contaminants.[15] The new policy paper *Environment Agency Strategy for Safe and Sustainable Sludge Use* supports an image makeover for sludge so that it is regarded as "a bioresource" rather than "an inconvenient waste," exploiting technical improvements in sludge treatment.[16] Nevertheless, the management of human sewage presents challenges due to the continued presence of traces of heavy metals and residues from oral contraceptives and antibiotics, accompanied by increasing levels of microplastics and more novel contaminants.

As sewage management has become a major political issue, the need to ensure that contaminants are neutralised when using sludge for agricultural purposes will be under much scrutiny. The use of human manure presents a particular quandary for organic production. It has been excluded from certification for organic and veganic food production due to potential residues of inadmissible contaminants. Hall and Tolhurst note the exclusion of human manure and urine but suggest a relaxation of the law for certified stockfree-organic systems, so long as the waste is carefully treated.[17] The Soil Association have recognised that problems of a deficit, as we near "peak phosphorus" in particular, can only be addressed by reintegrating most human sewage back into the agricultural system.[18]

Routine management through composting is viable in localised systems. Heat recovery systems, reed-bed filtration, and vermicomposting have all been used to treat sewage *in situ*, and mycoremediation—using fungi to decontaminate sewage sludge—is anticipated to have an increasingly helpful role.[19] Many modest-size houses with gardens could accommodate a homemade or commercially available compost toilet. Such conveniences could be phased in through new developments and incrementally retrofitted in place of, or addition to, flush toilets.

In highly centralised systems in urban areas, there are more logistical challenges, with much infrastructure and energy required to transfer the biosolids to the land where they are required in appropriate quantities for the needs of crops. The likely way forward is a combination of upstream solutions, entailing better waste management to reclaim potential nutrients through municipal infrastructure and local changes. Positively, more sophisticated methods for dealing with and monitoring toxic waste content are already being refined. Practically, the separation and use of more easily processed, and mostly sterile, urine as a source of phosphorus makes treatment much more effective and will be the easiest win. Using such separation, recent research on emerging methods in Germany is demonstrating highly effective and promising outcomes in the quest to balance the productive recycling of human waste with safety concerns respecting public health.[20]

There are potentially several significant wins here, yet currently there appears to be a lack of urgency in implementing change in the UK. This is due to a combination of political, economic, technical, and cultural obstacles. Any adjustment should seek to balance tighter control of the release of insufficiently treated and toxic sewage, while addressing barriers to the ecologically benign use of human waste. Human waste has an image problem. This must be overcome to move beyond the unwarranted and unsustainable loss of an invaluable resource. To achieve a transformation of the habitus relating to perceptions of ordure and urine is a formidable cultural task. It requires a reimagining from coprophobic associations with disgust as vectors of disease and as contaminants to precious elixirs of golden plant nutrients and phosphorus pearls as enriching fertilisers. Ecological sanitation demands a regenerative system to safely recycle sludge. Such a transformation is indispensable for any truly circular economy based on perpetual replenishment.

Notes

1   Graham Burnett, "Introduction to Permaculture," course held at Dial House, Epping, Essex (17–19 August 2018).
2   Bill Mollison, *Permaculture: A Designers' Manual*, 2nd ed. (Tyalgum, Aus: Tagari, 2002), 506.
3   Robert A. de J. Hart, *Forest Gardening: Rediscovering Nature and Community in a Post-Industrial Age*, rev. and updated ed. ([Totnes]: Green Books, 2009), 140. The UK's Permaculture Association also has a short webpage explaining social ecology: https://www.permaculture.org.uk/practical-solutions/social-ecology, accessed 10 February 2023.
4   Leahy, *Politics of Permaculture*, 99 and 187.
5   Mike Feingold, interview with the author, Royal Hill Allotments, Eastville, Bristol (8 August 2023).
6   Simon Fairlie, *Meat: A Benign Extravagance* (East Meon, Hampshire: Permanent Publications, 2010).
7   Hart, *Forest Gardening*, 40.

8   Monbiot, *Regenesis*, 95; their stockfree-organic systems are shared in Jenny Hall and Iain Tolhurst, *Growing Green: Organic Techniques for a Sustainable Future* [2006], rev. ed. (Altrincham: Vegan Organic Network, 2009).
9   Eric Toensmeier, Rafter Ferguson, and Mamta Mehra, "Perennial Vegetables: A Neglected Resource for Biodiversity, Carbon Sequestration, and Nutrition," *PLoS ONE* 15, no. 7 (2020): https://doi.org/10.1371/journal.pone.0234611.
10 Monbiot, *Regenesis*, 178–185.
11 Experimental Farm Network, "EFN Perennial Grain Sorghum Project," [c. 2021?], accessed 27 January 2023.
12 Fred Pearce presents a succinct overview from a global perspective, "Flushed with Success: Human Manure's Fertile Future," *New Scientist* (13 February 2013): https://www.newscientist.com/article/mg21729042-200-flushed-with-success-human-manures-fertile-future/.
13 My own university, UWE Bristol, has long been developing and expanding the use of microbial fuel cells to generate electricity from urine. See UK Research and Innovation website, "Spin-out Turns Urine into Electricity" (1 September 2022): https://www.ukri.org/news-and-events/responding-to-climate-change/developing-new-behaviours-and-solutions/spin-out-turns-urine-into-electricity/.
14 Phoebe Brathwaite, "The Long, Noble and Stinky Quest to Make Human Shit Useful," *Wired* (31 July 2018): https://www.wired.co.uk/article/human-faeces-poo-as-fertiliser.
15 Zach Boren, "The UK is Importing Sewage Sludge for Use on Farmland Despite Health Concerns," Greenpeace UK's *Unearthed* website (2 September 2020): https://unearthed.greenpeace.org/2020/09/02/uk-imports-sewage-sludge-agriculture/.
16 Environment Agency, *Environment Agency Strategy for Safe and Sustainable Sludge Use*, policy paper updated 1 August 2023: https://www.gov.uk/government/publications/environment-agency-strategy-for-safe-and-sustainable-sludge-use/environment-agency-strategy-for-safe-and-sustainable-sludge-use.

17 Jenny Hall and Iain Tolhurst, *Growing Green: Organic Techniques for a Sustainable Future*, rev. ed. (Altrincham: Vegan Organic Network, 2009), 69.
18 Soil Association, "A Rock and a Hard Place: Peak Phosphorus and the Threat to our Food Security," (Bristol: Soil Association, 2010)—unfortunately, this excellent 2010 report is no longer available from the Soil Association's own website, but can be accessed at https://worldveg.tind.io/record/39128/, accessed 7 February 2023.
19 Daniel Akira Stiebeling and Antje Labes, "Mycoremediation of Sewage Sludge and Manure with Marine Fungi for the Removal of Organic Pollutants," *Frontiers in Marine Science,* Sec. Marine Biotechnology and Bioproducts 9 (13 September 2022): https://doi.org/10.3389/fmars.2022.946220.
20 Franziska Häfner, Rodrigo Monzon Diaz, Sarah Tietjen, Corinna Schröder, and Ariane Krause, "Recycling Fertilizers from Human Excreta Exhibit High Nitrogen Fertilizer Value and Result in Low Uptake of Pharmaceutical Compounds," *Frontiers in Environmental Science* (2023): https://doi.org/10.3389/fenvs.2022.1038175.

AGROECOLOGICAL KNOWLEDGES

Safeguarding Adivasi knowledges

Indigenous knowledge is a living repository of incalculable value: dynamic wisdom, for the most part relating to tribes' intimate connections to the environments, within which their cultures have evolved. This rich heritage includes spiritual traditions, insights from ethnobotany, and agricultural know-how congruent with the future care of ecosystems in peril.

The tribal peoples of India—more than 700 ethnic groups, often known collectively as Adivasis—make up the largest population of Indigenous peoples in the world.[1] Their tribal traditions of gathering wild foods and agricultural practices make their cultural heritage a rich source of knowledge of the living world. Their lived experience has involved a highly elaborated set of skills, rituals, and sensory attunement profoundly nested within intergenerational folkways. Intimacy with place and ecological discernment has been essential to elicit the tools and garments, sweetness and colour, medicines, pleasures and protections, fruits, spices and vegetables, proteins, and grains necessary to sustain extended families in otherwise adverse terrains of mountain and forest.

Adivasis' ongoing reliance upon subsistence cultivation both ensures their deep awareness of strategies for resilience and food security, yet makes them particularly vulnerable to forms of development that exacerbate ecological stresses and displacement from the land. Such displacement is a double economic loss, since knowledge is an element of the means of production. As Felix Padel writes,

> One of the most painful aspects of displacement is the de-linking of people's economy from an all-round embeddedness in ecology that guarantees their food security.[2]

Colonial and post-colonial administrations alike have regarded the presence of traditional food-producing and craft societies as an impediment to high-impact developmental infrastructure and the imposition of industrial agriculture. However, alongside displacement, increasing burdens of debt, ecological stresses on soil health and water levels, and resource inefficiencies have exposed the costs of capital-intensive farming. In these circumstances, critics have looked to features of Adivasi communities, with their "symbiotic relationship with nature" and "need-based economic system," as inherently more stable and resilient, among potential pathways to alternative futures for tropical zones.[3]

The clash of worldviews was made apparent in strong Adivasi support for the successful Anti-Farm Laws alliance that emerged in 2020. Many Adivasis have long been organising to defend and conserve their forests and access to non-timber products to protect livelihoods without destroying the lands upon which they depend.[4] International recognition of, and solidarity with, Adivasi communities can help to support the cultivation of food using traditional practices compatible with agroecology, and its attendant ecological benefits. At the same time, ecological conservation is crucial to assure the survival of Adivasi tribal cultures. It is with some irony, then, that critics point to the role of the Forest Department in regularly taking possession of mineral rich, and supposed wilderness, areas, evicting and criminalising Adivasis for trespass in the name of wildlife conservation, often with military support.[5]

Given the range and complexity of the tribal peoples, it is difficult to ascertain the extent to which traditional methods of Adivasi food production survive in India. Development programmes and industrial agriculture have displaced millions, brought an end to their customs, and blighted the prospects for many more. It is not, however, entirely a story of decline. Many fresh programmes and experiments are underway to conserve the benefits of traditional cultivated varieties, the gathering of wild foods, and folk medicine.

Ashish Kothari is the co-founder of the ecological grassroots organisation Kalpavriksh and also a prominent speaker within the Global Tapestry of Alternatives, an initiative that seeks to connect a "pluriverse" of radical solidarity networks, including those such as the Kurdish and Zapatista movements following social-ecology-type principles. Kothari confirms that a countervailing resurgence has been underway:

> In many parts of India, Adivasis continue to use their traditional agricultural methods, seeds, knowledge etc. [...] in many these are not fully intact, but elements [of Indigenous farming practices and food gathering] continue [...] and in many, people are bringing them back, as evidence of the problems of Green Revolution, [with its] homogenous methods [of production] increases.[6]

The India Alternatives group Vikalp Sangam and Kothari point to many examples of networks and initiatives working to promote practices and wisdoms in the cause of food sovereignty. These include the Deccan Development Society, the Timbaktu Collective, Living Farms in Odisha, the seed guardians of the North East Network in Nagaland, MAKAAM, or Mahila Kisan Adhikaar

Manch (Forum for Women Farmers' Rights), the Food Sovereignty Alliance, and the efforts of Local Futures to maintain and relocalise food economies in Ladakh.[7] Despite the low recognition of such organisations in the West, the way that India sustains its population matters since, as it becomes the world's most populous country, it is at the forefront of food sovereignty issues.

While ambitious projects have been undertaken to document the stunning diversity of India's edible plants, the tribal populations, with their deep understanding of the uses of these species, are still being forcibly severed from the lands where they grow.[8] For this reason, the collection and recording of ancestral knowledge has been seen as an urgent task to improve the prospects for both cultural diversity and ecological integrity. Satyapriya Singh et al., for example, call for the creation of "a strong and information-rich data bank" to record Indigenous horticultural practices.[9] Such a collection would be a repository of knowledge relating to pest management, species, and varieties best suited to local geological and climatic conditions, nutritional and medicinal value, and maintaining production without reliance on imported fertilisers.

As Adivasi cultures evolve, it is important to protect the benefits of empirical knowledge of local ecosystems and food systems, the peer-review process of generations. As Singh et al. suggest, food production could be enhanced by "the amalgamation of age-old practice with novel advanced technology."[10] Social ecologist and "organic revolutionary" Grace Gershuny attributes the founding of modern organic systems to Albert Howard, who learned of the "Indore" method of soil improvement from his work with peasant farmers while serving with the Indian Raj during the 1930s and 1940s and was scrupulous in crediting their role.[11] In the present, it may be that low-input, open-source agroecological methods such as the System of Crop Intensification might at once raise yields and complement traditional polycultures.[12] Such approaches could potentially assist small producers, including Adivasis, to retain autonomy on their traditional lands, while avoiding the model of credit dependency that has been a consequence of the Green Revolution and corporate dominance through strategies such as genetic modification.

Notwithstanding the importance of collating traditional horticultural knowledge, vigilance is necessary to ensure that inventories of accumulated knowledge relating to Indigenous skills and practices are protected in the common domain, not appropriated and enclosed under the mechanism of prohibitive and exclusive intellectual property rights. Such a threat is not merely hypothetical. Vital Indian plants neem and turmeric have become contentious instances of alleged appropriation or "biopiracy," where prolific patenting has been applied to derivatives, leading to hot debates about corporate exploitation of such crops.[13]

Efforts to protect access to knowledge and rights to cultivate traditional varieties and to retain economic benefits and agency for Indigenous communities are enshrined in the Nagoya Protocol (2014).[14] When the collation of Indigenous knowledge is monetarised for commercial purposes, a horticultural and ecological matter becomes a political issue. Initiatives to exploit the neem tree and the wider cornucopia and pharmacopeia of traditionally cultivated species may be well-intentioned. Nevertheless, as Emily Marden concedes, as neem becomes "India's new cash crop," the conventional profit-driven monocultural model typically involves the displacement of the small farmers who, it is claimed, might benefit from the exploitation of such crops.[15]

In the context of asymmetrical neo-colonial economic relationships, compromises with the system of private patenting—which privileges individualistic and corporate concepts of innovation over the collective, and regards traditional varieties and modes of use as ripe for legal enclosure—is likely to jeopardise the future of Indigenous communities in Adivasi ancestral lands and elsewhere.[16] Ashish Kothari and Priya Das have called for the application of community intellectual rights to safeguard traditional horticultural varieties from commercial exploitation and to retain rights to propagate them within the public domain.[17] Food sovereignty activists are struggling to protect the immense variety of rices, since there were as many as 200,000 varieties in India alone before the Green Revolution, according to the often quoted estimate of Radhelal Herlal Richharia and Shanker Govindaswamy.[18] The substantial depletion in both the number of available varieties, and traditional growers retaining the expertise to best select and cultivate them with sensitivity to local conditions, indicates the way that the productivity gains of the Green Revolution and subsequent developments in genetic modification have also come at the cost of a retreat from the kind of abundance that could ensure the future adaptability and resilience that is necessary to feed the sub-continent's vast population.

As well as conserving the robust lore accrued from ancient texts and oral traditions, it will also be critical to revivify Indigenous knowledge within the educational system.[19] The finer nuances of such understanding are often retained in mother tongues, which are frequently excluded from mainstream schooling. Farming and Adivasi cuisine will need to be included in school curricula in rural settlements if the next generation is to develop the skills necessary to produce food for economic resilience, and retain some of the distinct cultural heritages their forebears have passed on. There are endeavours to cherish and develop living horticultural traditions in several Adivasi districts. Misra and Mishra, for example, discuss a Gandhian primary school called Puvidham in Tamil Nādu, where respect for "dignity for farming" is integrated into the taught curriculum, agricultural knowledge being "interwoven" within science, mathematics, and language lessons.[20] The Adharshila Learning Centre was started in 1998 to stimulate ecologically and community-centred schooling in Madhya Pradesh.[21] Within such cultures, it is hoped that practices of horizontal knowledge sharing will nurture a flourishing store of practical horticultural skills and principles of care for the living world to continue for years to come.

Citizen science: Food literacy and democratising research

Improvements in public education about farming and food literacy are also in demand at home. Greater awareness about how nutritional food is produced and can be best sourced, prepared, and enjoyed is necessary if better health outcomes are to be achieved.

The "National Food Strategy" makes a warm and persuasive plea for the full inclusion of food into schools' lifeways, through a "whole school approach," meaning not only that culinary education is truly embedded in curricula from early years, but holistically "treating the dining hall as the hub of the school, where children and teachers eat together" and cooks are visible and valued members of the staff team.[22] Relatedly, the Landworkers' Alliance alert us to what they perceive is the "cultural bias against land-based work in the education system," and call for education and training to "build skills and knowledge," about agroecology.[23]

Within and beyond the educational context, there is scope to expand the application of citizen science relating to food and agriculture. Since, seemingly, there is a dearth of research, Ryan et al.'s rare venture into this under-researched theme is a valuable if lonely article on the overarching application of citizen science in this area.[24] This US study finds that only a tiny proportion of citizen science is concerned with food, yet also indicates the potential benefits of promoting and extending community participation. This contrasts with the long tradition of amateur science in fields such as astronomy and meteorology, where, for instance, knowledge of microclimates or air pollution has been informed by data from neighbourhood monitors.

It has been previously argued that there is vast wisdom relating to horticulture and the culinary arts, which has been peer-reviewed by generations, and that it is empowering that this intellective horn of plenty, overspilling with popular understanding, is conserved and developed within the public domain. In the tradition of radical pedagogy, it is argued that open-access knowledge is a renewable source of power. Commoning knowledge-sharing and connected research to make contributions in this area is therefore rich with opportunity. Where the vast resources of the state and mighty power of commercial interests, each with the capacity to exploit big data, have been unable and unwilling to frame and answer fundamental questions, food and land justice activists have sometimes stepped in to tackle the groundwork.

We have seen that Kenneth Mellanby addressed the question "Can Britain feed itself?" back in the 1970s, a line of enquiry Simon Fairlie revisited in 2009, after finding "no evidence that anyone with the necessary qualifications and stipend to do justice to the subject has been inclined to take it on." Similarly, Guy Shrubsole, allied with data journalist Anna Powell-Smith, set the task of revealing "Who owns England?" observing that the issue remains "our oldest, darkest, best-kept secret," and suggesting that this is because "concealing wealth is part and parcel of preserving it."[25] So, information about food and land is locked up for commercial interests, destroyed, or simply lost, sometimes due to tacit conspiracies of silence, but equally due to cock-ups or the vacillations of policy. It may not fit the funding priorities and constraints of research and development budgets, but perhaps just as often it was never deemed to be expedient or profitable enough to collect the relevant information in the first place. In the UK, Margaret Thatcher's removal of minimum nutritional standards for school meals became a particularly notorious example of abolishing guidance based on inexpedient public information.[26]

Yet, it does not have to be exclusively "big picture" research to contribute to community knowledge. Micro-level input can also form the collective detail vital to broader insight. Throughout this book, several areas are touched upon where community production and sharing of knowledge could enhance people's lives and livelihoods. Specific examples include Indigenous knowledges, information about urban gardening and potential yields, experiments on radical materials science, and the need for surveys and analyses to supply data to better understand soil health, alongside, unfortunately, also the impacts of erosion, contamination, and climate change. The quantity and quality of such information can be collated, interpreted, and communicated at scale through increased collaboration between universities, small businesses, and cooperatives, and the efforts of community associations and dedicated individuals. Ryan et al. point to the scope for further integration of such research with living-world application into the education system, with mutual advantages, including opportunities to connect with under-represented communities.[27] Such research could have an important role in advancing agroecological systems, given the substantial gap between investment in research to support agribusiness, and that seeking to advance more sustainable farming practices.[28]

Some citizen science initiatives have already contributed relevant knowledge. Citizen participation in a nationwide survey of non-native species through the iNaturalist platform have already proved their worth in the United States.[29] In the UK, allotment holders collated and submitted details of their inputs to a study that sought to better understand resource consumption in urban horticulture.[30] Similarly, the MyHarvest project has been set up to gain better data about fruit and vegetable production by gardeners and allotment holders. This demonstrates how digital technologies are enabling citizen contributors to supply data that can be coordinated and aggregated to evidence and potentially inform policy.[31] When assessing two recent voluntary science initiatives based on the identification of bumble bees, the need for careful guidance and expert verification has arisen, although image upload, together with Geographic Information System software, can help to ensure data accuracy.[32]

Citizen scientists and small research networks, such as Garden Organic's research groups and Scotland's Soil Regenerative Agriculture Group, are already making valuable contributions to the horticultural knowledge store. Relevant areas of people's research include surveying plant landraces and heritage varieties and populating seed banks for improved food sovereignty, biodiversity counts, tracking pests and pathogens but also pollinators, nutrition and food hygiene, and the monitoring of habitat loss due to land grabbing and deforestation.[33] Democratising knowledge production in areas of agroecology—where research and development are limited or framed for profit-making, rather than social and ecological ends—could have considerable benefits for driving forward food justice.

Notes

1. Priya Priyadarshini and Purushothaman Chirakkuzhyil Abhilash, "Promoting Tribal Communities and Indigenous Knowledge as Potential Solutions for the Sustainable Development of India," *Environmental Development*, 32 (2019): https://doi.org/10.1016/j.envdev.2019.100459. "Scheduled Tribes" is the state's descriptor for this category of approximately 104 million people.
2. Felix Padel, 49 in "How Best to Ensure Adivasis' Land, Forest and Mineral Rights?," *IDS Bulletin* 43, no. S1 (July 2012), 49–57: https://doi.org/10.1111/j.1759-5436.2012.00346.x.
3. Gladson Dungdung, "A Vision for Adivasis," 594–612 in Ashish Kothari and K.J. Joy, *Alternative Futures: India Unshackled* (New Delhi: AuthorsUpFront, 2017), 601.
4. For example, Adivasi women's protests and defence of the commons led to the foundation of the Mahila Arthik Samoosh (Women's Economic Society) to administer the trade in non-timber forest produce in a district in central India, as told in Mahdu Ramnath, *Crossing Boundaries: Adivasi Women & Forest Produce – A Story from Central Bastar, Chattisgarh, India* ([s.l.] Coonoor Printing, 2004).
5. According to the discussion Peace in Kurdistan Ecology Network webinar presented by Ashish Kothari, Hemant Dalpati, and Felix Padel, "Grassroots Movements in India Today, and Ecological Alternatives" (23 April 2023), produced by Open Protest Network: https://www.youtube.com/watch?v=aQ6Hv-L6EDk.
6. Ashish Kothari, personal e-mail to the author, 5 May 2023.
7. Deccan Development Society: http://www.ddsindia.com/www/default.asp; the Timbaktu Collective: https://timbaktu.org/; Living Farms

FAARM Project: https://livingfarms.wordpress.com/project-overview/; North East Network: https://northeastnetwork.org/; Mahila Kisan Adhikaar Manch: https://makaam.in/; Food Sovereignty Alliance https://foodsovereigntyalliance.wordpress.com/about/. Since 1978, Local Futures have been making efforts to maintain and relocalise food economies in Ladakh: https://www.localfutures.org/programs/ladakh/. Founder member Helena Norberg-Hodge was supportive and inspirational when we set up Eco-Futures in Bath as a branch of the International Society for Ecology and Culture (ISEC) during the early 1990s.

8   For example, in the National Institute of Science Communication and Information Resources [CSIR], Undated (a multi-volume encyclopedia on India's biological wealth) and other sources cited by Bharat Mansata, Kavitha Kuruganti, Vijay Jardhari, and Vasant Futane in "Anna Swaraj: A Vision for Food Sovereignty," 228–249 in Ashish Kothari and K.J. Joy, *Alternative Futures: India Unshackled* (New Delhi: AuthorsUpFront, 2017), 230.

9   Satyapriya Singh, Biswajit Das, Anup Das, Sujan Majumder, Hidangmayum Lembisana Devi, Ranjeet Singh Godara, Alok Kumar Sahoo, and Manas Ranjan Sahoo, "Indigenous Plant Protection Practices of Tripura, India," *Journal of Ethnobiology and Ethnomedicine* 17, no. 50 (2021), 2: https://doi.org/10.1186/s13002-021-00476-7.

10 Singh et al., "Indigenous Plant Protection Practices, 14.

11 Gershuny, *Organic Revolutionary*, 15.

12 Erika Styger, "The System of Rice Intensification and Its International Community of Practice," *Patterns of Commoning* website: https://patternsofcommoning.org/the-system-of-rice-intensification-and-its-international-community-of-practice/, accessed 2 May 2023.

13 Emily Marden, "The Neem Tree Patent: International Conflict over the Commodification of Life," *Boston College International and Comparative Law Review* 22, no. 279 (1999): https://lira.bc.edu/work/ns/8fd5aa58-f4d5-4e7f-83ed-1cc54eddf3b7; Palpu Pushpangadan, Varughese George, Thadiyan Parambil Ijinu, and Manikantan Ambika Chithra, 9 in "All India Coordinated Research Project on Ethnobiology and Genesis of Ethnopharmacology Research in India Including Benefit

Sharing," *Annals of Phytomedicine* 7, no. 1 (2018), 5–12: https://api.semanticscholar.org/CorpusID:133810282. The All India Coordinated Research Project on Ethnobiology was a government-sponsored inventory of traditional varieties conducted from 1982 to 1998. It identified and gathered data on up to 10,000 plants in their cultural context.

14   Pushpangadan et al., "All India Coordinated Research Project on Ethnobiology," 9–10.
15   Marden, "The Neem Tree Patent," 285.
16   President Ali Hassan Mwinyi of Tanzania in Marden, "The Neem Tree Patent," 288, cited from Craig D. Jacoby and Charles Weiss, "Recognizing Property Rights in Traditional Biocultural Contribution," *Stanford Environmental Law Journal* 16, no. 74 (1997), 89–91 [accessed via Heinonline].
17   Ashish Kothari and Priya Das, "Local Community Knowledge and Practices: Implications for Biodiversity," *Selected Papers on Congress* TST 95, 3—Biodiversity, 31 [1990s paper kindly shared by Ashish Kothari].
18   A. Mohammed Ashraf and Subbalakshmi Lokanadan, 349 in "A Review of Rice Landraces in India and its Inherent Medicinal Values—The Nutritive Food Values for Future," *International Journal of Current Microbiology and Applied Sciences* 6, no. 12 (2017): 348–354. https://doi.org/10.20546/ijcmas.2017.612.042.
19   The heart-warming survival of four Indigenous children in the jungle for 40 days following a plane crash in Colombia, was a practical outcome of their botanical intelligence, not a lucky miracle: AFP, "Colombia Plane Crash: Children Survived 40 Days Eating Seeds," Al Jazeera website (11 June 2023): https://www.aljazeera.com/news/2023/6/11/colombia-indigenous-children-survived-40-days-eating-seeds-roots.
20   Girishwar Misra and Rishabh Kumar Mishra, "Ethnopsychological Perspectives on Education for Adivasi Children in India," *Indian Educational Review* 56, no. 1 (January 2018), 65.
21   Adharshila website: https://adharshila.yolasite.com/, accessed 19 August 2023.
22   Department for Environment Food and Rural Affairs, "National Food Strategy: Independent Review. The Plan," Government-commissioned,

independent review into the food system chaired by Henry Dimbleby (London: DEFRA, 2021), 149: https://www.nationalfoodstrategy.org/. The government partially responded to this recommendation in its "Government Food Strategy," although there are doubts as to whether its support will be sufficiently funded. See Sustain, "Government Food Strategy – Which NFS Recommendations were Passed, Failed or are on their Way?" (14 June 2022): https://www.sustainweb.org/blogs/jun22-which-nfs-recommendations-included-in-government-food-strategy/.

23 Georgie Styles, Isobel Talks, and Holly Tomlinson, "The Attraction of Agroecology and the Barriers Faced by New Entrants Pursuing Agroecological Farming and Land Work" (Landworkers' Alliance, 2022), 30: https://landworkersalliance.org.uk/new-report-the-attraction-pf-agroecology-2022/.

24 S.F. Ryan et al., "The Role of Citizen Science in Addressing Grand Challenges in Food and Agriculture Research," *Proceedings of the Royal Society B Biological Sciences* 285: 20181977 (21 November 2018): http://dx.doi.org/10.1098/rspb.2018.1977.

25 Guy Shrubsole, *Who Owns England? How We Lost Our Green and Pleasant Land and How to Take it Back* (London: William Collins, 2019), 1.

26 Under the Education Act 1980.

27 Ryan et al., "Role of Citizen Science in Addressing Grand Challenges in Food and Agriculture Research," 7.

28 Pablo A. Tittonell estimates this gap in research funding to be 90–95% in *Farming Systems Ecology: Towards Ecological Intensification in World Agriculture* (16 May 2013): https://www.wur.nl/upload_mm/8/3/e/8b4f46f7-4656-4f68-bb11-905534c6946c_Inaugural%20lecture%20Pablo%20Tittonell.pdf.

29 Adin L. Ring, "Harnessing Citizen Science and Collections Data for Invasive Plant Surveillance," EliScholar—Yale University Digital Platform (2023): https://evst.yale.edu/node/36881.

30 Miriam C. Dobson, Philip H. Warren, and Jill L. Edmondson, "Assessing the Direct Resource Requirements of Urban Horticulture in the United Kingdom: A Citizen Science Approach," *Sustainability* 13, no. 5: 2628 (2021): https://doi.org/10.3390/su13052628.

31 Jill L. Edmondson, Roscoe S. Blevins, Hamish Cunningham, Miriam C. Dobson, Jonathan R. Leake, and Darren R. Grafius, "Grow Your Own Food Security? Integrating Science and Citizen Science to Estimate the Contribution of Own Growing to UK Food Production," *Plants, People, Planet* 1, no. 2 (2019): 93–97.

32 Steven Falk, Gemma Foster, Richard Comont, Judith Conroy, Helen Bostock, Andrew Salisbury, Dave Kilbey, James Bennett, and Barbara Smith, "Evaluating the Ability of Citizen Scientists to Identify Bumblebee (Bombus) Species," PLoS ONE 14(6): e0218614 (2019): https://doi.org/10.1371/journal.pone.0218614.

33 Ryan et al., "Role of Citizen Science in Addressing Grand Challenges in Food and Agriculture Research," 4.

LIBERATORY
TECHNOLOGY

One of the core principles of social ecology has been the concept of liberatory technology. First set out in the extended eponymous essay of 1965, this idea has been developed and refined by Bookchin and others in the light of the rapid technological changes of the intervening decades. Discussion in one of Bookchin's final works, *Social Ecology and Communalism*, published posthumously in 2007, shows that he still advocated a similar human-scaled approach to the adoption of ecotechnologies. Here he continued to promote technologies powered by renewable energy, organic agriculture, and the production of high-quality goods characterised by their durability. In the tradition of William Morris and John Ruskin, he championed the human elements of creativity and craftspersonship in the productive process. Above all, he insisted that technology must have emancipatory potential "based on an ethics of complementarity," freed from the "grow or die" dynamics of industrial capitalism.[1] It is the context within which such ecotechnologies are developed and adopted, and the social interests that they serve, that determine whether their impacts can be malign or, rather, enabling of social betterment.

With a new scramble for rare-earth minerals and biofuels underway, it is apparent that substituting "renewable" technologies within the existing substantially fossil-fuelled energy grid, which continues to rely upon expansionist models of extraction and consumption, does not represent a credible means to shift to a regenerative economy. In what follows, discussions about the implementation of some potentially liberatory technologies in the present day are introduced, including vertical gardening, biopolymers, agrivoltaics, and the recent debate that has erupted around the efficacy of the use of grasslands to produce "green gas." It makes the case for applying a set of holistic and emancipatory criteria derived from social ecology principles when evaluating emerging technologies. The tacit premise that it is challenging to nurture and direct human talent and to allocate the resources and develop liberatory technology in a society which is far from liberated should also be acknowledged.

Hydroponics and vertical farming

Forms of hydroponics or soilless growing have been undertaken since the seventeenth century and became popular in the 1970s, when members of the counterculture sought alternatives to the already apparent stress-points of the military-industrial complex.[2] In the present, vertical farming is seen as a growth area, and is already attracting much attention and investment as a seeming quick win during an era of food crisis.[3]

What are the benefits and constraints of what is being called, in technical jargon, "Controlled Environment Agriculture" as a solution? It is necessary to navigate exorbitant claims gritted with abrasive scepticism relating to this growing phenomenon. There is a case that adapted forms of vertical farming could increase food production with several attendant ecological benefits for sustainability. Yet, there are important criteria to be factored in for such ventures to become liberatory on a social-ecology model. Indoor vertical growing demands and affords means to precisely control ambient conditions through careful monitoring of humidity, temperature, lighting, ventilation, and atmospheric gases, such as carbon dioxide. For proponents, attendant benefits include less susceptibility to vacillations in weather conditions; protection from traditional pests, removing the need for pesticides; and substantially reduced demand for those precious resources water and soil. Potentially, it is a form of high yield and intensive yet sustainable organic production near to the homes of its enjoyers, thus reducing emissions from shipping and transport.

There are, however, concerns about the impact of "Controlled Environment Agriculture" that should be considered when promoting such technology. Some—such as the limited number of mostly herbs and salad crops or "microgreens" that are currently suitable for harvesting—may be surmountable as ongoing experimentation and development make greater diversity possible. This widening of the nutritional cline would be especially valuable if imported protein-rich sources such as soya beans and water lentils could be cultivated, yet research into such indoor horticulture is in its infancy. Due to high-energy inputs, it seems unlikely that it will be viable to produce such popular charismatic tropicals as bananas, avocados, or pineapples.

The high start-up and operating costs such ventures require represent an obstacle to the adoption of indoor urban growing. They are capital-intensive and call upon considerable technical expertise, especially if cultivation and harvesting processes are automated. Where disused glass office blocks could be repurposed, the facilities might represent a significant enhancement in land use, although it would be difficult to retrofit them to a standard where they could be as efficient and productive as purpose-built buildings. Yet there are three energy impacts that effect the life-cycle of purpose-built vertical systems that could potentially offset their sustainability benefits: the oblique and unquantifiable sources of consumption, invariably entailed in the realisation of the initial capital; the embodied energy used in construction processes and materials, such as prestressed metals and plate glass; and the ongoing inputs required for maintaining the operation.

Within the constraints of current market forces, whereby land is designated as "real estate," urban sites are at a premium and command high prices. Such laws of supply and demand would tend to work against the production of proliferating abundance for a solidarity economy, since supply is controlled and restricted to keep prices high. In such circumstances, market demand diverges from need, being primarily driven by shareholders' return on investment, privileging, for example, niche luxury commodities targeted at affluent consumers and even production for biofuels, outbidding popular needs for accessible high-quality foods.

Once land and building for vertical or other forms of indoor urban farming are secured, the energy use of these operations is another challenging factor for their sustainability—one that researchers who have undertaken primary comparative studies and modelling have claimed is "typically underappreciated."[4] The implications of high consumption of energy generated at a distance make the real economic benefits questionable. Several factors are at play: not only whether the facilities are energy-intensive to run, but also the source of the energy and the extent to which it is low-carbon and renewable, and the distance from use, with accompanying transmission losses.[5]

Further challenges include concerns about the growth of mildews and other diseases or infestations in the indoor gardening facilities. While it is true that controlled, closed-circuit production of this kind makes it difficult for such biological threats to reach the growing trays, totally hermetically sealed microenvironments are unlikely and undesirable. Claims that there will be no diseases in scaled-up indoor farming are dubious, and it is probable that persistent organisms or pathogens will occasionally penetrate through to the crops, which is a particular problem for monocultural production. The absence of natural pollinators in the systems likewise presents a potential obstacle to diversifying and scaling up production.

Matters of agency and power are typically marginal to the entrepreneurial calculations of the prospects for vertical farming that make up most current literature.[6] Yet beyond such cost-benefit and logistical analyses, such aspects are central to social-ecology approaches. On the current business model, we could expect to see start-up entrepreneurs pioneering an expanding food industry, the unsuccessful of which will go bust, while the more prosperous will sell out to monopolistic corporations, dominating the market with vast economic and political power. In his discussion of "radical or reactionary tomatoes," Nick Hildyard argues that the underlying social relations at play are crucial to determining whether food production—in the form of rooftop gardens, greenhouses, or vertical farming—is exploitative and entrenches existing patterns of exclusion and injustice or can be liberatory, realising more equitable and harmonious exchanges based on mutual aid.[7] In this context, the control of the production and allocation of food, and relevant big data, could feed existing oligopolies. By contrast, there may, for instance, be shared initiatives with existing worker and consumer cooperatives.[8] Ideally, compatible ancillary and support services could federate to support other regional initiatives.

If we had a free rein to imagine, what synergies might be possible without the constraints of the present, seemingly unsustainable social and economic relationships and modes of exchange? Food growing could conceivably be a creative and productive means to repurpose some of the square metres of empty office-block assets, beached by the tide of speculative construction. Such neo-Brutalist millennials, bright with the bling of 24-hour illuminated glass, are uselessly stranded in most city centres. Other more modest possibilities are to grow extra food in glasshouses mounted on top of existing structures or to create "green walls"—edible versions of the "green façades" of a kind that are already growing on buildings in experimental forest cities, the prototypes for which are Milan's Bosco Verticale and the Liuzhou Forest City in China.[9] Or, if structures are to be purpose-built, they should be designed to last a few centuries as a gesture of goodwill and generosity for future generations, and so be culturally regenerative in a literal sense. We could foresee a powerful reclaiming of both the nineteenth-century legacy of that imperial botanical conveyance the Wardian case and the drab utilitarian office block of the twentieth century, repurposed in the service of social abundance.[10]

Imagine a future in which the stately octogenarian grandchildren of Generation Alpha promenade past hydroponic crystal palaces. Economically, now decolonised, they would enjoy the democratisation of the means of production. Aesthetically, such structures could be liberated from the monotony of international corporate style. Possibilities that come to mind are cathedral-like glasshouses harking back to Joseph Paxton's fabulous hothouses at Kew or their counterparts at Paris's Jardin des Plantes, or forward to town centres where abandoned car parks have been replaced with Edenic biomes supplying nourishing fresh vegetables in beautiful shimmering pleasure domes, multi-tiered glass pagodas fusing beauty and purpose by making available succulent shoots for a food-depleted world, sprouting neo-Hundertwasserian dwellings which host tree tenants producing fruit and nuts, or new, as yet unimagined or foreseen, vernaculars. If this production is to be liberatory, there will be democratic decision-making involving growers, eaters, and other people affected by its outcomes. In this respect, lessons from design thinking and charrette processes may help to nurture authentic inclusion. Apprenticeships would be required for this inner horticulture with reskilling and new crafts making livelihoods attractive as means for exploration and self-development, not wage drudgery.

So, what is reproducible and sustainable, what is speculative and experimental, and what is outright fantasy? Advances in renewable energy, such as energy-efficient LEDs, and hydroponics make possible abundance not available to earlier generations. Several existing processes, and those under development, could make further enhancements to the feasibility of indoor food production—for example, rain harvesting to make the systems more water efficient and on-site integrated microgeneration through solar or wind power (careful back-ups are a prerequisite to prevent the risk of harvest loss due to power cuts). Geothermal energy could be used where geologically feasible. Further harmonies could involve the combination of indoor growing with the use of spaces that are already lit and heated year-round, such as railway station hothouses (Madrid's Atocha Station, for example, boasts luxuriant foliage and resident terrapins) and hospital atria.

Already, experiments have been underway to grow food in the eateries where it is served, adding edible decoration and reducing transportation to zero.[11] Indoor farmers' markets for fresh produce could be set up in the premises where food is grown. While transport costs are a modest proportion of the carbon footprint of food production, this minimal supply chain would have several other advantages. Such local origin would help to ensure that food is connected into communities and visible, aesthetically attractive, and not imposing silos in privatised zones separated from the neighbourhoods where they are situated so that sociality is cultivated alongside crops.

Some of the advantages of indoor growing, such as insulation against seasonality, should also give us pause. The loss of seasonality, and other characteristics beloved of the real food movement such as provenance and terroir, are considerations that may be addressed. The prospect of insomniac 24-7 vegetables severed from diurnal and celestial biorhythms in their efforts to meet their key performance indicators could auger hidden abiotic stresses and further processes of alienation from organic evolution. Rotational growing could maintain some of the value of seasonality. With a renaissance of neighbourhood production, it is hoped that provincial cultural specialities could emerge, akin to the highly locally distinctive rhubarb forcing sheds of West Yorkshire's Wakefield triangle.

Due to ground-level pressures, attention for possible sites for urban farming is swivelling skywards and pivoting underground. I would conclude that expanded indoor farming is far from being a universal solution to the food crisis, but there are realistic benefits that could valuably contribute towards the localisation and diversification of production, and hence mitigate food security risks. As we have seen, the large purpose-built prototype facilities that are currently underway are capital- and energy-intensive operations. Distributed vertical farming could be safer but with some loss of economies of scale. If the production is kept within existing structures, the additional costs and even energy consumption may be marginal. However, if sustained at this minimal level, the contribution to food production may also be marginal.

In a socially oriented context, early adopters must share knowledge with creative commons-type protections to enable emerging benign technologies to evolve and flourish free from patent restrictions, or prohibitive expense, due to reliance upon technical expertise and automation dependent upon substantial borrowing and debt. The intriguing and innovative Open Source Ecology project, for example, is already proving to be a promising strategy for pioneering designs in farming and construction technologies.[12] New developments in vertical farming need to be transferable and accessible where food insecurity is most critical.

At its dystopian worst, Controlled Environment Agriculture has the propensity to develop as a resource-hungry biotechnology further alienating commodified food from its eaters, an unappetising form of intensified and privatised neo-enclosure, gated communities of microgreens where abseiling robots conduct Fordist horticulture in plant factories. At its ecotopian best, resurgent indoor gardening could represent a more tantalising prospect of dual-use transparent buildings, with integrated cultivation where foliage complements human design for more loveable neighbourhoods. Such initiatives may bring forth forms of sustainable localised production that kindles kindness and plenty that reconnect and humanise growing processes.

Energy gardens of tomorrow

Another possible way forward is to use agrivoltaics to optimise land use by combining food production with solar generation. It has long been recognised that the sun supplies abundant energy to power human needs. Yet, there have been constraints in collecting, storing, and distributing this energy. The hippy generation worked hard and experimented hard to realise their dream of gentle Prometheanism, through freeing people's power, showcasing the results at events such as the 1970s Comtek festivals.[13] One-time Bath Arts Workshop member, the actor and comedian Rob Llewellyn pointed out that they helped to promote advances in renewable technologies that presently contribute up to 25% of the country's energy.[14] Today, solar farms are making a significant and growing contribution to the national grid, with solar power generating around 14 gigawatts of energy per annum according to government figures.[15] Potentially, agrivoltaics could enable more efficient solar harvesting and allocation for social goods, while also maintaining food production. This would help to ease austerity and remove current grotesque inequalities in fuel poverty, making it possible to envision a future where energy is plentiful and free for life's essentials.[16]

However, there are legitimate concerns about the impact of many solar farms as currently arrayed. It is commonly objected that, rather than use land to generate solar power, there should be a rapid expansion of roof-mounted systems. Indeed, solar generation on buildings is increasing, incentivised by rising energy prices, falling installation costs, and due to design innovations, such as photovoltaic tiles. However, currently, panels are estimated to be installed on just 4.1% of UK homes.[17] Approximately a third of solar energy comes from panels on roofs, while two-thirds is generated at ground-level on solar farms.[18] Aesthetic objections to mega-solar farms can be justified. Anecdotally, there are winners and losers in terms of biodiversity, with, for example, some animals like hares finding the cover afforded by tilted panels a means to better evade predators and flourish, while others experience disruption—such as bats, whose echolocation can be disoriented. The ecological and social impact of initial production of the panels and associated hardware, as well as the transmission costs, are serious considerations. Like all large-scale industrial production, solar-energy infrastructure is currently based on manufacturing processes that are energy intensive, involve damaging mineral extraction, and produce hazardous pollutants. Most panels are produced in China, using plastics derived from fossil fuels and exploitative labour practices.[19] Since most large-scale energy generation has negative environmental impacts, informed decision-making must evaluate use holistically, considering demand as well as supply.

As ever, the ecological and social aspects of bringing together regenerative horticulture and energy cultivation are intimately entwined. Appeals by eco-socialists such as Aaron Bastani and Max Aji to decolonise and socialise green technologies are well made. Aji, for example, summarises his advocacy for a "People's Green New Deal" as redistributive democracy in the context of a publicly owned means of production, respect for the natural world, and the "decommodification of life," while Bastani calls for a project to unleash technically advanced modes of sustainable abundance able to surpass neoliberalism.[20] Institutional appropriation of, and political obstruction to, the emancipatory potential towards a regenerative economy should not be underestimated. First, technologies are typically monopolised to constrain supplies to maintain prices and boost profits. Second is the backlash from vested interests in the fossil-fuel and nuclear industries, who have amassed capital and built power upon the monolithic edifice of old power infrastructure (both in the sense of energy as a form of power and political power) that they will not relinquish easily. Corporate media offensives bolster this control, critical of zero-carbon policies and sceptical about green technologies. Rhetoric about free-market forces and deregulation notwithstanding, there are already new UK government incentives for oil (especially for the Jackdaw and Rosebank oilfields), gas, and nuclear power. By contrast, while in his previous role as the first Secretary of State for Energy Security and Net Zero, Grant Shapps signalled scepticism about renewable energy. Insulation programmes have also suffered from long-term lack of investment and policy vacillations.

Not to dampen excitement, innovations in agrivoltaics remain a promising way forward for a regenerative economy. Advances in design are revealing novel possibilities. By contrast to the now familiar first generation of static ground-level solar farms, vertical bifacial solar units are being constructed on stilts.[21] These panels leave space to grow crops or graze animals beneath, and have comparable generation capacity, together with technical advantages such as less dirt build-up and that they allow rain to reach the vegetation below. Alley cropping of fruit bushes or other crops then becomes viable under the heightened panels. Greenhouses or polytunnel structures are also being developed with photovoltaic capacity.

If the technical challenges are approached with a liberatory and ecological mindset which aspires to bringing abundant "power to the people" with "virtually free, limitless energy," then unleashing the visionary prospect of the kind of "fully automated luxury communism" invoked by Bastani, and dreamed of by utopian radicals for decades, becomes easier to envisage and implement.[22] The development of solar energy then becomes not so much an act of technological substitution and upgrading within a static social system, but a truly socially transformative process. There are already several authentic innovations that may enable more regenerative operations. What happens if such advances can be synthesised and activated? There are several potential directions for such synergies. Can the production of panels be onshored to domestic workshops?[23] Can solar panel and battery components be made from recycled oil-based plastics or with biopolymers, substantially mitigating the initial production and disposal impacts?[24] Could the solar power be stored as hot water or to generate green hydrogen, avoiding the toxic impact of cadmium, nickel, and lithium batteries?[25] Could locally generated solar power reduce transmission loss and ensure a more variegated landscape, with the possibility of local energy gardens producing free power for the commonweal through community supported agriculture? Agrivoltaic energy gardens could also be a source of plant or animal-based insulation materials. Experiments, research and development in each of these areas are already happening. A people's agrivoltaics, therefore, has potentially far-reaching benefits for social well-being, both through the rational and democratic management of energy, land, and food, and through open-sourcing the knowledge commons.

Point–Counterpoint: Herbal lays for green gas

The use of land for energy has controversial aspects as instanced by the spat between high-profile anti-climate-change activists and allies, Dale Vince and George Monbiot. Vince, founder of leading green energy company Ecotricity, advocates the use of grasslands freed up by reduced ruminant grazing as a source of biomass to supply "green," and vegan, gas through anaerobic digestion. An outline in Ecotricity's 2022 report, "Green Gas," suggests that this could have several advantages, including the following:

- absorption of greenhouse gases by sequestering carbon dioxide through increased vegetation in the form of mixed organic herbal leys
- adaptation of central heating boilers and other existing gas infrastructure, rather than replacement with heat-pump technologies
- increased biodiversity
- reduced reliance on imported gas or that from North Sea gas fields and fracking
- cheaper energy costs for householders
- regenerating livelihoods[26]

However, the approach has several critics who are sceptical. First, in the unlikely scenario that the proposed green gas scheme could be scaled up and implemented to its maximum extent, it would be immensely land-hungry. In particular, Monbiot, in a wider attack on the use of land to produce biofuels, singles out the Ecotricity plan for green gas as the "worst land use proposal I've ever seen in the UK."²⁷

To meet the UK's annual natural gas demand (with 20% hydrogen blended in), Ecotricity's own figures suggest that 10.14 million hectares would be required.²⁸ This is quantified on the 2020 demand, surely atypically representative due to the disruption caused by the coronavirus pandemic. This would be equivalent to nearly all the available pastureland.²⁹ Access to this amount of pastureland would rely upon a major switch to a plant-based diet. While this may be desirable to reduce greenhouse gases from ruminant grazing, a critical report by Biofuelwatch suggests that the more likely outcome would be either a substantial increase in imports of meat and dairy or in imported feed for factory farming.³⁰ The other chief objection that Almuth Ernsting of Biofuelwatch presents is the technical problem of biomethane leakage during processing; given the potency of methane as a greenhouse gas, this could be a significant factor.³¹ Ecotricity's 2022 report acknowledges that there could be between 0.001% to 5.5% leakage of biomethane. This factor is therefore accorded a wide parameter. If leakage can be contained to the former proportion, this problem would be minimal; if the emissions tend towards the latter, it could undermine the programme's viability.

It would also seem that the impact of free-market forces upon likely outcomes have not been sufficiently considered in the proposals as they stand. An ecologically responsible company like Ecotricity is committed to the use of organic herbal leys to produce biomethane. If the programme were to be scaled up nationally, it is hard to see how they would maintain a monopoly. If it proves profitable, then competitors would take over the market and be tempted to cut corners by growing chemical-based grass monocultures for more biogas, resulting in less benefit for biodiversity.³² Furthermore, use for transport or other purposes may attract higher prices for the biomethane, thereby potentially outbidding supply for domestic central heating.

For these reasons, claims for the future of green gas should be moderated. While they may form part of the solution, they are unlikely to have the reach that Ecotricity hope for. Several figures in the "Green Gas" assessment are based on hypothetical and speculative assumptions that are not fully warranted, perhaps rendering the report unduly optimistic about the prospects. The central claim, for example, that "6.46 million hectares of suitable grassland" theoretically exists, is not to say that it is practically available to power "5,400 Green Gas Mills."[33] Rather than one giant, elegant solution, therefore, a mixed approach to the repurposing of pastureland is more likely to optimise outcomes.

Given that grasslands are the single largest part of the UK's land surface area, the question is urgent. In much of Wales and the West Country, for example, the land is predominately pastoral and often unsuitable for arable farming. That Monbiot's research and analysis in *Regenesis* does not tackle this issue head-on is a surprising omission. Agrivoltaics could lead to a smarter use of pastures, working on some land to produce electricity alongside food or other production. Green gas could make a valuable contribution to replacing fossil fuel gas when used to supply UK's domestic heating needs for central heating, hot water, and cooking, if combined with other measures such as insulation and retrofitting, and the development of green hydrogen. Other land could be upgraded for arable use according to Tolhurst's pioneering techniques, for producing green manures and mulches, or for cultivating wood, nuts, and other non-timber forest products. For Monbiot, Tolhurst's work represents the most promising way to bring lower-grade land into production. Jenny Hall, Tolhurst's co-author, tackles the issue directly, investigating "strategies that can enable marginal soils used for grazing to be converted into productive food growing systems."[34] Other grasslands, especially hilly uplands, would be best given over for extensive rewilding with far-reaching benefits for returning biodiversity and drawing down carbon dioxide. There is no such thing as marginal land. Every acre must be managed, or conserved to look after itself. There are constraints upon the amount of land that could be rewilded, given the need to increase food production for domestic consumption without relying upon imports from ghost acres elsewhere. There are likely to be valuable synergies in considering food and energy production holistically, with democratic decision-making and the integration of community supported agriculture the best safeguard to ensure that advances in this area have broad social benefit.

Radical materials science

There are several crops that are also being used in design to make the stuff of everyday life more ecologically sustainable. This is the hopeful proposition that social goods can be harvested rather than extracted through mining, drilling, and blasting. Already, experimentation in what I am going to term radical materials science is producing durable yet biodegradable substances that are sufficiently versatile to transform the composition of textiles, crockery, architectural supplies, and even computer processing circuits.

There is an unsung timeline of citizen designers and scientists from the late 1960s onwards who have been quietly influential in researching and creating regenerative alternatives to fossil-fuel based energies and petrochemical polymers. These include the New Alchemy Institute, the Centre for Alternative Technology, and twenty-first-century contributions from Alex Steffen's *Worldchanging* (2006); and the tinkerers, permaculturists, and neo-commoners that Chris Carlsson celebrated in *Nowtopia* (2008). During the mid-1970s, many alternative-technology tribes and collectives such as Undercurrents, Street Farm, and the Radical Technology Unit convened at Bath for the Comtek (community technology) festivals. Street Farmer Graham Caine constructed the first intentionally designed eco-house, synthesising an elaborate system of renewable energy and food production, and trialled bamboo architecture.[35] Other contributors to *Radical Technology* (1976)— the major compendium of alternative-technology ideas—such as Alan Dalton, were starting to consider the prospects for biobased materials such as seaweed to provide alternative products from those derived from synthetic hydrocarbons.[36] The phase out and substitution of fossil-fuel based products will be essential if we are to meet social needs within ecological constraints. The following will outline the potential benefits of a triad of biobased materials being refined within emerging radical materials science—seaweeds, fungi, and hemp—and, also, some challenges to the development of these seemingly utopian options.

Many advocates can be messianic about the potential for hemp, so it is important to scrutinise the claims behind the hype. Even with its psychoactive properties (THC) bred out, hemp is something of a miracle plant. Its ecological benefits are many, being one of the fastest growing crops due to its exceptionally efficient photosynthesis—making it also suitable as an in-between or catch crop—high-yielding, drought resistant, and requiring only modest irrigation. It is mostly grown organically since it needs negligible fertiliser and no herbicides.

Hemp can produce an astonishing cornucopia of materials. Alongside the traditional uses of varieties of cannabis sativa—such as rope and netmaking, and of course as a euphoriant—in the twenty-first century, a new generation of hemp-based materials includes textiles, biodegradable plastics, medicines, new food products, and perhaps more controversially, biofuels. Hemp concrete or hempcrete has attracted particular attention since hemp sequesters carbon dioxide emissions, making it a promising alternative to the conventional concrete industry, globally a significant source of greenhouse gases.[37]

Eco-buildings can achieve high operational performance in energy efficiency but may have a significant ecological impact in their capital costs and in the carbon dioxide embodied in their construction processes and materials. There is increasing recognition, therefore, that impact evaluation needs to assess the emissions embodied in the entire process cycle. Considerable energy is expended, for example, in the production of concrete and fibreglass insulation materials. While the lime used with shives (hemp's fibrous by-product) to make hempcrete initially requires energy-intensive production, life-cycle assessment indicates a substantial net benefit in reduced emissions compared to conventional concrete production.[38]

Careful evaluation is necessary when growing hemp as a biofuel for energy-profligate uses, although the use of hemp waste is more viable. In all cases, supply-side calculations should not be severed from the assessment of demand. A present concern for English and Welsh farmers is the government's licensing restrictions, which present a major obstacle to domestic production.[39] The Industrial Hemp Licence needs urgent reform.[40] Promising present-day research on hemp growing in Wales suggests that a relaxation of the restrictions on the cultivation of this all-purpose crop could be a valuable part of a "wider green recovery," to repurpose pastoral land for food and medicine, energy, and other sustainable materials.[41]

Seaweeds are also a class of plants that grow rapidly without fertilisers and that efficiently absorb carbon dioxide. Their cultivation requires neither agricultural land nor fresh water. Such properties are an exceptional advantage. Seaweeds are another wonder crop harvested for food, which also have extensive further uses including bioplastics, fertilisers, and biofuels. Recent research supports claims that the consumption of seaweed or algae-based supplements can significantly reduce methane produced by cattle, sheep, and other ruminants, an effect attracting attention due to its potential to mitigate emissions from farming.[42] Nonetheless, even seemingly benign solutions must be implemented with caution. Here, a social-ecology perspective can help to ensure that human and ecological well-being are at the heart of democratic initiatives to implement research and design and production in a way that is genuinely transformative. Julia Lohmann, artist and designer at the Department of Seaweed, presents an inspiring, visionary account of algae's amazing properties and potential.[43] Nevertheless, as biotech start-ups try to monetarise the ecological crisis, there are risks that opportunities will be stifled and marginalised, or even that further ecological destruction can be unleashed in the cause of the so-called green economy.

While developments in the new material sciences with the content of biofabrication and the form of biomimicry have promise, there is a risk and likelihood of appropriation of yet more life forms and knowledge as part of a commitment to business as usual.[44] A greenrush to produce biofuels for transport could lead to accelerated extraction as part of the colonisation of the seabed. Furthermore, while rapid growth and resilience are intrinsic to seaweed's immense vitality, this needs to be balanced against the risk of the proliferation of some species at the expense of aquatic biodiversity.[45] Species such as wakame have been causing ecosystemic disruption and have been categorised as one of the world's worst "invasive species."[46] The emotive term "invasive species" has been challenged. American restoration scientist Jessica Hernandez, for example, suggests the notion of "displaced relatives" as more holistic and preferable, since such species are of course native to habitats elsewhere, yet does not dispute the ecological need to remove such outcompeting species.[47]

While successful enterprises bring profits to entrepreneurs and investors, where such unintended consequences occur, too often negative outcomes fall to the rest of society and other species as externalities. Non-profit organisations such as Bioneers are providing a valuable focus on these issues, uniting cutting-edge science with Indigenous perspectives, climate justice activism, and eco-philosophy. Despite an uplifting title, however, a Bioneers forum on "Creating A Future Less Disposable Than Our Plastics" becomes the occasion for a dispiriting discussion.[48] Without profound social change and democratisation, confronting the systemic barriers to that change with a paradigm shift in mindset and practice, the implementation of solutions falls back on a consumer appeal to multinational corporations and becomes problematic for all the reasons that the participants in the conversation acknowledge.

Nevertheless, seaweed harvesting, and the development of new materials, has potential to contribute towards the creation of a regenerative economy for coastal communities. It would also provide an incentive to protect kelp forests, a significant carbon store.[49] The Sustainable Inshore Fisheries Trust provide a nuanced assessment of the opportunities and risks of seaweed cultivation, or algaculture.[50] The virtuous circle of such a cyclical economy demands an end to the dumping of toxic waste and raw sewage into the seas and, also, enables macro-algae to undertake their role in cleaning, reconditioning, and oxygenating the waters.

Fungi are the sources of some of radical materials science's most dramatic and encouraging developments. There is an urgent demand to use biodegradable alternatives to petrochemical polymers to convert to a truly regenerative economy, an accomplishment which would undoubtedly call upon the assistance of fungal mycelia. Like hemp crafters and seaweed gatherers, the makers who are charming fungi into new forms are revealing an astonishing realm of imaginative multifunctionality. Drawing upon Indigenous and folkloric practices, the *puhpowee* of radical mycology out of the underground scene dates from the 1970s.[51] Merlin Sheldrake particularly attributes the movement's emergence to late psychedelic neo-shaman Terence McKenna and Paul Stamets, joined more recently by hip-hop artist Peter McCoy.[52] In addition to some species' psychoactive properties, fungi's special twin talents for composition and decomposition are enabling conspicuous contributions to the evolving field of radical materials science. Since the ecological crisis has moved beyond the stage where it is enough to conserve the living world, it is necessary to reverse the damage to ecosystems by proactively reclaiming despoiled environments. We have already seen that residual contaminants complicate the reclamation of some growing spaces. The seminal science of mycoremediation is developing to better understand and cultivate the capacity of fungal enzymes to break toxins down into less harmful forms. Experiments and practical applications are demonstrating the astonishing capacity of fungi to absorb and decontaminate biohazards from oil spillages, forest fires, war zones, agricultural land laden with pesticides and other synthetic chemicals, and toxic industrial and domestic waste.[53]

Research on the creative potential of fungal materials in university labs and maker spaces is starting to attract the attention of larger players in business and industry. The germination of fungi to produce alternatives to leathers and PVC materials has been a promising avenue of interest since the early 2000s.[54] Such a breakthrough is in demand, due to the damaging ecological impact of abattoirs, the tanning industry, and petrochemicals alike. Both animal leather, typically a factory farming by-product, and PVC substitutes are sources of greenhouse gas emissions. PVC-type plastics, by-products of petrochemical-based industries, generate emissions and other pollutants through their production and as a consequence of their incineration. Yet both leather and PVC are firmly locked into all aspects of twenty-first-century living in an existential way, fundamental to how we present ourselves to the world, and also protect or even conceal ourselves. People support revolutions in utility and taste when something better comes along; time will tell whether sartorial fungal-wear will become that something, gaining favour by becoming more convenient, affordable, and aesthetically appealing than cow hides or extracts from fossilised plants. The future, too, will confirm whether even more outlandish propositions may become a reality. The intriguingly titled Unconventional Computing Laboratory at my own institution, UWE Bristol, for example, is even experimenting with fungal microprocessing.[55] Furthermore, while the foregoing has considered three separate crops—hemp, seaweeds, and fungi—in practice, the benefits may be combined, for instance, by using hemp shives as a base for growing fungal mycelia.

By definition, a social-ecological perspective must assess the implementation of any material or technology in terms of its consequences for society and ecological well-being. Godfrey Boyle—musing over the definition of what has been variously called radical, alternative, or liberatory technology—noted that its aspiration was not only to be "green" but also to include a social dimension—for example, to "foster increased equality between people and nations."⁵⁶ We need to ask some critical questions if a green transformation is to adopt novel biodegradable materials.

Bookchin's notion of liberatory technology provides a helpful lens with which to holistically evaluate the implications of the apparently utopian material technologies that may be used to overturn the hegemonic values embodied in industries such as petrochemicals, concrete, and factory farming. While set out in 1965, a significantly different material and cultural era, Bookchin's three questions to ask of nascent material technologies are as pertinent as ever:

> What is the liberatory potential of modern technology, both materially and spiritually? What tendencies, if any, are reshaping the machine for use in an organic, human-oriented society? And finally, how can the new technology and resources be used in an ecological manner – that is, to promote the balance of nature, the full development of natural regions, and the creation of organic, humanistic communities?⁵⁷

To address these overarching questions, supplementary questions are called for. How can the cultivation of plants incorporated into radical materials science be used to meet individual and social needs and help nurture a liberatory imaginary, embracing qualities such as freedom and autonomy, participatory democracy, and self-realisation? Can a mushroom or mould contribute towards sustainable abundance and resilience, enabling access to the goods humans need to ensure a decent quality of life and enhancing agency, while reducing dependence upon unreliable state institutions and corporate interests? Commercial interests tend towards monopoly, restricting supply through prohibitive patenting rather than liberatory abundance. The inequitable distribution of the COVID-19 vaccines showed how current market mechanisms work for the benefit of wealthy clients in high-income countries, rather than those in need in the Global South.⁵⁸ Research and development are driven by risk-averse investors looking for dependable income streams. In this conservative context, "innovation" tends to follow existing channels; capital flows resemble water memory, pouring towards familiar opportunities, while failing to irrigate new imaginative territory.

How might communities ensure that the means of production and distribution and benefits are shared and not locked up behind patents, proprietary control, and other intellectual property constraints that ensure any bonanza is restricted to shareholders? What incentives can be instilled to push forward development and dissuaders to avoid the corporate theft and capture of the fruits? The struggles behind such enquiries are underway across the planet.

Bookchin's ecological question must also be taken seriously. However benign such crops, there will be a negative impact upon biodiversity if they are grown exclusively as biofuels, which social ecologist Brian Tokar describes as "a leading symbol" among the "capitalist false solutions of the global climate crisis."[59] The fecundity and promise of rapidly growing plants such as farmed seaweeds also represent ecological threats, since they are potentially "invasive," with the capacity to displace other species, and in the case of fungal mould types, to be vectors of disease.

The risk of unintended consequences, therefore, demands awareness and invites caution. Nevertheless, the development of crops such as hemp, seaweeds, and fungi potentially meets criteria for high-yield, ecologically sustainable approaches. They are not reliant upon substantial irrigation, herbicides, or fertiliser. They are highly nutritional as foodstuffs, with all parts of the crops being usable. They are durable but ultimately biodegradable, reducing the creation of damaging toxic wastes. This is not to endorse single-use products, since it is nearly always better to reuse, and if this is not possible, to recycle. However, it seems to me to be a priority to promote the development of such resources within the commons of land and sea, and within the domain of open-source knowledge, and to distribute any benefits in a scalable and accessible manner.

This is a journey to bring forward materials through savvy and enabling design that avoids the need for expensive capital investment and does not ultimately rely upon high levels of technical expertise and costly equipment. In a democratically controlled society, there would be an interest in avoiding planned obsolescence, replacing goods and infrastructure only when they are worn out and something better comes along. In the field of durable bioplastic products, this would involve a standardisation of sizes, components, and fittings to foster easier accessibility, longer use-life and exchanges across regions—this should not preclude aesthetic and stylistic diversity.

Presently, developments in renewable energies and biodegradable materials, such as biopolymers, tend to be parallel, but research into the potential for convergence—for instance, the production of bioplastic solar panels—would be welcome. Such technologies could extend individual and community agency by making local autonomy more realisable through reducing dependence on centralised and precarious global sources. This could address the kind of "social fatalism" that Bookchin warned about in 1965, a major factor currently, and bring nearer the libertarian dream of radical technology or fully automated luxury communism. The emergence of radical materials science, therefore, constitutes a significant potential for growers to enable society to advance beyond the fossil-fuel economy in a way that meets key needs within an equitable regenerative economy.

Notes

1   Murray Bookchin, *Social Ecology and Communalism*, with an introduction by Eirik Eiglad (Oakland, CA: AK Press, 2007), 44–48.
2   For example, Stefan A. Szczelkun, *Survival Scrapbook #2: Food* [1972] (New York: Schocken Books, 1973), [unpaginated]; James Sholto Douglas, "The Answer Lies in Solution," 37–41 in *Radical Technology*, ed. by Geoffrey Boyle and Peter Harper (London: Wildwood House, 1976).

3   It is, for example, an area of innovation recommended in DEFRA, "National Food Strategy: Independent Review. The Plan," 159 and 241, although not a form of future food production that is given emphasis or even discussed. The case for the new technologies from within the industry is made, for example, by Derek Stewart of the Advanced Plant Growth Centre, "Food Security Rests on the Growth of Farming Indoors," James Hutton Institute website (13 October 2022): https://www.hutton.ac.uk/news/food-security-rests-growth-farming-indoors.

4   Till Weidner, Aidong Yang, Florian Forster, and Michael W. Hamm, "Regional Conditions Shape the Food–energy–land nexus of Low-carbon Indoor Farming," *Nature Food* 3, 206–216 (2022): https://doi.org/10.1038/s43016-022-00461-7.

5   Andrew M. Beacham, Laura H. Vickers, and James M. Monaghan Vertical Farming: A Summary of Approaches to Growing Skywards," *The Journal of Horticultural Science and Biotechnology* 94, no. 3 (2019), 277–283: https://doi.org/10.1080/14620316.2019.1574214. The Swedish agri-tech company Plantagon has been experimenting with recovering the energy from LEDs, according to Angeli Mehta, "From Vertical Farms to New Proteins: Innovating to Feed the Planet," *Reuters Events* (22 February 2018): https://www.reutersevents.com/sustainability/vertical-farms-new-proteins-innovating-feed-planet.

6   Kurt Benke and Bruce Tomkins, "Future Food-production Systems: Vertical Farming and Controlled-Environment Agriculture," *Sustainability: Science, Practice and Policy* 13, no. 1 (2017), 13–26, https://doi.org/10.1080/15487733.2017.1394054.

7   Nicholas Hildyard, "Radical or Reactionary Tomatoes? Organizing against the Toxic Legacy of Capital's Environmentalism," 61–73 in *Ecological Solidarity and the Kurdish Freedom Movement: Thought, Practice, Challenges, and Opportunities*, ed. by Stephen E. Hunt (Lanham, MD: Lexington, 2021). Specifically in terms of issues of inclusion and the justice system, the outcomes of the aeroponic container farm that the Bristol enterprise LettUs Grow has recently set up as part of a rehabilitation programme at HM Prison Hewell in Worcestershire will be of interest. See School of Biological Sciences, University of Bristol,

"Sustainable Bristol Student Start-up Branches into Prison Partnership to Aid Rehabilitation," (24 August 2022): http://www.bristol.ac.uk/biology/news/2022/sustainable-bristol-student-start-up-branches-into-prison-partnership-to-aid-reh.html; LettUs Grow website, "HMP Hewell Case Study": https://www.lettusgrow.com/hmp-hewell-case-study," accessed 21 January 2023. The Severn Project, a social enterprise polytunnel growing project set up to provide employment for ex-offenders in the Bristol area, went into liquidation in 2019, after just under a decade. Hannah Baker, "Bristol Farm that Helped Prisoners Rebuild Lives Goes Bust," *Bristol Post* (8 February 2019): https://www.bristolpost.co.uk/news/business/severn-project-bristol-farm-business-2519272.

8   A pioneering experiment is underway in Sweden, where Coop Butiker and Stormarknader has started a partnership with vertical gardening enterprise Swegreen to pilot an in-store growing system. See "Coop and Swegreen Announce Partnership, Introducing In-Store Vertical Farming Units in Three Locations," Swegreen website (12 June 2023): https://news.cision.com/swegreen-ab/r/coop-and-swegreen-announce-partnership--introducing-in-store-vertical-farming-units-in-three-locatio,c3783996.

9   Manfred Köhler, "Green Facades—A View Back and Some Visions," *Urban Ecosystems* 11 (2008), 423–436: https://doi.org/10.1007/s11252-008-0063-x; Beacham, Vickers, and Monaghan, "Vertical Farming." The forest cities are design projects of Stefano Boeri Architetti.

10 Jen Maylack, "How a Glass Terrarium Changed the World," *The Atlantic* (12 November 2017): https://www.theatlantic.com/technology/archive/2017/11/how-a-glass-terrarium-changed-the-world/545621/.

11 Michele Butturini and Leo F.M. Marcelis, "Vertical Farming in Europe: Present Status and Outlook," Chapter 4 in *Plant Factory: An Indoor Vertical Farming System for Efficient Quality Food Production*, ed. by Toyoki Kozai, Genhua Niu, and Michiko Takagaki, 2nd ed. (London: Academic Press, 2020): https://doi.org/10.1016/B978-0-12-816691-8.00004-2. One such venture in Bristol, Suncraft, was short-lived; seemingly, it opened just before the global coronavirus pandemic and ceased to do business due to the subsequent disruption.

12 Open Source Ecology homepage, accessed 25 October, 2023, https://www.opensourceecology.org/.
13 David Elliott, *Renewable Energy in the UK: Past, Present and Future* (Cham, Switzerland: Palgrave Macmillan, 2019). Godfrey Boyle (1945–2019) co-editor with Peter Harper of *Radical Technology* and of *Undercurrents* magazine was a key figure within Comtek in Bath, and then through its relocation to Milton Keynes. He founded the Energy and Environment Research Unit at the Open University, consulted by the Labour government when it began to channel funds into the research and development of renewable energies in the years after the Oil Crisis.
14 Robert Llewellyn as chair of "Past, Present, and Future of Community Energy," event at Museum of Bath at Work (20 June 2019). The National Grid was shortly to proclaim "2020 Greenest Year on Record for Britain," National Grid website (12 January 2021) in Terms of Electricity Production: https://www.nationalgrid.com/stories/journey-to-net-zero-stories/2020-greenest-year-record-britain.
15 Department for Business, Energy and Industrial Strategy, *Policy paper: British Energy Security Strategy* (updated 7 April 2022): https://www.gov.uk/government/publications/british-energy-security-strategy/british-energy-security-strategy#renewables. The target is for solar technologies to produce 70 gigawatts by 2035, Department for Energy Security and Net Zero, *Powering Up Britain: Energy Security Plan* (March 2023): https://assets.publishing.service.gov.uk/government/uploads/system/uploads/attachment_data/file/1148252/powering-up-britain-energy-security-plan.pdf.
16 Although it is important to avoid the negation of these advances through unsustainable demand-side increases through aviation, cars, and other forms of power-hungry transport.
17 Beth Howell, "Solar Panel Statistics 2023: Everything You Need To Know," The Eco Experts website (26 January 2023): https://www.theecoexperts.co.uk/solar-panels/solar-statistics#link-what-percentage-of-the-uks-renewable-energy-is-solar.
18 In the UK, the vast majority of rooftop solar panels are on domestic rather than commercial buildings (about 1.1M out of 1,265,000

registered solar power installations), according to Gareth Simkins, "Rooftop Solar Power Installations Double in a Year," Solar Energy UK website (24 February 2023): https://solarenergyuk.org/news/rooftop-solar-power-installations-double-in-a-year/.

19 My trade union, Unison, is campaigning to expose, and avoid reliance upon, the forced labour of Uyghur workers, "Clean Dirty Energy – Sourcing Solar Energy Without Uyghur Forced Labour," (August 2022): https://www.unison.org.uk/content/uploads/2022/08/Clean-dirty-energy-1.pdf.

20 Bastani, *Fully Automated Luxury Communism* and Max Aji, *A People's Green New Deal* (London: Pluto, 2021), 200. Despite common ground, eco-socialist faith in the efficacy of state planning distinguishes such programmes from social-ecology tendencies.

21 Pietro Elia Campana, Bengt Stridh, Stefano Amaducci, and Michele Colauzzi, "Optimisation of Vertically Mounted Agrivoltaic Systems," *Journal of Cleaner Production* 325 (2021): https://doi.org/10.1016/j.jclepro.2021.129091; Matt Ferrell provides an interesting overview of the issues involved, "Solar Panels Plus Farming? Agrivoltaics Explained," *Undecided with Matt Ferrell*, YouTube video (5 October 2021): https://www.youtube.com/watch?v=lgZBlD-TCFE&list=RDCMUCjtUS7-SZTi6pXjUbzGHQCg&start_radio=1&t=757s.

22 Bastani, *Fully Automated Luxury Communism*, 102.

23 It is worth recalling that renewable technology producers in the UK were dismantled and the technology was off-shored, a notable instance being the Vesta Wind Systems factory on the Isle of Wight in 2009. Matthew Weaver and Steven Morris, "Staff Occupy Isle of Wight Wind Turbine Plant in Protest Against Closure," *The Guardian* (21 July 2009): https://www.theguardian.com/environment/2009/jul/21/wind-turbine-factory-occupation.

24 Kishor Kumar Sadasivuni, Kalim Deshmukh, T.N. Ahipa, Aqib Muzaffar, M. Basheer Ahamed, S.K. Khadheer Pasha, and Mariam Al-Ali Al-Maadeed, "Flexible, Biodegradable and Recyclable Solar Cells: A Review," *Journal of Materials Science: Materials in Electronics* 30 (2019), 951–974: https://doi.org/10.1007/s10854-018-0397-y; Andreea Irina Barzic, "An Introduction to Engineering Applications

of Bioplastics," 3–22 in *Handbook of Bioplastics and Biocomposites Engineering Applications*, eds Inamuddin and Tariq Altalhi, 2nd ed. (Hoboken, NJ and Beverly, MA: Wiley, Scrivener Publishing, 2023), 10–11.

25 As described in this recent Chinese report, Ying Zhou, Ruiying Li, Zexuan Lv, Jian Liu, Hongjun Zhou, and Chunming Xu, "Green Hydrogen: A Promising Way to the Carbon-Free Society," *Chinese Journal of Chemical Engineering* 43 (2022): https://doi.org/10.1016/j.cjche.2022.02.001.

26 Gbemi Oluleye and Semra Bakkaloglu, "Green Gas: The Green Economy Under Our Feet" (May 2022), Ecotricity website: https://www.ecotricity.co.uk/our-green-energy/green-gas.

27 George Monbiot, "Why are we Feeding Crops to Our Cars When People are Starving?," *The Guardian* (30 June 2022): https://www.theguardian.com/commentisfree/2022/jun/30/crops-cars-starving-biofuels-climate-sustainable.

28 Oluleye and Bakkaloglu, "Green Gas," 20.

29 Rae, "A Land Cover Atlas of the United Kingdom," 5; Oluleye and Bakkaloglu, "Green Gas," 13.

30 Biofuelwatch, "How Green is Ecotricity's 'Green Gas from Grass'?," (December 2016), 3: https://www.biofuelwatch.org.uk/2016/grass-biomethane-report/.

31 Almuth Ernsting, "It Beats Fracking – But Can we Believe Ecotricity's Vision of 'Green Gas from Grass'?," *The Ecologist* (27 January 2017): https://theecologist.org/2017/jan/27/it-beats-fracking-can-we-believe-ecotricitys-vision-green-gas-grass.

32 This is in addition to the concerns of Biofuelwatch that to reach the levels of productivity that the scheme requires, there would be two or three mowings a year, unlike permanent pasture, resulting in disruption that would tend to undermine biodiversity. Biofuelwatch, "Conversation with Ecotricity about Their 'Green Gas from Grass' proposal" (2017): https://www.biofuelwatch.org.uk/2017/ecotricity-conversation/.

33 Oluleye and Bakkaloglu, "Green Gas," 9.

34 Jenny Hall, "Alternatives to Commercial Grazing: A Guide for Farmers in an Age of Climate Emergency and Public Goods," The Vegan Society

[2020]: https://www.vegansociety.com/sites/default/files/uploads/ Alternatives%20to%20Grazing.pdf.

35 Attracted by its properties as a light, fast-growing, strong variety of grass that has proved to be so versatile that it can be used to make anything from socks to musical instruments to housing structures. See Stephen E. Hunt, *The Revolutionary Urbanism of Street Farm: Eco-Anarchism. Architecture and Alternative Technology in the 1970s* (Bristol: Tangent, 2014).

36 Alan Dalton, "Skeptikal Chymist," 182–185 in *Radical Technology*, eds Peter Harper, Godfrey Boyle, and the editors of *Undercurrents* (London: Wildwood House, 1973).

37 Tom Woolley, *Natural Building Techniques: A Guide to Ecological Methods and Materials* (Ramsbury, Crowood Press, 2022), Chap. 6.

38 This is accounting for the carbon dioxide absorbed by hemp cultivation, and also believed to be sequestered through a process of carbonation as the lime gradually reverts to limestone, according to a detailed analysis in Y. Florentin, D. Pearlmutter, B. Givoni, and E. Gal, "A Life-cycle Energy and Carbon Analysis of Hemp-lime Bio-composite Building Materials," *Energy and Buildings* 156 (2017), 293–305: https://doi.org/10.1016/j.enbuild.2017.09.097.

39 Lucinda Dann, "Why Hemp is an Attractive Alternative Crop to OSR," *Farmers Weekly* (17 June 2020): https://www.fwi.co.uk/arable/crop-selection/market-opportunities/why-hemp-is-an-attractive-alternative-crop-to-osr.

40 To avoid incidents like the destruction of the crop produced by the non-profit cooperative, Hempen, as detailed in "Grow Hemp," 26–30 in *With the Land: Reflections on Land Work and Ten Years of the Landworkers' Alliance* ([s.l.]: Landworkers' Alliance, 2023).

41 Welsh Government, *Sustainable Farming and Our Land: Proposals to continue and simplify Agricultural Support for Farmers and the Rural Economy: Summary of Responses including Welsh Government Responses* (November 2020): https://www.gov.wales/sites/default/files/consultations/2020-11/sustainable-farming-summary-of-responses.pdf.

42 Robert D. Kinley, Gonzalo Martinez-Fernandez, Melissa K. Matthews, Rocky de Nys, Marie Magnusson, Nigel W. Tomkins, "Mitigating the

Carbon Footprint and Improving Productivity of Ruminant Livestock Agriculture Using a Red Seaweed," *Journal of Cleaner Production* 259 (20 June 2020): https://doi.org/10.1016/j.jclepro.2020.120836; Sandra Vijn et al., "Key Considerations for the Use of Seaweed to Reduce Enteric Methane Emissions From Cattle," *Frontiers in Veterinary Science* (23 December 2020): https://doi.org/10.3389/fvets.2020.597430; Christopher R.K. Glasson et al., "Benefits and Risks of Including the Bromoform Containing Seaweed Asparagopsis in Feed for the Reduction of Methane Production from Ruminants," *Algal Research* 64 (May 2022): https://doi.org/10.1016/j.algal.2022.102673,

43 Julia Lohmann, "We Know Too Much and Do Too Little," video on YouTube (15 February 2020): https://www.youtube.com/watch?v=Jzml_O64CtI.

44 For instance, a blog on the *Treehugger: Sustainability for All* website cites improvements for city offices and jets among the benefits of biomimicry. Shea Gunther, "8 Amazing Examples of Biomimicry: How Designers and Engineers Look at Nature for Solutions" (21 July 2022): https://www.treehugger.com/amazing-examples-of-biomimicry-4869336.

45 The most famous and notorious example of a natural solution going catastrophically wrong is surely the introduction of the cane toad as a so-called biological control for cane beetles in Australia. Surprisingly, the cane toad is still not classed as an invasive species in Australia, according to Queensland Government, "Cane Toad," Business Queensland website: (updated 19 May 2023): https://www.business.qld.gov.au/industries/farms-fishing-forestry/agriculture/land-management/health-pests-weeds-diseases/pests/invasive-animals/other/cane-toad, accessed 19 August 2023.

46 *Wakame Watch* website, accessed 24 October 2023, http://wakamewatch.org.uk/, citing the International Union for Conservation of Nature's Invasive Species Specialist Group.

47 Jessica Hernandez, "Invasive Species as a Metaphor for Colonization," *Rewilding* website, accessed 24 October 2023, https://www.rewildingmag.com/invasive-species-as-a-metaphor-for-colonization/.

48 Bioneers, "Creating A Future Less Disposable Than Our Plastics," *Bioneers* website (2018): https://bioneers.org/creating-a-future-less-disposable-than-our-plastics-ze0z1709/.

49 World Wildlife Fund, "Land of Plenty," 10.
50 Sustainable Inshore Fisheries Trust, *Seaweed Cultivation in Scotland: A Guide for Community Participation in Seaweed Farm Applications* (March 2021): https://www.sift.scot/wp-content/uploads/2021/03/SIFT-Seaweed-Guide.pdf, accessed 29 August 2022.
51 A popular and fabulously onomatopoeic borrowing from Native American culture, reputedly being a Potawatomi word derived from the force with which a mushroom pushes through the soil overnight.
52 Merlin Sheldrake, *Entangled Life: How Fungi Make Our Worlds, Change Our Minds, and Shape Our Futures* (London: Vintage, 2021), 200.
53 Rahul Bhadouria, Somenath Das, Ajay Kumar, Rishikesh Singh, and Vipin Kumar Singh, "Mycoremediation of Agrochemicals," Chapter 22 in *Agrochemicals Detection, Treatment and Remediation: Pesticides and Chemical Fertilizers*, ed. M.N.V. Prasad (San Diego: Elsevier Science and Technology, 2020).
54 Mitchell Jones, Antoni Gandia, Sabu John, and Alexander Bismarck, "Leather-like Material Biofabrication Using Fungi," *Nature Sustainability* 4, (2021), 9–16: https://doi.org/10.1038/s41893-020-00606-1; Laurie Donaldson, "Leather Substitutes Derived from Fungi Show Promise," *Materials Today* 41 (2020), 1–2: https://doi.org/10.1016/j.mattod.2020.10.019.
55 Andrew Adamatzky, Anna Nikolaidou, Antoni Gandia, Alessandro Chiolerio, and Mohammad Mahdi Dehshibi, "Reactive Fungal Wearable," *Biosystems* 199 (2021): https://doi.org/10.1016/j.biosystems.2020.104304; Andrew Adamatzky, Phil Ayres, Alexander E. Beasley, Alessandro Chiolerio, Mohammad M. Dehshibi, Antoni Gandia, Elena Albergati, Richard Mayne, Anna Nikolaidou, Nic Roberts, Martin Tegelaar, Michail-Antisthenis Tsompanas, Neil Phillips, and Han A.B. Wösten, "Fungal Electronics," *Biosystems* 212 (2021): https://doi.org/10.1016/j.biosystems.2021.104588.
56 Godfrey Boyle, "Radical Technology – Yesterday, Today and Tomorrow," paper at Radical Technology 2.0 Conference, Bristol (2–4 September 2016).
57 Murray Bookchin, "Towards a Liberatory Technology [1965]," 85–139 in *Post-Scarcity Anarchism* (London: Wildwood House, 1974), 86.

58 Simar Singh Bajaj, Lwando Maki, and Fatima Cody Stanford, "Vaccine Apartheid: Global Cooperation and Equity," *The Lancet* 399, no. 10334 (23 February 2022), 1452–1453: https://doi.org/10.1016/S0140-6736(22)00328-2.
59 Tokar, "Biofuels and the Global Food Crisis," 121–205 in *Agriculture and Food in Crisis,* ed. Magdoff and Tokar, 124.

RIGHT LIVELIHOODS

Sadly, and ironically, the most vital work for society is typically the least well remunerated for the workers tasked with producing, delivering, and servicing the goods and needs necessary to thrive. It would be an error to separate future food production from pressing concern for the prospective welfare of agricultural producers. In the UK, most workers are employed in the processing, distribution, retail, and hospitality part of the food industry, rather than in growing and producing food.[1]

Consequently, perhaps, primary producers receive scant mention in the "Government Food Strategy." The apparent expectation for the short to medium term is that seasonal migrant workers will harvest crops until automation incrementally takes over the task. This is in a context in which the NFU reports that growers are "currently struggling to find the skilled workforce needed," and in which NFU Cymru, for example, has long expressed the view that "finding reliable workers from within the UK workforce is impractical."[2]

However, a recent Landworkers' Alliance report exposes the reality of working conditions for visitors with temporary access under the Seasonal Workers' Visa scheme.[3] Exploitative circumstances in which, for example, workers in the soft fruit and poultry sectors are rewarded a tiny proportion of profits for working days likened to modern slavery—where bullying and intimidation is rife, unfair third-party brokerage costs are embedded in the system, and debt operates as a mechanism of control and coercion—characterise such arrangements.

As it stands, there is limited detail in the current government policy outline to substantiate how the situation might change to meet its objective to "ensure that by 2030, pay, employment and productivity, as well as completion of high-quality skills training will have risen in the agri-food industry in every area of the UK."[4] The NFU, using similar language regarding "levelling up" in the rural economy, calls for investment in education, training, and infrastructure. In the meantime, many rural labourers continue to endure long working hours, subsisting on the minimum, or living wage (or worse, for those in the informal economy).[5] Furthermore, there were "months of extensive NFU lobbying" of Farming Minister Mark Spencer to scrap a 60p pay uplift for seasonal workers.[6] While some agricultural workers are members of Unite, the sector remains largely un-unionised.[7] Vicki Hird of Sustain has also noted that protections afforded by the Agricultural Wages Boards were lost when the Cameron administration abolished them in 2013, and has called for their reinstatement.[8]

Agriculture remains, at best, poorly paid, and at worst, an "at-risk" sector for human trafficking, unlicensed labour providers (or "gangmasters"), and abuse. In such circumstances, land work is not an appealing or even viable prospect for domestic workers. Furthermore, small farmers' organisations and critics persistently claim that new entrants attempting to find livelihoods as growers face formidable barriers.[9] Despite the emphasis upon the importance of food production across the current reports on UK agriculture, there continues to be a perception of "physical taint" associated with labour that involves getting soiled by working on the land and with animals, which contributes to its low occupational prestige.[10] The Landworkers' Alliance points to the "stigma and stereotypes attached to farming and land work,"[11] while Tim Lang also acknowledges food workers' "low-wage image problem."[12]

The high costs of entry, coupled with constraints newcomers face in gaining access to land, help to explain the ageing demographic profile of the shrinking farming profession, with a current median age of 60 years old.[13] The impact of uneven access to education, training, and knowledge serves to bolster existing hierarchies. Relatedly, current trends in agribusiness are seeing larger landowners and corporations control enterprises, combining capital-intensive technologies and deskilled, minimum-wage labour.[14] Farmers and their employees are also often held responsible for agriculture's negative ecological impacts, yet lack agency to determine the means of their production in the context of the world market. Achieving improved models of food production, therefore, calls for a profound shift, upgrading the status of agricultural work through improved representation and understanding of such roles through the media and education, and challenging cultural and organisational hierarchies.

Critics argue that inequalities and structural balances particularly impact women in agriculture.[15] Social ecology emphasises a socioeconomic analysis of ecological outcomes. Gender equity is a core tenet of democratic confederalism and, consequently, has been inseparable from many of the agricultural concerns in this book. Applying social-ecology ideas to farming and food production raises multiple discussions about the way that social hierarchies are expressed and experienced in practice. Questions about who makes decisions, and how, are fundamental to any advance towards a democratic and inclusive future.

Within the realm of food production, this is connected to additional factors relating to the gendered division of labour and differentiation of roles within production and supply chains. Accumulative patterns of historic social expectation and reward have served to entrench inequalities over time and have a determining impact upon generations to come. Critics have noted that while in many regions women have been taking a greater share in food production due to the "feminization of agriculture," traditional disadvantages have persisted in terms of lower wages and less favourable access to land, finance, resources such as seeds and fertilisers, and agricultural extension services.[16] In England, while 55% of family farm workers are women, only 16–17% are registered as landowners or farm managers.[17] Radical agriculture, therefore, demands that the democratisation of the economy should address longstanding exclusion or barriers to women's fair participation in the agricultural system.

As we have seen, liberatory technology asks not whether the implementation of agricultural technologies will boost profits, but poses wider questions about working conditions and livelihoods, such as whether they have an emancipatory function in upskilling and empowering the workforce, and reducing disparities based on class, gender, and ethnicity. For such reasons, social ecologists hold that technological innovation should not be assessed separately from considerations of gender inequalities, power imbalances, economic opportunities, and other social factors.

Current contrasting perspectives upon labour and technology signify competing visions of agricultural production. Substantial subsidies have long been disproportionately directed towards large agribusiness enterprises, best able to invest in the implementation of capital-intensive technology. In the post-Brexit environment, the NFU and DEFRA are supportive of "Agri-tech," and respectively call for, and promise investment in, for example, agri-robotics and the deregulation of genetic technologies.[18] Linked to concerns about job losses and demoralisation in the agricultural profession, however, the Sustainable Food Trust argue that there is a wider sense of alienation from growing processes and that "the high-tech nature of most farming systems has led to us becoming increasingly distanced from agriculture and, consequently, the story behind our food."[19]

Utilitarian approaches to profit-driven production may dissuade new entrants who might otherwise be attracted by the creativity, artisanship, and autonomy that long-term growers have found to be so satisfying.[20] There are, therefore, different, indeed contested, "stories" about new technologies' impacts upon food production, especially genetic modification, agri-robotics, and artificial intelligence. These jarring narratives in present-day reports reflect older arguments about labour and technology. So-called cornucopians (techno-optimists) have expressed confidence about the progressive thrust of technological development *per se* in driving prosperity for the benefit of all.

Critics of modernising tendencies have spanned the spectrum from countercultural back-to-the-land advocates seeking simpler, more authentic lifestyles to feudalist right-wing anti-modern movements, which reached their apogee in the Nazi era, when the "glorification of rural peasant values" became of a piece with notions of racial purity and anti-Semitism.[21] By strong contrast, social ecologists have taken a forward-to-the-land position: a more deliberative approach that weighs specific technologies in the context of their social implications and effects upon the living world.[22] Advanced "agri-tech" often increases dependency on precision engineering and reduces affordable access to commercially patented seeds. There are concerns, therefore, that it has a propensity to concentrate monopoly production, undermining the bargaining power of smaller producers and new entrants into the field, or excluding them outright. Calls for ethical responsibility are difficult once technology has been generally released beyond democratic control. Liberatory technology is committed to progressive change in the here and now, and the betterment of prospects for future generations.

Few writers have been more eloquent in evoking the fulfilment and profound self-realisation experienced through active participation in land work than the agricultural sage John Stewart Collis, who spoke passionately of the "new vision of the field" in his 1946 account, *The Worm Forgives the Plough*.[23] This, he largely attributes to the "agricultural habit of mind," entailing routine problem solving and "endless improvisation."[24] As to labour, Collis permits himself a utopian reverie:

I continually have day-dreams of a time when lots of people would come out into the fields and love working with their hands, and also love working with the mind, their manly heritage, and make such jobs as these go quickly and delightfully. It will be a sad criticism of life if we have to say that such a dream is futile. Anyway I wouldn't ask much more than this of my utopia.[25]

An important lesson of history is that coercion regarding matters of rural labour rarely ends well. This applies to both driving people off the land and forcing them back to the land. Yet Collis's "day-dreams" suggest, rather, a more life-affirming perspective upon manual labour. At least in Collis's utopian imaginary, people would do well to undertake the work of food cultivation as art, craft, and science, as a source of purposeful pleasure, pursuing their common interests experienced as sociability and self-development.

It is relevant that Collis was writing as a member of the land army during the 1940s, when commercial imperatives were briefly suspended, and the drive for profit ceased to be the immediate priority. In banishing the "physical taint" of toil on the land, his celebration of emancipatory farming was made in the context of the successful national "Dig for Victory" campaigns of the time, in part a triumph of voluntary effort.

During the early 2000s, the American activist and economist Michael Albert put forward the idea of balanced job complexes as a part of his programme of participatory economics.[26] This involves a breakdown of the rigid forms of the division of labour so that workers undertake a variety of tasks. This would not, of course, mean that a teacher or bricklayer would work in a seed nursery in the morning before taking up their chosen profession during the afternoon, but could entail some seasonable variation in tasks to share roles more equitably, avoid monotony, raise horticultural and culinary literacy, and develop a broader skill-set and knowledge base.

In the tradition of Collis's "day-dreams"—and the concerns expressed about exclusion, inequality, and alienation in the present-day reports of the Landworkers' Alliance[27] and Sustainable Food Trust—a version of balanced job complexes could represent a more inclusive and less exploitative approach to food production and other forms of land management. Again, the proto-green Collis's musings while working as an agricultural labourer stand in contrast to the more productivist and profit-minded targets of the "Government Food Strategy." Regretting that "everyone must make a living rather than make a life,"[28] his writings return us to the theme of agriculture as a sacred activity and as a form of cultivation enabling of culture:

> There is an occupation which can engage nearly the whole man and which if there were time given for the development of the mind, would satisfy the needs of hundreds of thousands of people. This is agriculture. It could provide scope for bodily, mental and spiritual development. [...] What was agriculture for, it seemed to me, except that such a thing as [a] symphony and the playing of it should be made possible? To make bread so that it shall be possible for mankind to have more than bread and hear the scripture of the kings; to listen to a Beethoven, a Sibelius, a Tchaikovsky, uttering some far message of paradox and joy.[29]

Collis raises fundamental yet practical questions about farming, which are only implicit in present-day policy reports considering the implementation of technologies and rural labour. Despite the outmoded language of assumed masculinity, his writing is a valuable bridge back to the interwar transition from animal to motorised farm machinery, and evokes the role of farming in holding together human community and culture that Bookchin was later to celebrate in "Radical Agriculture."[30] In a meditation upon the combine harvester, Collis was dazzled by the new machine's ingenuity and power, yet uncertain as to its ultimate benefits and social consequences. Neither writer was anti-technology, but anticipated the debates about what Collis termed the coming "Leisure state," and Bookchin termed "post-scarcity," for human self-realisation. Neither were from farming backgrounds, and their trenchant rejection of instrumentalism perhaps reflects the perspectives of outsiders. Both realised that labour-saving technology was unlikely to be liberatory if those whose labour is displaced and were deskilled experienced loss of income and agency, leading to impoverishment and alienation. As Fairlie argues, where rural infrastructure is developed and working conditions are better, land-based work could be less seen as "drudgery" and more attractive—for example, in the horse industry, where employment by "well-heeled clientele" "pays people properly."[31]

Aspirations towards "levelling up," set out in the NFU's "British Farming" and in the "Government Food Strategy," are unlikely to be achieved without addressing the "systemic power imbalances" identified by Benton and Harwatt.[32] Initiatives such as universal basic income could potentially temper further displacement of rural livelihoods brought about by further automation of production but, in the UK, are not currently part of mainstream debate regarding the workforce. In addition to his relevant advocation of an "irreducible minimum," guaranteeing that basic needs be met for all, Bookchin's early discussion of liberatory technology is invaluable in explaining and providing flexible criteria for evaluating the implementation of technology, and for deciding which technologies are taken forward, and for whose benefit; the just distribution of goods; and potential ecological impacts.[33] It is the abolition of conditions of rural exploitation and coercion that is sought, not the replacement of manual labour. It is argued that there are desirable social benefits for human well-being where lifelong connection to part-time food growing is widely experienced, including purposeful physical activity, developing horticultural skills and knowledge, and cooperative working.

While the pains and pleasures of physical labour raise dilemmas as to the human experience of land work, we will now consider some of the spiritual and aesthetic aspects of growing and consuming food, starting with personal involvement working on a small farm dedicated to Japanese agriculture.

Notes

1. There are an estimated 471,000 agricultural workers on commercial holdings in the UK, DEFRA et al., "Agriculture in the UK 2022" (2023), 9 and 32. Forum for the Future suggest that the "asymmetric" power relationship between farmers and retailers is also a factor that undermines the position of the former when negotiating prices in the supply chain, in "Supply Chain Synergies: What is the Appropriate Role of Supply Chains in Achieving Responsible Production at Farm Level?," report commissioned by the Oxford Farming Conference (January 2023), executive summary available from https://www.ofc.org.uk/ofc-reports.
2. NFU, "Seasonal Agricultural Worker Scheme – Extra Visas a Step Forward," *NFU Online* (16 December 2023): https://www.nfuonline.com/updates-and-information/increase-in-seasonal-workers-visas-is-a-step-forward-nfu-says/; NFU Cymru and NFU, "Backing British Farming in a Volatile World: The Report" (2015), 3: https://www.nfuonline.com/archive?treeid=43617, accessed 29 November 2022.
3. Catherine McAndrew, Oliver Fisher, Clark McAllister, and Christian Jaccarin, "Debt, Migration, and Exploitation: The Seasonal Worker Visa and the Degradation of Working Conditions in UK Horticulture," report by New Economics Foundation, Joint Council for Welfare of Immigrants, Sustain, Focus on Labour Exploitation Landworkers' Alliance (2023): https://staging.landworkersalliance.org.uk/wp-content/uploads/2018/10/LWA-Debt-Migration-and-Exploitation-2023.pdf.
4. Department for Environment, Food and Rural Affairs, "Government Food Strategy" (June 2022), 9: https://www.gov.uk/government/publications/government-food-strategy.
5. Current set rates and limited protections are published by DEFRA as "Agricultural workers' rights" https://www.gov.uk/agricultural-workers-rights/pay-and-overtime. In practice, opportunities to secure fair pay, especially for workers on Seasonal Workers' Visas who make up

a large proportion of the workforce for harvesting produce, are highly precarious, according to McAndrew, Fisher, McAllister, and Jaccarin, "Debt, Migration, and Exploitation," 11–12. While figures are by definition uncertain, in 2020, the Office for National Statistics cites a total of 4.36% for agricultural workers in the informal sector: ONS, "Informal Employment in the Agricultural and Non-agricultural Sectors by Sex, Country, and Region of the UK: 2012 to 2020," (8 June 2021): https://www.ons.gov.uk/employmentandlabourmarket/peopleinwork/ employmentandemployeetypes/adhocs/13308informalemploymentintheagriculturalandnonagriculturalsectorsbysexcountryandregionoftheuk2012to2020.

6 NFU, "Seasonal Worker Wage to Revert to the National Living Wage," NFUOnline (24 February 2023): https://www.nfuonline.com/updates-and-information/seasonal-worker-wage-to-revert-to-the-national-living-wage/.

7 The National Farmers' Union is more akin to an employers' organisation than one that represents the interests of agricultural workers.

8 McAndrew, Fisher, McAllister, and Jaccarin, "Debt, Migration, and Exploitation," 44.

9 Styles, Talks, and Tomlinson, *The Attraction of Agroecology*.

10 For example, research has placed farmers in the category with the highest stigma of "physical taint," Roberta Rosa Valtorta, Cristina Baldissarri, Luca Andrighetto, and Chiara Volpato, 961 in "Dirty Jobs and Dehumanization of Workers," *British Journal of Social Psychology*, 58 (2019), 955–970: https://doi.org/10.1111/bjso.12315. It is ironic that life-sustaining soil is used as a pejorative verb "to soil."

11 Styles, Talks, and Tomlinson, *Attraction of Agroecology*, 5 and 26.

12 Lang, "Feeding Britain," 12 and 143.

13 DEFRA, "Agriculture in the United Kingdom 2021," 26–27.

14 The fear that global-power imbalances will be made worse is one of the aspects of "critical ethical reflection" on cutting-edge agri-technology revealed in one of the few research studies dealing directly with this issue, Simone van der Burg, Marc-Jeroen Bogaardt, and Sjaak Wolfert, "Ethics of Smart Farming: Current Questions and Directions for Responsible Innovation Towards the Future," *NJAS – Wageningen*

Journal of Life Sciences 90–91, no. 1 (2019): https://doi.org/10.1016/j.njas.2019.01.001.

15 Carolyn E. Sachs, Leif Jensen, Paige Castellanos, and Kathleen Sexsmith (eds.), *Routledge Handbook of Gender and Agriculture* (Abingdon: Routledge, 2021), 1.

16 Issues dealt with in Sachs et al., *Routledge Handbook of Gender and Agriculture.*

17 DEFRA / ONS, "Agricultural Labour in England and the UK: Farm Structure Survey 2016": https://assets.publishing.service.gov.uk/government/uploads/system/uploads/attachment_data/file/771494/FSS2013-labour-statsnotice-17jan19.pdf, accessed 19 August 2023.

18 NFU, "British Farming," 4, 7, 11; DEFRA, "Government Food Strategy," 20.

19 Robert Barbour, Patrick Holden, and Jez Fredenburgh, "Feeding Britain from the Ground Up" (Bristol: Sustainable Food Trust, 2022), 12.

20 The human and ecology-centred values cherished by respondents in Jeff Pratt and Pete Luetchford, *Food for Change: The Politics and Values of Social Movements* (London: Pluto, 2014), 186–187.

21 Biehl and Staudenmaier, *Ecofascism*, 7.

22 Clearly expressed, for example, in support for the French Confédération Paysanne's position on this issue by social-ecologist Chaia Heller, *Food, Farms, and Solidarity*, 94.

23 John Stewart Collis, *The Worm Forgives the Plough* [1946–47] (Harmondsworth: Penguin, 1975), 39.

24 ibid., 29.

25 ibid., 63. In his introduction to a recent edition of Collis's book, Robert Macfarlane finds him to be too grounded to fall for "Blood and Soil" mysticism, and absolves the common-sense Collis of the "taint" and "thoroughly repellent politics" of fellow "work-worshippers," such as his acquaintance, far-right traditionalist and revivalist Rolf Gardiner. Robert Macfarlane, "Introduction" in Collis, *The Worm Forgives the Plough* [1946–47] (London: Vintage, 2009).

26 Michael Albert, *Parecom: Life After Capitalism* (London: Verso, 2004). Although broadly supportive of the idea of balanced job complexes, Peter Staudenmaier, a prominent member of the Institute for Social Ecology,

provides a critique of participatory economics from a social-ecologist perspective in "Social Ecology and Participatory Economics," Institute for Social Ecology website (four articles, 2002). Post-capitalist economist David Schweickart also undertakes a comprehensive analysis of what he sees as the shortcomings of participatory economics, "Nonsense on Stilts: Michael Albert's Parecon," Loyola University, Chicago paper (16 January 2006): http://dschwei.sites.luc.edu/parecon.pdf.

27   Who emphasise the social value of agroecology as "purposeful work," in *Attraction of Agroecology*, 14.
28   Collis, *The Worm Forgives the Plough*, 39.
29   ibid., 127–128.
30   Collis at once admired the fine engineering and power of the tractor, but could also experience ploughing by horse as "the very top-notch of satisfaction," ibid., 2–3.
31   Fairlie, *Meat*, 296.
32   Benton and Harwatt, *Sustainable Agriculture and Food Systems*, 31.
33   It is timely and important to note here that Bookchin's shifting views and approach are contested within the domain of social ecology. In an extended corrective to what he considers to be shortcomings in later Bookchin's programme of libertarian municipalism, fellow and rival social ecologist John P. Clark argues that political projects are in continuous dialectical exchange with concrete historical processes and that social creativity should be based upon dispersed agency across a range of initiatives, not what *ought* to be the outcome from a particular conception of citizens' decision-making, in "Beyond the Limits of the City: A communitarian anarchist critique of libertarian municipalism," Ch. 10 of *The Impossible Community: Realizing Communitarian Anarchism* (New York and London: Bloomsbury, 2013), 247–290. As new biotechnologies appear in forms that Bookchin could not have foreseen, fresh questions are being asked about their ethical implications and impacts, for example, in van der Burg, Bogaardt, and Wolfert, "Ethics of Smart Farming."

QUALITY OF PRODUCTION, OF CONSUMPTION, AND OF LIFE

Shumei: Japanese natural agriculture the Wiltshire way

On Summer solstice 2022, I found myself cycling down a shady lane to a remote hamlet in Wiltshire to volunteer at Shumei, a Japanese natural agriculture project. I was brought up nearby, but I had not visited Yatesbury since my teenage years. This trip felt at once like a homecoming and a voyage into the unknown. Wheeling past downland flowers and serenaded by skylarks, I disrupted a buzzard enjoying its freshly caught breakfast, causing it to rear up crossly next to me and flap off with what appeared to be a weasel kit still dangling in its beak.

I had contacted Shumei's demonstration farm after hearing about it through a random conversation in a pub in Bristol. I didn't know what to expect—deliberately so, because I had carried out no previous research, wanting to approach Shumei with an open mind. Was it a cult? A highly ecological approach to food production to benefit humanity while protecting the Earth? A means to launder corporate wealth through nature? A practical scientific experiment in alternative methods of cultivation? We'll see.

Farm manager Shinya Imahashi set up the five-acre farm in 2010, renting from the neighbouring Yatesbury Home Farm, which, happily, is also run on organic and biodynamic principles. Shumei agriculture as practiced at Yatesbury rests upon the challenging proposition that natural production requires only extremely low-inputs, avoiding not just synthetic chemicals and pesticides, but, seemingly, even specially grown green manures—the mainstay of veganic production. Immediately available sources of biomass are used, especially grass mowings for mulch, but animal manure is not applied, and, more surprisingly, the farm has no compost bins for vegetable food waste.

When I ask Shinya the perennial question about how nutrients are replaced when harvests are removed, he smiles and patiently explains, "the soil revitalises itself." It seems that this is not somehow magically defying the laws of thermodynamics, but the self-sustaining power of plants to draw-down nitrogen and carbon dioxide from the air, as well as draw up nutrients from the ground.

John Stewart Collis had observed the peculiar fact of plants' ability to "eat the sky" during the 1940s, explaining that "those roots sucked gases from the earth, those leaves sucked gases from the sky, and the result was the visible, hard, concrete potato."[1] In this way, dependency upon large imports of fertiliser from elsewhere is avoided at the Natural Agriculture Farm.

My main companion and Shumei mentor, Masa Saruhashi, tells me that the farm has been created as a demonstration to model feeding the people of the world with pure and natural food. The question of output is often raised, given the current hard-fought debates about the merits of sharing and sparing the land for biodiversity, since, as Monbiot argues forcefully in *Regenesis*, farming with reduced yields increases the amount of land that needs to be under cultivation and can, therefore, exacerbate the impact of agriculture upon other species.[2]

Masa explains that their priority is to grow healthy and resilient plants so that ample yields will follow and that "If the result is not so good, we try to find the cause by thinking about what is not in harmony with nature."[3] This is done with attention to, and care of, the soil and crops and through regular mulching, weeding, seed-saving, conserving water usage, and using rain-fed sources.

The project has lasted 12 years and is still producing goodly yields of healthy, nutritious vegetables. To date, then, it is working. Seven weeks after my visit, when we transplanted tiny seedlings from plug trays in the greenhouse, Masa sent me a photograph of rows of healthy and robust-looking beetroot plants that had shot up and were clearly flourishing, despite record temperatures and droughts experienced in the heatwave of summer 2022.

Masa further explains the three core principles of Shumei: natural agriculture, a form of meditation practice called *Jyorei*, and the appreciation of beauty in art and nature. The philosophy of Shumei turns out to be based upon a syncretic new-age religious practice, particularly derived from elements of Shintoism, Buddhism, and Christianity. A short form of *Shinji Shumeikai*, Shumei descends from the ideas of Mokichi Okada (1882–1955), who launched a group that translates to Nature Farming, and had correspondence with Jerome Irving Rodale in the United States, an early advocate of organic farming who shared similar ideas. Now, Shumei operates as a practical spiritual toolkit to promote harmony for humanity within itself and with the natural world. Such idealism is represented by a centrepiece at the farm, consisting of avenues of lavender leading to flower-shaped beds of French marigolds, around a topiary representation of Mount Fuji and the words "World Peace," both cut into privet.

My brief experience of working at Shumei met my critical approval, with a warm welcome from Shinya and the four Japanese workers under his guidance. I found instant rapport with Masa, and the other co-workers, Kay, Tommy, and Aika, who formed the team at the time of my visit. Since all were learning English, there was plenty of opportunity for me to exchange conversational vocabulary for information about Japanese culture, such as *taiko*, the percussion music now practiced in Yatesbury Church each week.

Work consisted of gathering and applying mulches to rows of onions and curly and Russian kale varieties, planting out beetroot seedlings from three large polytunnels, sowing chard seeds, weeding, and netting. The cultivation methods were labour-intensive, combining the use of mini-tractors with considerable manual work (I never did get a satisfactory understanding as to why we didn't use hoes for weeding). The result is long hours for the dedicated Shumei practitioners, working full days and weeks with only occasional days off.

The farm was teeming with butterflies and other insect life, and generally seemed rich in biodiversity, with five red kites, a species now flourishing in Wiltshire, making their commotion above us, and a happy encounter with a hedgehog. The produce from Yatesbury is certified as organic through the Soil Association, and supplies two retailers in Bristol, Earthbound and Matter Wholefoods, and London's Shumei Centre.

Perhaps there were elements of all the things that I had hoped and feared when approaching Shumei, but the experience was overwhelmingly positive. Two insights come to mind when considering the wider significance of the practices at Yatesbury.

First, in utilitarian approaches to farming, one place is too often sacrificed to another, whether removing existing wildlife or as sites for the extraction, manufacture, and storage of fertilisers and other synthetic chemicals. Accordingly, the integrated methods of Shumei challenge the dichotomy between intensive and extensive forms of cultivation. The maxim that nothing is wasted is honoured. Transplanting Shumei from its native Japan, where rice is the main crop, has involved considerable adaptation, with the result that a diverse abundance of produce is cultivated. This again demanded a shift, since my immediate co-worker, who had arrived a little over 2 months previously, had yet to taste a parsnip or cauliflower.

Second, the spiritual aspect to Shumei, which provokes contemplation upon the intangible aspects of growing. Certainly, Masa and Aika offered the experience of *Jyorei* with respect and generosity, with no sense of cultish pressure. The Shumei growing process is grounded in intuitive observation and seasonality. Above all, the value of Shumei and its relevance is the priority it gives to the life-affirming and healing properties of food production.

In Julia Wright's thought-provoking and charming collection of essays *Subtle Agroecologies: Farming with the Hidden Half of Nature*, there is an exploration of the intangible aspects of growing, often reliant upon such invisible phenomena as the seasons, photosynthesis, and growth itself that are mostly evident through their effects.[4] This delightful expedition into the ethereal aspects of cultivation spans the gap between Indigenous, spiritual, and quantum scientific dimensions to biology. Its quest for holistic farming chimes perfectly with the Shumei emphasis on harmony to be found at Yatesbury. Japanese natural agriculture's faith in the ability of plants to self-care with a little tending, tapping into nutrients and building up their own defences against species that might attack them, rests on resilience. Resilience may be an uncountable noun, but it is a quality readily recognisable among the forty types of vegetables that have been grown on this modest Wiltshire acreage.

A party in your mouth:[5] *Commensality, or the pleasures of eating together*

I'd like to reflect on the pains, but much more the subtle, and sometimes not so subtle, pleasures of commensality, or eating together. Food can work as a wonderful host for networking, cultivating interpersonal relationships through its occasions for growing, preparing meals, and dining with each other. Folk history has always been nourished by the romance of food, from the medieval fantasies of the land of Cockaigne, harvest festivals, the Cries of London, and the lively exchanges of the street market and souk. My next call, therefore, is to reinvigorate public space with a new generation of affordable communal eating places. These could enhance the quality of life through their economic benefits and potential to address social alienation.

Much has been said about the death of the high street in recent years. As greengrocers and hardware shops retreat, leaving the dreary predictability of identikit franchises interspersed with empty boarded shops, ghost towns before dismalands of offices, ring roads, shed warehouses, and business parks at the periphery. Social malaise thrives in such environments. Yet new modes of eating together could help to address social isolation. Whether the phenomenon is attractive—inducing either traumatic memories or fond recollections—is partly conditioned by whether the language is appetising. If the terms commensality, social eating, conviviality, canteens, refectories, companionship, togetherness, "alimentary participation," were biscuits on a platter, which one would you reach for?[6]

It must be conceded that, for some people, the word "canteen" has mixed connotations. Canteens can bring to mind the horrors of the state confiscation of food and cooking utensils during Mao's Great Leap Forward and controversies over the extent to which police "canteen culture" may engender prejudices. Winston Churchill reportedly insisted that the communal eating establishments set up during the Second World War were to be called "British Restaurants," since he found the notion of canteens had distasteful associations with communism.[7] Present-day pains include introverts' fears of forced gregariousness or the experience of mealtime in the refectory as an occasion where schoolchildren establish who is to be included or excluded in fluid popularity stakes. Notwithstanding such reservations, the establishment of public refectories has the potential to extend community assets and forge new bonds between the producers and consumers of food.

The present cost-of-living crisis has brought to the fore longer-term trends towards mass homelessness and food poverty. In the wake of the dismantlement of welfare provision, austerity, and policies that have delivered increasing inequality, outdoor soup runs and food banks have become familiar sights in neoliberal Britain.[8] Grounded in principles of mutual aid and reciprocity, creating communal eateries could usher in a more joyful, less stigmatising alternative to the individualised and remedial charity of food banks. Today, however, canteens and refectories survive where catering has not been outsourced and replaced, yet tend to be visible mostly within the institutional worlds of schools, prisons, hospitals, a decreasing proportion of workplaces, universities, and youth hostels.[9]

There is also a long, radical tradition of communal eating; the social and potentially liberating implications of canteens has long been recognised. In 1894, socialist Robert Blatchford advocated such resources in his manifesto for *Merrie England*: "I would institute public dining halls, public baths, public wash-houses on the best plans, and so set free the hands of those slaves – our English women."[10] It was to be expected, then, that the Suffragette movement too would embrace the emancipatory potential of public dining, opening, for example, cheap restaurants in women's centres across East London to feed local people without the stigma of charity.[11]

Canteen-style mass catering was a cost-effective means to reduce the proportion of time spent preparing meals in the home. Sharing the workload in this way could save time and money incurred with domestic cooking by reducing household fuel use and food waste.[12] A single heat source, for example, can heat through a giant pan for twenty nearly as easily as a portion for a single dish. A single warm dining hall can accommodate a street's worth of otherwise centrally heated houses for an hour.

Sue Bruley's fascinating account of collective eating during the 1926 General Strike and miners' lockout found that the South Wales Miners' Federation's practice of channelling limited funds to a proliferation of self-managed canteens and communal soup kitchens not only enabled resources to go further, due to economies of scale, but had a vital role in maintaining community solidarity.[13] While class struggle was regarded as a priority over the cause of greater equality for women, Bruley tentatively concluded that the joint operation to run the miners' kitchens meant that roles shifted, and that in the "context of communal food preparation there is evidence of a breaking down of traditional gender segregation and increased fellowship between men and women," at least for the duration of the dispute.[14] The 1984–1985 Miners' Strike was to see a repeat display of mutual aid through improvised soup kitchens. Ken Loach pays homage to the social power of food in his 2023 film *The Old Oak*, celebrated in the memorable slogan "When We Eat Together, We Stick Together," which appears on a photograph that has survived from the Miners' Strike.

Many radical movements have since made use of mass catering to similarly benefit from economies of scale, to provide affordable alternatives to home cooking and private restaurants, and to sustain campaigns of direct action. I have happy memories of vegetable stew and fireside chat mingled with wood smoke as the sun went down on St Catherine's Hill, during the protest camp with the Dongas Tribe at Twyford Down. I was later pleased to find that a gigantic kettle, kindly serving treacly tea during the Newbury Road Protest Camps of the late 1990s, was a veteran of the women's peace camps at nearby Greenham Common.[15]

When there was a call out for folks to assist the Common Ground Collective in providing food and basic supplies during the Hurricane Katrina disaster, Food not Bombs members were the first responders.[16] Formed during the 1980s, the organisation now has a global reach, with groups on every continent. In recent years, a striking and impressive example has been the emergence of Food not Bombs Yangon, initiated in part by Yangon punk band Rebel Riot. Now active in other parts of Myanmar, the group has raised funds, distributed food, and organised collective eating for street children and those suffering from extreme weather events, before and after the 2021 military coup.

A further recent example is the appearance of the traditional Sikh community kitchen, known as the langar, as a means of sustenance to support the mass mobilisations of farmers during the Indian protests in 2021–2022. A supportive commentator, Bikrum Gill frames the inclusiveness of the langar as a visible rejection of hierarchical relations based on caste or divisions of faith. He suggests that setting up the community kitchens in this context is a practical demonstration of "a world in which food is grown, prepared, and served in common, in community, for the purposes not of profit but rather of sustaining community and earth in service of a higher power."[17]

The Common Ground Collective upheld the enabling principle of "solidarity not charity," and their forthright rejection of food aid as a form of condescension or even coercion is well made. The distribution of food proved to be an attractive bond for the Occupy movement's camps.

Occupy was just one instance where self-managed food provision merged into something of an improvised welfare service. The movement exposed the degree of social isolation in the twenty-first century's metropolitan centres. One of the chief benefits of communal eating is to help to address alienation.[18]

Brigida Marovelli's heartening study finds that contemporary food sharing initiatives are nurturing commensality and making efforts to build trust. Invitations to eat together are breaking down barriers of exclusion and hierarchical dynamics that may otherwise divide hosts and guests, donors and recipients, kitchen teams and diners. Amid the chink and tinkle of tines and blades, it is not only salt and ketchup that are passed around the table; shared ideas, contrasting perspectives, tips, jokes, and memories are the garnish and condiments of convivial conversation.[19] Such moments of intimate connection and uproariousness build social cohesion. They create chances for serendipity, affording opportunities to pool resources to help in other areas of life.[20] According to the adage that suggests it takes a whole village to raise a child, more social contact can build confidence. Even if mealtimes can sometimes be stormy, regular public dining can help to instil, for instance, social skills such as turn-taking, sharing, and the ability to articulate ideas, express feelings, and make sense of the world. In this way, commensality addresses the whole span of human needs, including nutrition and health, mental wellness, emotional literacy, social cohesion, and even spiritual gains.

As the rapid implementation of self-service technology advances in supermarkets, further undercutting small independent food outlets, the prospect of staff-free shops and the single-portion TV dinner fills the belly but leaves the mind lonely. In such a context, affordable communal eating seems not only a throwback to a more collective past society, but a priority for future sociability and well-being. The creation of democratic, self-managed canteens has the potential to contribute towards the much-needed reinvigoration of public space. If individuals spend more time in nurturing and stimulating collective spaces and enjoy a positive experience, then perhaps they are likelier to care about, and be oriented towards, wider society.

Notwithstanding the inspirational character and local successes of the projects that Marovelli describes, however, terms such as "surplus food," "temporary," and "meanwhile lease" perhaps give the impression that such community enterprises are scraps from the table, due to their uncertain tenure. Similarly, many instances of communal eating-with campaigns are tactical interventions and improvisations that do not endure beyond the defensive cause at hand. Like their predecessors, twenty-first-century collectives for self-managed canteens or refectories will need to federate and have a longer-term support strategy with permanent premises so that the benefits of retrofitting and microgeneration could be added—credit subscriptions, regular workers cooperating with compatible unions or municipalities (where this is possible and viable)—while protecting the integrity of the initiative. Links to compatible infrastructure for public food, such as community supported agriculture, street markets and farmers' markets, and local allotments could further strengthen such bonds.[21]

Moments of social progress come when the labour movement and countercultures start to take concrete measures in building infrastructure of change, lessons learned from the mechanics' institutes of the Victorian and Edwardian era, the projects for building societies and social insurance, to the experimental alternative societies of the 1960s and 1970s. Such reforms constitute the kind of transitional demands that build confidence and solidarity, expediting further change and igniting the kind of far-reaching and revolutionary transformation that social ecology envisions.

Point–Counterpoint: Farm animals in food production

My second point–counterpoint concerns contentions within social ecology about the contrastingly framed place of livestock or domesticated non-human animals (hereafter animals) within food production. The issue is crucial since it pertains to bodily sustenance, perhaps the primary social good and necessity, and the ecological implications of the human relationship with other species.

There have been significant skirmishes around this subject, provoked, particularly, by social ecologist Peter Staudenmaier's essay "Ambiguities of Animal Rights" (2003). Ethical approaches to the integration of farm animals into agricultural practice are largely determined by socially negotiated priorities and imperatives. Social-ecology principles would suggest that desirable aspirations would include abundant nutritional food to further social well-being and justice, more rewilding and biodiversity, protection and nurturing of healthy soil systems, and the reduction of animal suffering in factory farming. More metaphysical issues also arise relating to potential social evolution and liberation actualised in a deep future posed by the concept of "free nature."[22]

While the tensions between complementary but also competing aspirations can never be neatly resolved, the challenge to ameliorate such stresses is a philosophical journey that is dynamic and ongoing. Social ecology seeks to take a dialectical approach to such matters where the outer limits of intransigent moral absolutism or vague ethical relativism are unsatisfactory. In the harsh, amoral, commodifying, and conflictual context of neoliberalism, social ecology's insistence on posing such ethical questions stands as a powerful form of resistance.

Staudenmaier's essay "Ambiguities of Animal Rights," put the case against animal activism on the basis that he considers such thinking to be a "moral mistake and a symptom of political confusion."[23] While here is not the place to revisit the extensive philosophical debates around "animal rights," the points in Staudenmaier's essay relating to the consumption of animals as food are cogent and representative of a prevailing strand—perhaps most aligned to Bookchin's ideas—of social-ecological thinking on this divisive issue. By contrast, another social ecologist, Dayton Martindale, presents a counterpoint to what he considers to be the shortcomings of Bookchin and Staudenmaier's attitudes towards animals, in his 2019 essay "The Social Ecological Case for Animal Liberation."[24]

In keeping with Bookchin's dialectical naturalism, a conceptual framework by which *Homo sapiens* is uniquely accorded the status of "second nature," Staudenmaier stresses human distinctiveness.[25] Perhaps surprisingly, he does not explicitly invoke "second nature" or articulate what constitutes human distinctiveness. He contends humanity accrues moral claims through our capacity for moral agency that should only be granted to other species with caution. Staudenmaier's connected ethical concern is for ecological integrity, or the "well-being of a complex functioning ecological community." He rejects grounding ethical claims in the sentience of individual animals. Indeed, Staudenmaier asserts, rather, that "An ecologically and socially credible effort to take animal interests seriously will dispense with the notion that killing and harm are wrong per se." His argument rests in the idea that social ecologists should celebrate entire ecosystems rather than upholding rights or liberation discourses, deemed to be concerned with singular animals grounded in individualistic notions of sentience.

Martindale objects, however, that Bookchin and Staudenmaier's perspectives are based on "empirical misunderstandings about other animals." Refuting that claims for human uniqueness (based on tool-using, culture, symbolism, and so forth) constitute absolute distinctions, he suggests that current research in ethology and the nature of consciousness has tended to indicate greater appreciation of animals' sensibilities, during the 40 years since Bookchin introduced dialectical naturalism in his major work *The Ecology of Freedom*.[26] Martindale argues, therefore, that moral consideration is accorded due to assumptions about human exceptionalism that are not convincingly established, and even potentially contrary to social ecology's own philosophical tenets about "second nature," which posits that organic evolution tends to ever greater diversity, complexity, and subjectivity. He cautions that the underlying principles of dialectical naturalism should "counsel against human exceptionalism." Martindale suggests, moreover, that the difficulty in part rests in Bookchin's varying ideas about "second nature" and the inexact, rather metaphysical concept of "free nature," which can be "confusing."

This makes it more difficult to assess the implications of dialectical naturalism for guiding human relationships with the rest of the living world—and, in our case, in its treatment of farm animals. He is specifically uneasy about Staudenmaier's linkage of moral agency with entitlement to moral consideration. Relatedly, and even more troubling for Martindale, is that it is questionable whether Staudenmaier grants animals any kind of agency and that "morally, it appears that a cow or pig is closer to a plant than a human."

While on occasion Bookchin would speak of compassion and care in respect to other species, such ideas are absent from Staudenmaier's analysis. In a response to a critic, he alleges that animal rights or liberation ideas narrow down the application of compassion and "moral standing" to "sentient creatures." For

Martindale, this approach appears to obfuscate relevant differences between more complex biota and bacteria, or even rocks, in a way that risks their unwarranted and problematic exclusion from substantive ethical consideration. Fellow social ecologist Blair Taylor is also critical of the basis of Staudenmaier's arguments about animal rights, questioning whether "individual animals and the survival of species and ecosystems must be mutually exclusive aims."[27]

While humanity doubtless has distinct characteristics and attributes, Staudenmaier's omission in precisely securing what this uniqueness means for him makes it difficult for critical readers to evaluate whether it is philosophically and ethically robust. Staudenmaier's tendency to conflate killing and harm is also problematic. Death is not life's worse outcome; it is the most inevitable. Yet the infliction of intense suffering, fear, and pain and the extreme denial of self-directed existence arguably raise distinct ethical questions. While it is not difficult to imagine a scenario where killing a mammal may be justified for reasons of defence or subsistence, normative uses of the word "harm" entail forms of injury or violence to interests or oppression that have different ethical connotations.

While Staudenmaier's addition of "per se" somewhat modifies the statement, we do not know what contingencies might apply to mitigate the fear that not only is animal liberation under assault, but that the case for any kind of animal welfare is diminished. In seeming to emphasise that the substantive moral standing of vertebrates is attained by virtue of their membership of an "ecological community," and that both killing and harming individuals is not wrong, he risks diminishing them to their functions within an ecosystem and making them vulnerable to regressive Cartesian ideas characterised by the notion of the bête-machine.[28]

To further quote Staudenmaier, "The well-being of a complex functioning ecological community, with its soils, rocks, waters, micro-organisms, and animal and plant denizens, cannot be reduced to the well-being of those denizens as individuals."

It is true that, ecologically speaking, organisms should not be considered in isolation from the context of their habitats. However, Staudenmaier's elevation of the "ecological community" and relegation of the individual is problematic here for two relevant reasons. First, if he is reluctant to ascribe intrinsic moral standing to "denizens as individuals," then at what scale might ethical value be ascribed in a way that does not appear arbitrary? If, for instance, a partridge lacks claims as a single bird, what of a pair of partridges, or a nest with chicks, or a full covey, or an entire breeding population in a location? Second, moreover, if individuals only have value as functionaries in an abstract whole, this attempt to avoid reductionism sounds dangerously like a reversion to a totalising perspective, risking the introduction of an undifferentiated holism of a kind of which social ecologists accuse deep ecologists. For philosopher Timothy Morton, the notion that the "whole is greater than the parts" should be dismantled in favour of the idea that "the whole is *different* than its parts," a proposition he calls subsendence, which forgoes holism and individualism alike in rejecting deep ecology and neoliberalism.[29]

I would concede with Martindale that Bookchin's concepts "second" and "free" nature are not sufficiently delineated, perhaps inevitably given their speculative status. On the other hand, in critiquing Bookchin and Staudenmaier, it may be that Martindale obfuscates human uniqueness too much. There is a defining qualitative dimension to explain how a relatively weak species has come to dominate, to the extent that it is often conceived that we are living in the Anthropocene. In this context, it seems to me that highly elaborated abstract symbolism, enabling accumulative knowledge and culture, is the critical evolutionary trait, ultimately realising historical subjectivity.

While Martindale points to animal vocalisations as perhaps representing rudimentary languages, these seem to be qualitatively different from written records. However, it is true that instances of great apes and dolphins seemingly demonstrating competences with basic signifiers raises the tantalising prospect that humans may intervene to extend the cognitive abilities of other species. Nevertheless, even if Martindale persuades us that social ecology should more fully adapt dialectical naturalism to recognise that animals, including farm animals, have ethically relevant qualities such as sentience and forms of intersubjective intelligence, we are far from establishing consistent real-world consequences of such insights for their lives on farms, grazing lands, and smallholdings.

Relatedly, Staudenmaier strongly rejects the extension of the social-ecology critique of human hierarchy and domination to the moral consideration of animals on the grounds of speciesism as unwarranted. Not only is this based upon a "dubious analogy," it "undermines" the "humanist impulse" in, for example, the women's liberation and civil rights movements. As we have seen, opposition to social domination and hierarchy is a core principle of social ecology. Staudenmaier resists the inclusion of animals in calls for liberation, since he believes these are predicated upon humans' unique capacity to strive for freedom. He concludes by proclaiming the need for an ethical as well as political revolution to overturn institutions upholding domination, based on hierarchical structures, after which, it is claimed, people will treat each other and animals more humanely.

Again, Martindale challenges Staudenmaier's reasoning, citing counter-examples which demonstrate that tropes enabling the commodification of farm animals are comparable to those that promote the objectification of women. He responds that social ecologists should be sensitive and attuned to the logical continuities between the domination of colonialism and patriarchy and that of other species. Similarly, Erika Cudworth finds the exclusion of animals from social ecology's critique of hierarchy and domination anomalous. She argues instead that, if Bookchin's rigid "humanocentric" bias is relaxed, his work continues to stand as a strong basis for an intersectional understanding of overlapping forms of "co-constituting" oppression that can be extended to other animals.[30]

Another issue for Staudenmaier is that social injustice is a structural problem relating to liberal political economy and control of the means of production and, therefore, consumption-focused concern is at best misplaced, at worst a form of class elitism that stigmatises the diets of deprived communities in the West and the Global South alike. It follows, then, that decisions relating to diet fail to move beyond the limits of green consumerism—a middle-class fad firmly embedded within, and perpetuating of, capitalist market forces. Staudenmaier, therefore, dismisses the "seemingly inherent self-righteousness of food politics, where puritanism is often mistaken for radicalism." Elements of puritanism in food reform are disturbingly regressive and reactionary, both echoing Nazi preoccupations with hygiene and auguring incipient fascism for the future.

So, as we have seen, social ecologists diverge in their opinions about the relationship between humans and other animals. For Staudenmaier, the creation of a more humane, post-capitalist society based on social-ecology principles is the best hope for future improvements in the treatment of other species. Martindale sees it differently. With reference to the ideas of urban geographer Jennifer Wolch, he counters that sensitive attention to animals' species-being and their place in human society in the here and now could have emancipatory consequences in line with social-ecological aspirations, by enabling "environmental consciousness," "re-enchanting urban space," and "expanding 'political agency.'" He points to Cooperation Jackson's experimental "Freedom Farm" as a potential prototype for a socially inclusive alternative to the "destructive capitalist food system." There is, however, more substantial common ground when Staudenmaier recognises the current detrimental ecological impact of industrial agriculture incorporating animals, arguing that, in a profit-driven capitalist system based on commodification, "much of the current industrialized manufacture of animal products is socially worthless and ecologically disastrous." Such disagreements, therefore, have a bearing on current food systems and issues of diet.

WE MUST BEGIN WITH THE LAND

It is always helpful to consider foremost the problem that we are trying to solve. The present scale of industrial animal farming is without historical precedent and on a rapidly expanding trajectory. It seems to me that this is a lose-lose-lose trend. From a social-ecology standpoint, this situation represents three interlocking concerns affecting people, the living planet, and animals. The following data tell many stories:

- 80 billion animals are slaughtered each year for meat.[31]
- The number of animals consumed for meat has tripled during the past 50 years, while the human population has only doubled.[32]
- Globally, the consumption of meat proteins is projected to increase by 14% during the decade up to 2030.[33]
- Half of the planet's habitable land is used for agriculture, and of this 77% of global farming land is used either for directly grazing animals or for producing animal feed.[34]
- Livestock are estimated to be the direct source of 14.5% of anthropogenic greenhouse gas emissions.[35]
- Lobby groups highlight the detrimental impact of the factory-farming sector on the health and mental health of workers.[36]
- The UK has 235.8 million farm animals.[37]
- UK imports and consumption of animal feed exceeds £8 million.[38]
- Water contamination, air pollution, and the emission of greenhouse gases from intensive livestock farming units are recognised as significant local and global problems.[39]

Behind the statistics are people displaced from the land for food production and irrigation projects; workers in meat and dairy production and processing industries experiencing bleak and exploitative labour conditions; ecologically, and therefore economically, unsustainable food systems breaching planetary boundaries relating to climate change, the nitrogen cycle, and the loss of biodiversity; as well as the inevitable animal suffering entailed in systems where profit rather than welfare are paramount and species-being is severely constrained. Taken together, these clusters of issues, on a scale without historical precedent, call for an urgent reframing of what is supposedly realistic or idealistic.

Simon Fairlie's *Meat: A Benign Extravagance* advocates the inclusion of "default" meat, dairy products, and eggs within the food system from the perspective of agroecology. "Default livestock" production is a model whereby animals are integrated into agriculture that relies upon using pasture not readily cultivatable for arable purposes, live off wastes and residues, and that are used in their entirety for not only meat but products such as leather, tallow, and bonemeal. The book is a masterclass in critical thinking, data analysis, and entertaining prose. Fairlie's regenerative agriculture has strong affinities with permaculture, advocating a symbiotic approach in which the countryside is attractively transformed into a diverse landscape of pasturelands and woods.[40] While he leaves aside moral and health aspects, Fairlie's well-evidenced argument at once makes a reasoned case for the inclusion of animals within the agricultural cycle, and for a radical reduction in meat eating—perhaps neither pleasing consumers of average quantities of meat nor vegetarians. He does not exhort people to consume extravagant amounts of meat but that a "modest" amount is admissible as a "benign extravagance." Above all, Fairlie's approach is a counterblast against the model of intensive monocultural farming in which animals are fatted on purpose-grown feed—typically imported grains—and transported to urban populations.[41] The implications are that a dominant contemporary omnivorous diet would need to reduce meat consumption by around 50% to come within the bounds of what a sustainable "default livestock" system could reasonably produce—a figure Fairlie estimates to decrease to two-thirds of present consumption levels to accommodate the rising population level anticipated for 2050.

Fairlie is aware of the dilemma that, for most people in England and Wales, readily available and affordable meat and dairy products are not from agroecological systems but commodities from industrialised factory farming. For most communities locked into the dominant food system, such products cannot be sourced without time and expense. As Timothy Perrine argues, most consumers do not have a realistic option to buy meat from agriculture that is "heavily composed of pasture-forage sources."[42] Although I do not personally care to eat meat, I indirectly consume many animals. Habitats are cleared, animals are killed through pest-control measures, animal derivatives appear in all kinds of products beyond meat and dairy, edible or non-food upon which purchasers may, even unwittingly, spend money (indeed, even the banknotes used to make the purchase!), and, currently, even plant-based food is nearly always grown with manure or other inputs of animal origin, rather than in veganic permaculture systems.[43]

So, there are diverse combinations of three major options at play concerning animals in food systems, each of which is problematic for different reasons:

- A fully industrialised factory farming system, which is not only unpalatable to ecological humanists for its levels of suffering and pollution but largely dependent upon imported soy, corn, and other fodder, and ecologically/economically unsustainable on its present trajectory.
- A decentralised agroecology system based on "default livestock" that would involve the reduction of animals by a half to two-thirds, and which is against current production trends and beyond the reach of most consumers.
- An agriculture without farmed animals, which, while it might have some efficiencies, is dependent on veganic practices that require further research and development, so there are shortcomings in aspirations to an "absolutely" pure vegan diet.

No wonder there is much cognitive dissonance, inviting polarised opinions on diet-related matters! Given these circumstances, there have been calls for a culturally sensitive contextual or default vegetarianism or veganism.[44] In addition to individual and household lifestyle changes in recent years, in the UK there has been some collective and societal momentum towards pragmatically reducing the consumption of factory-farmed meat products.[45] A rethink presaging a global plateauing and reversal in the world farm animal population, and ameliorating conditions in which they are reared, would be welcomed for having positively mutually affirming outcomes for ecological sustainability, human health and well-being, and for the well-being of animals.[46]

While it is desirable to be compassionate towards other animals, it is not, of course, possible to relieve them from suffering in the wild (or rewilded environments) due to predation, disease, and the harshness of the natural environment, where it is unlikely that they will meet with an end that is gentle or dignified. The concern here from the perspective of ecological humanism, however, is with human behaviour, since, in the Anthropocene, that has the greatest impact on, and ramifications for, all life on Earth and can be consciously adjusted. Ethical responsibility comes with this power and agency, albeit the latter is variable and contingent upon social context.

Where animals are farmed, it seems to me that this extends to preventing animal suffering through fear, pain, and mitigating unwarranted coercion or constraints upon their species-being entailed in domestication. Such humane treatment in farming helps to uphold our empathy. Morton playfully describes a situation not where pigs "no longer existed," but rather to let "actually existing pigs get to enjoy themselves more, to go about their piggy business."[47] The more scope there is for animals to retain some autonomy in their lives, the better they are able to choose and self-actualise their species-being in their environmental context, adapting to which is the mechanism for organic evolution through natural and sexual selection.

While human intervention might act as a catalyst for evolution—through, for example, selective breeding—social ecology is emphatically not a project to subsume the biosphere and its organisms entirely within the human realm, extinguishing their autonomy and independent existence. It has an ethos of liberation, not tyranny, and would not seek to make unwarranted interventions such as to prevent predation, even if such an objective were to be attainable. In my reading, transcending disagreements of the kind represented by the counterpointing between Staudenmaier and Martindale, social ecology avoids infringements on animals' lives that would be irreconcilable with autonomous ecological existence. However, to make human systems of production more compassionate is within the bounds of, and in furtherance of, ecological humanism.

As we have seen, during the past 50 years there has been a tripling of global meat consumption as a greater proportion of populations adopt a global standard diet. Steady increases across the twentieth century were made possible in part by the introduction of new technologies such as refrigerators and integrated global transport systems during the late nineteenth century, and the conversion of vast tracts of agricultural land for feed production and development of larger feedlots. This reflects a shift away from traditional dietary habits where modest amounts of meat derivatives were consumed regularly—for example, in stock—while larger portions were an extravagance reserved for special occasions and feasts. Such patterns are similar to the "default livestock" models that Fairlie envisages. Social ecologists, represented above by Staudenmaier and Martindale, are divided on the issue of the treatment of animals and their use for food. However, social-ecology principles disfavour factory farming—the industrial system that produces by far the greatest quantities of meat to supply the global standard diet. As we shall see, apprehensions about the impacts of meat production upon the environment and human health are a topic shared across several reports on the future of the UK's farming and dietary needs, most of which call for policies to encourage a reduction in consumption.

Notes

1. Collis, *The Worm Forgives the Plough*, (1975), 222.
2. George Monbiot, *Regenesis: Feeding the World Without Devouring the Planet* (London: Allen Lane, 2022).
3. Masa Saruhashi, personal e-mail to the author, 17 February 2023.
4. Shumei is referenced in *Subtle Agroecologies: Farming with the Hidden Half of Nature*, ed. Julia Wright, Advances in Agroecology (Boca Raton: CRC Press, 2021), 14.
5. I am borrowing this phrase from my colleague Jane Saville, who spoke of her enjoyment of a tasty meal in a Lebanese restaurant in Bristol as "eating there felt like having a party in your mouth," personal conversation with the author, 21 November 2022.
6. Marsha Smith and John Harvey, "Social Eating Initiatives and the Practices of Commensality," *Appetite* 161 (1 June 2021), 6: https://doi.org/10.1016/j.appet.2021.105107.
7. Winston Churchill, "Memo to Minister of Food," 21 March 1941, Churchill 1950: 663, cited in P.J. Atkins "Communal Feeding in War Time: British Restaurants, 1940–1947," in *Food and War in Twentieth Century Europe* (Farnham: Ashgate, 2011), 141.
8. Brigida Marovelli, "Cooking and Eating Together in London: Food Sharing Initiatives as Collective Spaces of Encounter," *Geoforum* 99 (2019), 192.
9. Henry Dimbleby, Director of the National Food Strategy, speaks of how he was won over to the idea of school kitchens and refectories as community restaurants when witness on the Environment, Food and Rural Affairs Committee ("Food Security," 18 October 2022), *Parliament Live TV*: https://parliamentlive.tv/event/index/bc3c87fc-3732-4ff1-b3bc-653eb241a24f.
10. Robert Blatchford, *Merrie England* (London: Clarion Office, 1894), 43.
11. Sarah Jackson and Rosemary Taylor, *East London Suffragettes* (Stroud: History Press, 2014), 61.
12. Smith and Harvey, "Social Eating Initiatives," 4.
13. Sue Bruley, "The Politics of Food: Gender, Family, Community and Collective Feeding in South Wales in the General Strike and Miners' Lockout of 1926," *Twentieth Century British History* 18, no. 1, (2007), 63: https://doi.org/10.1093/tcbh/hwl045.

14   Ibid., 77.
15   Stephen E. Hunt, "The Echoing Greens: The Neo-Romanticism of Earth First! and Reclaim The Streets in the U.K.," *Capitalism Nature Socialism* 24, no. 2 (2013), 88, https://doi.org/10.1080/10455752.2013.784526.
16   scott crow, *Black Flags and Windmills: Hope, Anarchy, and the Common Ground Collective*, 2nd ed. (Oakland, CA: PM Press, 2014), 120.
17   Bikrum Gill, 14 in "The 2020 Indian Farm Laws in an Emergent Global Financial-AgriTech Accumulation Regime," *Sikh Research Journal* 6, no. 2 (Fall 2021), 4–20: https://sikhresearchjournal.org/wp-content/uploads/articles/Vol.%206%20No.%202_SRJ_V6N2.pdf?fbclid=IwAR0JkavNKUgteo-i-BxTegvDonVSBzzBlwg_G73CnxMC2nS97nnL6bmyk3A.
18   Smith and Harvey, "Social Eating Initiatives," 3.
19   It was not coincidental that weighty volumes of table talk—wisdom fuelled, it is supposed, by a good repast and cordial company—became a favourite published sub-genre, particularly during the late eighteenth, early nineteenth centuries due to heightened interest in the biography of self. Contributions by Samuel Johnson, Napoleon Buonaparte, Johann Wolfgang von Goethe, Samuel Taylor Coleridge, William Hazlitt, and Samuel Rogers were among the more renowned.
20   A process enabling the extension of what Richard D. Putnam and others have popularised as "social capital."
21   Several of these could afford opportunities for connecting conversations, potentially facilitating farm visits for diners.
22   As previously outlined under the principle of "respect for ecological integrity."
23   Peter Staudenmaier, *Ecology Contested: Environmental Politics Between Left and Right* (Porsgrunn: New Compass, 2021), Chapter 4. This essay was first published in *Communalism: International Journal for a Rational Society* in 2003, then posted as a blog on the Institute of Social Ecology website in 2005, provoking a heated exchange in the accompanying comments.
24   Dayton Martindale, "The Social Ecological Case for Animal Liberation: Towards an Interspecies Communalism," *Harbinger* issue #1 (2019):

https://harbinger-journal.com/issue-1/the-social-ecological-case-for-animal-liberation/; an earlier version of Martindale's challenge to Staudenmaier's argument was published as Dayton Martindale / Symbiosis Research Collective, "Animal Liberation from Below: Toward a Radical Interspecies Municipalism," *The Ecologist* (2018): https://theecologist.org/2018/aug/06/animal-liberation-below-toward-radical-interspecies-municipalism. All following references to Martindale's ideas are to the 2019 essay.

25   Again, see previous account of dialectical naturalism under the principle of "Respect for ecological integrity."

26   Such as Peter Godfrey-Smith, *Other Minds: The Octopus and the Evolution of Intelligent Life* (London: William Collins, 2016); Martindale grounds his case in Michael Tye's arguments for extended sentience in *Tense Bees and Shell-Shocked Crabs: Are Animals Conscious?* (New York: OUP, 2017).

27   Blair Taylor, "Book Review: Ecology Contested by Peter Staudenmaier," Institute for Social Ecology website (2022): https://social-ecology.org/wp/2022/01/book-review-ecology-contested-by-peter-staudenmaier/.

28   The cuddly embrace of "community" is beloved of nearly everybody, including myself, but also used as a weapon of exclusivity by the far right.

29   Timothy Morton, *Humankind: Solidarity with Non-Human People*. London: Verso, 2017), Chapter 3.

30   Erika Cudworth, "Intersectionality, Species and Social Domination," 93–107 in *Anarchism and Animal Liberation: Essays on Complementary Elements of Total Liberation*, eds Anthony J. Nocella II, Richard J. White, and Erika Cudworth (Jefferson, NC: McFarland & Company, 2015), 96.

31   Hannah Ritchie, Pablo Rosado, and Max Roser, "Meat and Dairy Production," *Our World in Data* website (2017; rev. 2019): https://ourworldindata.org/meat-production#livestock-counts.

32   Ritchie, Rosado, and Roser, "Meat and Dairy Production."

33   OECD-FAO, "Agricultural Outlook 2021–2030": https://www.agriculture.gov.au/sites/default/files/sitecollectiondocuments/abares/agriculture-commodities/AgCommodities201903_MeatConsumptionOutlook_

v1.0.0.pdf, accessed 9 August 2023; M. Henchion, A.P. Moloney, J. Hyland, J. Zimmermann, and S. McCarthy, "Review: Trends for Meat, Milk and Egg Consumption for the Next Decades and the Role Played by Livestock Systems in the Global Production of Proteins," *Animal* 15, Supplement 1 (2021): https://doi.org/10.1016/j.animal.2021.100287.

34 Hannah Ritchie, "Half of the World's Habitable Land is Used for Agriculture," *Our World in Data* website (11 November 2019): https://ourworldindata.org/global-land-for-agriculture.

35 It is hoped that this can be mitigated by improved practice, according to FAO, "Major Cuts of Greenhouse Gas Emissions from Livestock Within Reach," (26 September 2013): https://www.fao.org/news/story/en/item/197608/icode.

36 Matthew Chalmers, "Factory Farming: The Impact of Factory Farming on Workers," Humane League United Kingdom website (27 May 2022): https://thehumaneleague.org.uk/article/the-impact-of-factory-farming-on-workers.

37 According to government figures that include cattle, pigs, sheep, and poultry, but exclude other animals such as goats, rabbits, and farmed fish. DEFRA, "Livestock Populations in the United Kingdom at 1 June" [2022] (updated 3 May 2023): https://www.gov.uk/government/statistics/livestock-populations-in-the-united-kingdom/livestock-populations-in-the-united-kingdom; 2022 statistics note a slight increase in sheep and lamb numbers to 33 million, with decreases of cattle and calves to 9.6 million, pigs to 5.2 million, and poultry to 188 million animals: DEFRA et al., "Agriculture in the UK 2022" (2023), 27–28.

38 DEFRA et al., "Agriculture in the UK 2022" (2023), 12; Emma Bedford, "Animal Feed Import Value in the United Kingdom (UK) 2003–2021," *Statista* website (20 July 2023): https://www.statista.com/statistics/316185/animal-feed-import-value-in-the-united-kingdom-uk/.

39 Livestock, Environment and Development Initiative / FAO, "Livestock's Long Shadow: Environmental Issues and Options" (2006), 273 and 281: https://www.fao.org/3/a0701e/a0701e.pdf.

40 Fairlie, *Meat*, 250.

41 Fairlie's support for a reversal of the trend from urban to rural living is presented as a social ecologist's perspective in *Meat*, 147.
42 Timothy Perrine, "Default Vegetarianism and Veganism," *Journal of Agricultural and Environmental Ethics* 34, no. 13 (2021), 13: https://doi.org/10.1007/s10806-021-09856-1.
43 Of which Fairlie gives a fair assessment in *Meat*, 103.
44 Australian ecofeminist philosopher Val Plumwood first proposed the concept of contextual vegetarianisms in "Integrating Ethical Frameworks for Animals, Humans, and Nature: A Critical Feminist Eco-Socialist Analysis," *Ethics and the Environment* 5, no. 2 (2000), 285–32; Brian Dominick makes a case for aspirational rather than prescriptive veganism in "Anarcho-Veganism Revisited," 23–39 in *Anarchism and Animal Liberation: Essays on Complementary Elements of Total Liberation*, eds Anthony J. Nocella II, Richard J. White, and Erika Cudworth (Jefferson, NC: McFarland, 2015).
45 Cristina Stewart, Carmen Piernas, Brian Cook, and Susan A. Jebb, "Trends in UK Meat Consumption: Analysis of Data from Years 1–11 (2008–09 to 2018–19) of the National Diet and Nutrition Survey Rolling Programme," *The Lancet Planetary Health* 5, no. 10 (October 2021): https://doi.org/10.1016/S2542-5196(21)00228-X.
46 Peter Scarborough, Michael Clark, Linda Cobiac, Keren Papier, Anika Knuppel, John Lynch, Richard Harrington, Tim Key, and Marco Springmann, "Vegans, Vegetarians, Fish-eaters and Meat-eaters in the UK Show Discrepant Environmental Impacts," *Nature Food* 4, 565–574 (2023): https://doi.org/10.1038/s43016-023-00795-w.
47 Morton, *Humankind*, 144.

PART 3
BRITAIN: LOCK-IN AND UNLOCKING

British Agribusiness: Is it "a great story"?

While setting out some possible ways forward, it is necessary to consider current thinking about British farming. Several recent reports provide a detailed picture of contemporary policy-thinking and aspirations.

As the sector's most prominent organisation, with 55,000 members and covering two-thirds of the agricultural land in England and Wales, the National Farmers' Union, brands itself "the voice of British farming."[1] Alongside the Country Land and Business Association (28,000 members), the NFU represents the *ancien régime* of landed power but also the young entrepreneurial disrupter for biotech farming in the United Kingdom.[2] Its promotional report, "British Farming: A Blueprint for the Future" (2022), largely an intensification and extrapolation of current norms and trends, therefore expresses mainstream industrial agricultural policy.

Further relevant reports offering insights about the state of, and prospects for, farming include *The National Food Strategy* (2021), the Food, Farming, and Countryside Commission's *Farming for Change* (2021), the Chatham House research paper *Sustainable Agriculture and Food Systems* (2022), the Royal Agricultural Society of England's *Farm of the Future* (2022), the Sustainable Foods Trust's *Feeding Britain from the Ground Up* (2022), and the World Wildlife Fund's *Land of Plenty* (2022).[3] These reports are invaluable in assessing current ideas about feeding the people of England and Wales, and attempts to grapple with the challenges of economic uncertainty, climate change, and population increase. Using the lens of social ecology to analyse some key issues within these reports helps to illustrate where some of the fundamental alternative perspectives and priorities lie.

While NFU's ebullient report insists that its current farming practices, predominantly based on agribusiness, has a "great story to tell," others are less certain about the predicament of domestic and world agriculture.[4] Is it sustainable or even efficient to boost yields by increasing capital and energy inputs? While output per acre has increased, yields comparative to energy and capital input have decreased. What follows critically considers some of the competing narratives about the direction of British farming.

Decolonising food security thinking

Food security and the case for greater self-sufficiency are rising concerns among policymakers. While total self-sufficiency for England and Wales is neither a realistic nor worthwhile aspiration, recent global volatility suggests that a greater proportion of domestic production would be beneficial. The Government's current "Food Strategy" is not inspiring in this respect, since its objective is to "broadly maintain the current level of food we produce domestically."[5]

The National Farmers' Union's aspirations regarding self-sufficiency are similarly unambitious; namely, that it is seeking to "work with government to develop a commitment to maintain, and ideally increase, our current food production self-sufficiency of 60%."[6] The NFU's pronouncement sounds less upbeat when placed in context. According to DEFRA figures, the UK imports food, feed, and drink to the amount of £48 billion, while it exports only £21.4 billion by value.[7] Whisky, chocolate (not home-grown!), cheese, and salmon top the list of high-value luxury exports, helping to mitigate the balance-of-payments deficit.[8]

In contrast to the NFU's emphasis, the Food, Farming and Countryside Commission (FFCC) frames the situation as "the UK imports almost half of its food needs."[9] Although a 2015 NFU report had expressed concern that "for three decades the UK's self-sufficiency has insidiously declined," and called for a reversal in the trend, two more percentage points have been lost since.[10]

The "National Food Strategy" also records an overall decrease in self-sufficiency in recent decades, down from nearly 80% during the mid-1980s, when the unpopular Common Agricultural Policy (CAP) maximised production and protected markets.[11] However, the CAP has been seen to have incurred significant costs in terms of subsidies, the environment, and food waste. Consequently, while widespread food shortages have been averted in Europe since its implementation in the early 1960s, diverse critics have variously regarded the CAP as an anti-competitive barrier to fairer world trade, enabling of ecologically destructive farming methods, over-centralised and bureaucratic to administer, beneficial to large landowners to the detriment of small-scale farmers, productive of food quantity over quality, and as a burden on the taxpayer.

Since the 1980s, self-sufficiency has been reduced overall in the UK, with a slight downwards trajectory for several years—a trend continuing after Brexit in 2020, which has triggered the phasing out of the CAP's Basic Payment Scheme. Currently, produce such as vegetables and fruit, which could be grown in greater quantities in the UK, are more often imported.[12] To complicate matters, home production is not straightforwardly an indication of self-sufficiency, because the meat and dairy industries rely upon substantial imports of grains and other foodstuffs for animal feed. We should be troubled by the mismatch between production and consumption since it is a trend also seen across other countries to the extent that, under a "business-as-usual" scenario, it is anticipated that self-sufficiency will become the exception rather than the norm.[13]

Moreover, threats of shortages that had been nascent in supply-chain interruptions following the coronavirus pandemic and Brexit, when the "National Food Strategy" was being compiled in 2021, have since come to be more regular occurrences after the Russian invasion of Ukraine, which has destabilised the global distribution of several key food commodities—notably, wheat, maize, and sunflower products.

Risks such as climate change also look to have an even more negative impact upon crop yields, since the 27th United Nations Climate Change Conference ("CoP27") at Sharm El Sheikh, in Egypt, failed to make progress with binding measures to hold temperature increases to 1.5 °C above pre-industrial levels. More hopefully, the "National Food Strategy" report suggests that the trajectory towards diminishing self-sufficiency could be reversed, using only two-thirds of current land use, assuming that three auxiliary goals could be met, namely "Halving food waste, increasing crop yields by 15% and eating 30% less meat."[14] Such a change in direction would be a welcome advance if achieved.

Consideration of the position of England and Wales, and indeed any other countries, from the perspective of social ecology requires a cooperative and internationalist approach. Following principles of alter-globalisation leads to a radically different set of assumptions about successful strategies and desired outcomes. In the context of current global-supply chains, over-dependence on imports for food security is a potentially dangerous strategy to feed domestic populations. The UK's relatively wealthy status ensures that it can afford to secure produce on the world market (despite recent fluctuations in its balance of payments) for the foreseeable future. However, should wholesale food inflation continue to translate into higher prices on retailers' shelves, the purchasing power of those already suffering food insecurity will be further diminished.

It is also unethical to allow the invisible hand of the market to reap so-called "ghost acres," outbidding less wealthy countries by offshoring food production and speculating upon an immense amount of land overseas. As the title "British Farming" would lead readers to expect, the NFU report emphasises "British" and "Britain," words used 72 times. The promotion of "Brand Britain," combining nationalism and globalism, contrasts with perspectives from social ecology, which tend rather to support local accountability, favouring municipalism and regionalism, alongside a commitment to internationalism.

Ecologically speaking, there is no intrinsic reason why buying British is preferable. Why, for example, should Londoners favour produce grown or reared in the Dundee area or County Antrim, over goods from nearer Breton fields or Norman orchards? Local production helps to shorten supply chains and can afford better accountability and traceability, although this depends upon how it is produced and who is producing it. The NFU claim, therefore, that "locally produced food gives people confidence in standards and provenance," is partially true. It may do, but there is a logical inconsistency here; since all food produced is local to somewhere, it does not follow, of course, that all is of fine quality or ethically produced.[15]

A distinction that matters, and a point of agreement or even consensus, is where a home jurisdiction upholds higher standards than others. As the NFU report argues, "As a country, we must avoid simply displacing our domestic food production with imports from countries which do not adhere to the same values or environmental and animal welfare standards that our farmers and growers do."[16] The "National Food Strategy" also largely endorses this stance, arguing that "There is no point making UK farmers do all the hard work necessary to reduce carbon emissions and restore biodiversity only to open up the market to cheap food produced to lower standards abroad."[17] This is supported by comparing the rearing of UK farmed animals with that of other potential trade partners, which for the most part reflects well on domestic welfare standards.[18] Over the longer term, whether post-Brexit Britain will necessarily be best at feeding its population while protecting the living world, or whether this is merely "a great story," remains to be seen.

More broadly, ethical issues relating to environmental protection have an uncertain position in international free trade agreements. The WTO at once cautiously holds environmental measures to be admissible in some circumstances, yet also fears that they could inhibit free trade as "disguised protectionism," and consequently deemed to be anti-competitive.[19] In this twilight world of subtle ambivalence, the dominant national and corporate economic interests behind the WTO fail to take appropriately robust measures to protect the living world. For this reason, progress towards addressing the ecological crisis and transitioning to an authentically regenerative economy faces challenging, likely insurmountable, barriers within the present multilateral policy infrastructure.

Benton and Harwatt's research paper on "Sustainable Agriculture and Food Systems" offers the objection that there are formidable systemic obstacles to achieving authentic agroecological production across the planet. They recognise that "a single country cannot transform its food system while existing in a liberalized global trading system, as 'sustainable production' in the domestic system will be undermined by imported food produced more cheaply at lower standards."[20] The blocks to the way forward along a sustainable agroecological path, therefore, appear in this analysis to be primarily political rather than scientific. Yet the consequences of the unsustainability of the world food system are socially and ecologically unthinkable. To advance to a mode of production that could work for the longer term, all countries would be "required to move in step."[21]

While this is offered as a "critique," the argument corroborates social-ecologist views that the failures of current geopolitical governance prevent the kind of international cooperation that is essential to implement solutions to the food and ecological crises. For social ecologists, therefore, a model such as democratic confederalism is a priority over the drive for national and corporate competition and capitalist imperatives to grow the economy regardless of the consequences.

Again, while investment in food production and processing is, for the most part, to be welcomed as a social good (depending on the nutritional value of the products), the NFU's call for "increasing British farming's share of markets" does not of itself advance the security or quality of world food supplies.[22] For this reason, present-day social ecologists such as Yavor Tarinski go further in making the case for the democratic control of the economic sphere, and advancing the idea of a solidarity economy.[23] Such calls favour democratic oversight of shorter, more localised supply chains and production cycles, as part of a radical shift towards social and ecological priorities.

Ecological integrity and climate change

Positively, the NFU have set out a "roadmap" for the UK to be net-zero in terms of greenhouse gas emissions by 2040, and its commitment to "climate-friendly farming" is a prominent and welcome part of its blueprint for the future.[24] Its showcase report on "British Farming," however, is unconvincing. Is its narrative really a "roadmap" or just a "story"?

There is a lack of consensus about not only the priorities for more sustainable farming but even the direction of travel. The NFU's propositions are no exception and are questionable, since in several cases they could potentially be drivers of, rather than solutions to, climate change. Growing biomass for bioenergy is particularly controversial, and its impact depends on several variables, including its end use. Increasing home production to reduce food miles is less contentious, although recent data suggesting that transport averages at 13–19% of the food supply chain's carbon footprint serves to moderate expectations that this could be a decisive saving.[25]

The NFU's championship of meat and dairy production is out of step with most other recent reports, except the allied Royal Agricultural Society of England's "Farm of the Future"; although it should be recognised that the lobby group represents a larger membership and, as the voice of agribusiness, has greater political influence with DEFRA than the other UK organisations that have put forward recommendations for agricultural futures.[26] There is a case that the UK does comparatively well in terms of animal welfare standards and low greenhouse gas emissions (two factors that are not necessarily complementary). Most reports, however, place a contrasting emphasis, suggesting that the meat and dairy industries remain significant sources of greenhouse gas emissions.

The more independent and nuanced account of the "National Food Strategy," for example, sets out some of the complexities of the environmental impact of meat production, arguing that "Our taste for ruminants [...] is a major contributor to climate change," and recommends a substantial reduction in meat consumption of 30% by 2032 (in comparison to 2019).[27] The "Sustainable Agriculture and Food Systems" report also notes the high impact of meat consumption, although conceding that there are cultural barriers to widespread dietary change, while the WWF's "Land of Plenty" also speaks of the "mitigation potential" of dietary shift and of the need for a "drop in demand for meat of all types."[28] In this context, the NFU report's cited data from the Parliamentary Committee on Climate Change "that greenhouse gas emissions from beef production in the UK are about half the global average" is perhaps misleading without acknowledging that the Committee also places a markedly different emphasis, recommending "a 20% reduction in meat and dairy by 2030 and 35% reduction for meat by 2050, eating better meat and plant-based alternatives."[29] Despite this recommendation, references to policies regarding meat consumption are absent from the current "Government Food Strategy."

The NFU's "British Farming" proceeds to celebrate the 4.1 billion visits to British farmland annually. While this is no doubt profitable, it is unclear how this contributes towards tackling climate change. Electric vehicles could help reduce emissions depending on how the electricity is generated, while the outline report claims, yet does not demonstrate how, biotechnology and agri-robotics might drive down greenhouse gas emissions. Furthermore, the NFU's highlighting of advances in diminishing emissions from sugar production as the key example of a "British business success story" in this area seems an odd choice, since this directly contravenes parallel health policies to reduce sugar intake due to its low nutritional value.[30] The lobby group's position on protecting the living world was thrown into further uncertainty in September 2022, when its current President, Minette Batters, called for delays to the implementation of the Environmental Land Management Schemes to support environmentally sustainable production.[31]

A combination of habitat loss and environmental degradation has led to a critical decline in biodiversity.[32] Sadly, the evidence of recent decades does not bear out NFU's bucolic claim that "British farmers are proud to produce climate-friendly food while maintaining and protecting the great British countryside, its air, water, soils and its wildlife."[33] While many farmers are certainly mindful of nature conservation and making great efforts to this end, wildlife has not been successfully protected within the prevailing system of industrial agriculture.

Bird populations are a key indicator for biodiversity on farmland. The picture for the UK is a melancholy one, ushering in springs that, while thankfully not silent, are considerably less melodious than the immediate post-war era. The standard measure, the Farmland Bird Index, shows a consistent decline in bird numbers since the 1970s.[34] Claiming that "wildlife numbers are crashing," the FFCC report adds concerns about the critical loss of pollinators, and cites a scathing report from the Royal Society for the Protection of Birds, "A Lost Decade for Nature," that the "UK will miss nearly all its commitments for nature made in 2010" as a signatory of the UN Convention on Biological Diversity.[35] Tanya Steele too, introducing the World Wildlife Fund's (WWF) report "Land of Plenty," repeats that the UK is "one of the most nature-depleted places in the world."[36]

Additionally, in outsourcing much of its food production, the UK has a damaging impact upon ecological integrity beyond its shores, albeit less visible and difficult to measure. More positively, proponents of sharing land with wildlife, such as the Sustainable Food Trust, point out that "nature-friendly" land use, based on sensitive agroecological farming, can have benefits for biodiversity in a long-cultivated landscape such as that of England and Wales.[37] Encouragingly, too, biodiversity is now a consideration in most assessments of British farming.

Lock-in and unlocking

Surrounding the challenges of producing food in a sustainable way are the hard realities of the market context for agribusiness and agroecology alike. This means that even leading players, such as the NFU, must deftly negotiate dissonant economic tensions. They champion competitive free trade to ensure healthy exports and access to raw materials, while lobbying for state subsidies for farming and being aware that unshackled market forces threaten parts of the domestic sector.

Due to institutional inertia, caused by the concentration of economic and political power in the hands of those that it serves and who control the means of production and information, there are immense obstacles to the implementation of the agricultural transition that is necessary to address the ecological crisis. Some of the reports seeking workable solutions hint at organisational and political impediments to change. Benton and Harwatt, for example, acknowledge that within the current system, attempts to attain sustainable farming practices will likely not be guided by science:

> Rather, it will depend on the primacy of the role given to the market and its drivers, and, as such, will be the outcome of a political and ideological process, enabled or disabled by incumbent power relationships and the political economy.[38]

Several commentators, such as Tim Lang, hint at the way that policy "lock-in" acts as a powerful impediment to the transformation necessary for the reform of food systems, and to address regional and planetary threats such as climate change and biodiversity loss.[39] The Centre for Alternative Technology similarly speaks of the problem of both "carbon lock-in," being the commitment to consuming the fossil-fuels that are embedded within existing infrastructure, and the degree to which the concentration of political and economic power and the ideology of neoliberalism are entrenched.[40]

Observations relating to vested interests and media bias are well founded. Unfortunately, in the short term, those with the most power to effect change have the greatest incentives to thwart it. However, even these reports perhaps understate and underestimate the extent and paradoxical nature of the problems that stand in the way of transformational change of a magnitude to match the task. The perverse dynamics of the profit motive mandate that we are all locked-in and dependent upon a system that destroys our own livelihoods. This is not so much a failing of individual ethical greed, but a key contradiction of capitalism. From the materially comfortable, enjoying well-being and security, to the poorest members of society with some hope of uplift in future and for the next generation, we rely upon and benefit from the eco-destructive and exploitative practices that at once provide hope for better times and recklessly squander our prospects. Notwithstanding whether we applaud or critique capitalist growth, its perpetuation is a boon for the sake of our benefits, wages, or pensions, even as that accumulation destroys the foundation upon which such value depends, since, as ecosocialist Joel Kovel argued, it permeates into every aspect of our life-worlds.[41]

The foregoing included a brief survey of report proposals for the future of UK farming and food production, all of which purported to be socially beneficial and better for the environment. Current mainstream approaches, exemplified by the National Farmers' Union, largely favour a continuation and intensification of current trends, looking to expand exports to the world market and to implement more "agri-tech" in the form of biotechnologies and agri-robotics. Present government policy broadly endorses this direction, and, indeed, critics point to the physical location of DEFRA and the NFU in adjoining buildings in London as an indication of proximity, all too readily tending to policy alignment. More independent assessments of the way forward have sought to make an accommodation between agribusiness and agroecology, seeking to synthesise the benefits of both.

The major "National Food Strategy," for example, settles for a three-compartment approach to agriculture, combining high- and low-yield agriculture and semi-natural land—a pragmatic, although not wholly convincing, attempt to straddle different paradigms of land use. Its report is probably the most comprehensive assessment of the current state of the UK's farming and food sectors, making several sound recommendations relating to better nutrition and food education, land use, and participation in growing food. Unfortunately, these are largely dependent upon agreement and funding from a Conservative government that is often ideologically opposed to allocating the resources and making the endorsements that could bring such improvements about.

Although the "NFS" asserts it is making "concrete proposals" and "not a wish list," these will remain just that if the prevailing neoliberal statist paradigm is not challenged and changed.[42] Key recommendations proposed in the 290-page report were absent in the response, the 2022 "Government Food Strategy," especially those relating to poor health outcomes due to the prevalence of cheap processed salty, fatty, and sugary foods, reduced meat and dairy consumption, and addressing decreasing biodiversity and other damaging ecological impacts from current agricultural practices. Quasi-autonomous research teams of this kind frequently find themselves in a contradictory and invidious position, enjoying a limited privilege to comment independently, since they do not need to turn a profit, yet having an advisory mandate that is at once outside and inside dominant political and economic power structures. We also see, however, that discussions of agroecological approaches have increasingly moved into the centre of debates about British agriculture.[43] Social ecology represents a conceptual framework and set of principles that attempt to unlock such dilemmas in favour of the thoroughgoing systemic shift that is necessary.

It is by forging alliances and strategies for what Australian social ecologist Stuart Hill terms "world system change"—through a collective combination of practical, concrete, and achievable measures and an ambitious paradigm of democratic confederalism— that he and others direct their energies and place their faith. Such grassroots alliances are grounded in efforts to enhance political self-determination alongside cooperation, increasing the effectiveness of local food production in fairly distributing plentiful nutritious food while maintaining ecological integrity. These entail concern not just for ethical or "green" consumerism, but also to sustain purposeful and rewarding livelihoods for food producers.

Another important factor is the intersection between agriculture and other sectors. It is impossible to consider the future of the UK's food production in isolation from stark inequalities in land allocation and competing claims upon its use, such as transport, housing, and industrial development. To this end, continuing to better map the land surface, particularly linking to current patterns of ownership, as Guy Shrubsole has advocated, would be constructive. This would help to inform democratic decisions relating to land ownership or stewardship, access, and use, since, as Shrubsole shows, the publicly funded Land Registry often fails to serve the common interest by sometimes acting to obfuscate rather than reveal possession.[44]

The government estimate that 71% of land is used for agriculture.[45] The greatest proportion is currently pasture land, although key voices such as the "National Food Strategy" and Monbiot call for a reduction of at least 20% for other forms of food production and biodiversity. Changes to transport infrastructure and behaviour could potentially deliver substantial ecological wins, but is also an area confronted by a significant issue of lock-in, due to the staggering number of private cars, averaging well over one per household, and the social priority for motoring that this affords. In the foregoing discussion of Kleingärten, for example, we saw that up to 25% of car parking spaces could be made available for urban gardening and other uses. Additional benefits for neighbourhood enhancement would include freeing up land for food growing and other purposes, and vast public health improvements by boosting physical activity and reducing air pollution. Such practical opportunities to shift the relationship to land use and land work and to alter material circumstances, demand a groundswell of voluntary coordination and participation by the substantial swathes of the UK's population already committed to social and ecological transformation.

Notes

1   "About Us," National Farmers' Union webpage: https://www.nfuonline.com/archive?treeid=265, accessed 24 November 2022.
2   "About the CLA," Country Land and Business Association webpage: https://www.cla.org.uk/about-cla/, accessed 27 February 2023.
3   The high-profile lead advisor on the National Food Strategy, Henry Dimbleby, resigned in March 2023 due to profound disagreements with the direction of government strategy.
4   "A great story to tell" is a [common/prevalent etc. rather than "popular" = well-liked] phrase in the NFU's "British Farming" report.
5   Department for Environment, Food and Rural Affairs, 'Government Food Strategy" (June 2022): https://www.gov.uk/government/publications/government-food-strategy.
6   National Farmers' Union, "British Farming: A Blueprint for the Future" (2022): https://www.nfuonline.com/media/ag2djfgn/british-farming-a-blueprint-for-the-future.pdf.
7   Department for Environment, Food and Rural Affairs, "United Kingdom Food Security Report 2021: Theme 2: UK Food Supply Sources" (updated 22 December 2021): https://www.gov.uk/government/statistics/united-kingdom-food-security-report-2021/united-kingdom-food-security-report-2021-theme-2-uk-food-supply-sources.

8   Gwen Ridler, "UK Food Exports Reach Record Highs in 2022," Food Manufacture website (3 March 2023): https://www.foodmanufacture.co.uk/Article/2023/03/03/uk-food-exports-reach-record-highs-in-2022. DEFRA et al. reported a widened trade gap in food, feed, and drink of up to £33.2 billion for 2022, "Agriculture in the UK 2022" (2023), 13.

9   Food, Farming and Countryside Commission, "Farming for Change: Mapping a Route to 2030" (January 2021), 9: https://ffcc.co.uk/library/farmingforchangereport. The report is similarly referencing DEFRA statistics: Department for Environment Food and Rural Affairs. "Agricultural Statistics and Climate Change," 10th ed. (2020): https://assets.publishing.service.gov.uk/government/uploads/system/uploads/attachment_data/file/941991/agriclimate-10edition-08dec20.pdf.

10 NFU Cymru and NFU, "Backing British Farming in a Volatile World: The Report" (2015), 3: https://www.nfuonline.com/archive?treeid=43617, accessed 29 November 2022.

11 DEFRA, "National Food Strategy: Independent Review. The Plan," 39; data from Food Chain Analysis Group, Department for Environment Food and Rural Affairs, "Food Security and the UK: An Evidence and Analysis Paper" (2006), National Archives. Available at: https://www.ipcc.ch/apps/njlite/ar5wg2/njlite_download2.php?id=8916.

12 Just over 50% of the UK's vegetables are home produced, but only 16% of fruit. Department for Environment, Food and Rural Affairs, "United Kingdom Food Security Report 2021: Theme 2: UK Food Supply Sources" (updated 22 December 2021): https://www.gov.uk/government/statistics/united-kingdom-food-security-report-2021/united-kingdom-food-security-report-2021-theme-2-uk-food-supply-sources. Fruit output also decreased 12% by value in 2021, in part due to poor weather conditions, according to Department for Environment, Food and Rural Affairs, "Agriculture in the United Kingdom 2021" (14 July 2022, last updated 21 October 2022), 12, 43–44, and 94–95: https://www.gov.uk/government/statistics/agriculture-in-the-united-kingdom-2021. The overall productivity of vegetables and horticultural output continued to decrease in 2022 (by 4.9%), although rises in production by value were recorded due to price inflation, DEFRA et al.,

"Agriculture in the UK 2022" (2023), 10–11 and 60. Fruit production figures saw a slight uptick of (0.6%), DEFRA, "National statistics. Horticulture statistics - 2022" (updated 13 June 2023), Section 2: https://www.gov.uk/government/statistics/latest-horticulture-statistics/horticulture-statistics-2022.

13 Areidy Beltran-Peña, Lorenzo Rosa, and Paolo D'Odorico, "Global Food Self-Sufficiency in the 21st Century Under Sustainable Intensification of Agriculture," *Environmental Research Letters* 15 no. 9 (2020), 4: https://iopscience.iop.org/article/10.1088/1748-9326/ab9388.

14 DEFRA, "National Food Strategy: Independent Review. The Plan," 110, data from NFS analysis based on Poore, J. and Nemecek, T. (2018) and de Ruiter, H. et al. (2017). See "National Food Strategy Evidence Pack," 42 and 56, for details. Available from https://www.nationalfoodstrategy.org/. The "National Food Strategy" also notes an astonishing increase in the UK's self-sufficiency from 30% to 75% during WWII, a time when large tracts of countryside were ploughed for food and households were famously encouraged to "Dig for Victory."

15 Raj Patel shares a salutary example of a buy-and-eat local public relations offensive relating to the grape growing industry in 1960s California, used to undermine a United Farm Workers' boycott campaign which aimed to challenge exploitation and economic injustice, *Stuffed and Starved*, 77–78.

16 NFU, "British Farming," 3.
17 DEFRA, "National Food Strategy: Independent Review. The Plan," 11.
18 ibid., 139.
19 World Trade Organization, "Harnessing Trade for Sustainable Development and a Green Economy," (2011), 1: https://www.wto.org/english/res_e/publications_e/brochure_rio_20_e.pdf.
20 Benton and Harwatt, "Sustainable Agriculture and Food Systems," 31.
21 Both quotations are from Benton and Harwatt, "Sustainable Agriculture and Food Systems," 31.
22 NFU, "British Farming," 7.
23 Yavor Tarinski, *Concepts for a Democratic and Ecological Society* (Winchester: Zer0 Books, 2022), 10–11.

24 NFU, "British Farming," 4; NFU, "Achieving Net Zero: Farming's 2040 Goal" (September 2019): https://www.nfuonline.com/media/jq1b2nx5/achieving-net-zero-farming-s-2040-goal.pdf.
25 Food miles account for 13% of UK food emissions according to DEFRA, "National Food Strategy: Independent Review. The Plan," 74. Globally, this figure is rising, with a 2022 research article attributing an estimated 19% of total food emissions to transport, Mengyu Li, Nanfei Jia, Manfred Lenzen, Arunima Malik, Liyuan Wei, Yutong Jin, and David Raubenheimer, "Global Food-miles Account for Nearly 20% of Total Food-Systems emissions," *Nature Food* 3, 445–453 (2022): https://doi.org/10.1038/s43016-022-00531-w.
26 Royal Agricultural Society of England, "Farm of the Future: Journey to Net Zero" (8 March 2022), 97: https://vm-01-crm02.altido.com/clients/rase-c3c5ffc2133a3eed/uploads/documents/website-report/FARM%20OF%20THE%20FUTURE-%20JOURNEY%20TO%20NET%20ZERO.pdf. Critics point out that the NFU's headquarters is next door to DEFRA in London, allegedly a close working relationship that effects or even directs the levers of power regarding food policy.
27 DEFRA, "National Food Strategy: Independent Review. The Plan," 81–82 Department for Environment Food and Rural Affairs, "National Food Strategy – Chapter 16 Recommendations," (London: DEFRA, 2021), 2: https://www.nationalfoodstrategy.org/.
28 Benton and Harwatt, "Sustainable Agriculture and Food Systems," 28; the WWF recommends a reduction in meat and dairy consumption of 30% by 2030 and 50% by 2050, "Land of Plenty," 22, 34, and 36.
29 Climate Change Committee, "Government's Food Strategy 'A Missed Opportunity' for the Climate," (13 June 2022): https://www.theccc.org.uk/2022/06/13/governments-food-strategy-a-missed-opportunity-for-the-climate/.
30 NFU, "British Farming," 5. The "Government Food Strategy" aims to reduce sugar consumption, while conceding that its voluntary programme has made "mixed progress" to date (p. 22). The "National Food Strategy" has a target to reduce the consumption of foods with high fat, sugar and/or salt content by 25% by 2032, DEFRA, "National Food Strategy: Independent Review. The Plan," 142.

31 Claire Marshall and Malcolm Prior, "Government Review of ELMS Farming Subsidies Stokes Anger," BBC News website (26 September 2022): https://www.bbc.co.uk/news/science-environment-63029266, accessed 3 January 2023. The three ELMS schemes—namely the Sustainable Farming Incentive, Countryside Stewardship, and Landscape Recovery—are being phased in in a rolling programme from 2022 onwards.
32 DEFRA, "National Food Strategy: Independent Review. The Plan," 41 and 97.
33 NFU, "British Farming," 6.
34 Statistics from the British Trust for Ornithology/Royal Society for the Protection of Birds as published by DEFRA, "Agriculture in the United Kingdom 2021," 139
35 FFCC, "Farming for Change," 8, citing RSPB, "A Lost Decade for Nature" (2020), 2: https://rspb.org.uk/globalassets/downloads/pa-documents/a-lost-decade-for-nature-2020.
36 Foreword to World Wildlife Fund, "Land of Plenty," 4. As we have seen, this was a claim made in the House of Commons paper on "Biodiversity in the UK."
37 Barbour, Holden, and Fredenburgh, "Feeding Britain from the Ground Up," 14.
38 Benton and Harwatt, "Sustainable Agriculture and Food Systems," 27.
39 Lang, "Feeding Britain," 13.
40 Centre for Alternative Technology, "Zero-Carbon Britain: Making it Happen," Centre for Alternative Technology website (2017), 43: https://cat.org.uk/info-resources/zero-carbon-britain/research-reports/zero-carbon-britain-making-it-happen/, accessed 19 September 2022.
41 Joel Kovel, *Enemy of Nature*, 52–53.
42 "National Food Strategy," 143.
43 For example, the Forum for the Future report "Supply Chain Synergies."
44 Shrubsole, *Who Owns England?*, 264.
45 Department for Environment, Food and Rural Affairs and Government Statistical Service, "Agriculture in the UK Evidence Pack" (September 2022 update): https://assets.publishing.service.gov.uk/government/uploads/system/uploads/attachment_data/file/1106562/AUK_Evidence_Pack_2021_Sept22.pdf.

CONCLUDING THOUGHTS

The tacit premise of *We must begin with the land* has been to encourage enquiry into practical possibilities for a circular economy of nutritious food as an essential human need and desire. Can the straight trajectory of relentless economic growth be bent into the spiralling plenty of truly regenerative production? Is what Mark Fisher termed "capitalist realism," the belief that capitalism is the only way to meet such human needs, indeed without alternative?[1] As he well understood, posing this question invites contemplation of other, plural visions of the future. The notion that advanced capitalist post-industrial societies provide the sole and inevitable template for "progress" looks to be excessive capitalist naivety when countries such as the United Kingdom, with its much-proclaimed knowledge economy, does not know how to feed and dress itself. As we have seen, it imports up to 50% of its food, often using "ghost acres" in debtor nations, yet still experiences widespread food insecurity. As fewer countries achieve food self-sufficiency, this appears to be a doubtful model to follow.

Social ecologists take a step back to consider the deep roots of the present malaise and the underlying, systemic barriers to change. They then endeavour to take a step forward by presenting a transformational vision of the future. Put simply, if future systems for food production are not sustainable, then—to be obvious and blunt—they will not sustain. And currently, there are well-founded projections that anticipate they will not.[2] It will not be possible to keep calm, decarbonise, and carry on. However, "lock-in" to the prevailing paradigm of capitalist modernity is an intractable obstacle to change. Stuart Mills "suggests the following:"

> It is easier to imagine the end of the world than the end of capitalism because it is easier to imagine death, fire and destruction than it is to imagine supply chains, innovation and institutions functioning in a post-capitalist world.[3]

In 2023, a year of record temperatures and headlines about widespread forest fires, and fears about harvest failures across the major regions of food production, we do not need to leave such fiery scenes to the imagination.[4] Responding to this sense of urgency, social ecology helps innovative thinking by addressing obstacles to far-reaching change. Sympathisers with social ecology, such as Grace Gershuny, have been attracted by its authentic commitment to put forward a non-dogmatic reconstructive programme, proposing "a free, ecologically harmonious, and liberatory society."[5] Here, deep change has been considered as a profound social metamorphosis beyond those clichés of recent decades, "reform" and "modernisation." Too often the latter are an intensification of what is already happening, and bywords for the acceleration of dispossession and the plunder of natural resources, or cuts to public services and job losses. By contrast, social ecology attempts to seed an alternative social imaginary by envisioning change grounded in practical pathways. While reference to such potentialities may sound utopian, it is intended to be a utopianism tempered by pragmatism. As Ruth Levitas, philosopher of utopia, argues, utopian projects need enough detail to be tangible and viable, yet enough flexibility so as not to be dogmatic in the context of a dynamic and fluid world.[6]

A pressing challenge for social ecologists, however, as for other proponents of revolutionary transformation, is that any emerging social imaginary is constrained, since incumbent power structures condition and police the borders of what is supposedly politically feasible and realistic. While social ecology embeds problems of power and control throughout its critical analysis, awareness of such issues does not, of course, resolve this quandary. Capitalism is a powerful and brilliant incentiviser. It sets the rationale for decision-making at both macro and micro levels. However, as the Kurdish thinker Abdullah Öcalan observed, the capitalist free market is not the same thing as the economy in the real world of lives and things, and, paradoxically, even uneconomic in its wastefulness. Critics of Gross Domestic Product as an economic measure have pointed to the irony that it values resources by consuming and wasting them, typically discounting negative impacts as externalities. Heroic deeds and car crashes, apprenticeships and redundancies, bountiful harvests and food scarcity alike are equivalents so long as they contribute towards profitable outcomes.

Here are three relevant instances from the sources that have already been cited. The "National Food Strategy" has found it difficult to make the case for the take up of measures to reduce the promotion of foods high in refined sugar, salt, and saturated fats because "Company bosses do not dare to stop investing in these foods, in case they lose their competitive edge."[7] Meanwhile, the WWF has insisted that "Governments and businesses need to support farmers and growers to transition to sustainable practices, rewarding and incentivising them to deliver societal benefits," yet such subsidies remain contentious in the present ideological climate.[8] The son of a farmer interviewed for Jumana Manna's "Wild Relatives" documentary commented that it had proven far more profitable to host refugee camps than it would be to continue to grow food on his family's land (while ironically prevailing economic forces continue to perpetuate the mass displacement of communities). So, while capitalism undoubtedly constitutes a forceful set of incentives and dissuaders, we could no doubt endlessly multiply instances where it is failing to encourage the adequate provision of social goods and ecological well-being and to prevent unsustainable practices.

This book hopes to contribute to conversations about change based on the principles of social ecology. It has gleaned widely in the fields of current literature, but also harvested ideas from personal exchanges and experiences. Through its proposals, it seeks to place itself within a radical tradition that does not aim to uproot but rather to re-root, to put down deep tap roots for a more secure future. In promoting endeavours for progress towards a more equitable, democratic, ecologically benign society, issues relating to food, farming, and care for the land and sea are at its heart, and are inseparable from attaining well-being in health, education, and shelter. There is a growing weight of evidence that multiple planetary boundaries are being breached, and that stress and trauma characterise the lived experience of a substantial proportion of the world population.

Radical change is, therefore, imperative to ensure liveability and the survival of humans and non-human species. I have sought to suggest practical changes that are achievable at the collective and community level, without having to wait for politicians and CEOs of corporations to deliver more robust policies. Their support would help, but does not emerge easily within the hierarchical statist and capitalist paradigm, so far counter to a regenerative solidarity economy. The underlying assumption is such change is unlikely to be, and should not be, socially engineered from above. In this sense, the foregoing approach positions itself not as "top-down," or even "from below," but alongside, in the spirit of ecological solidarity. Its commitment is to social agency through mutual aid to implement and provoke far-reaching transformation.

The principles for implementation can be conceived as potential points for a charter—which hopefully could be taken forward at the individual, community, or municipal levels—of inclusive policies that can be scaled across to an accountable democratic federation with worldwide reach.[9] As we have seen, multiple networked organisations large and small, with a social-ecology dimension relating to food production, from La Via Campesina to the Transition Movement to Green Tress, already exist in contrasting contexts. Such initiatives need to extend, to be further developed, refined, consolidated, and scaled across. It is hoped that social-ecological efforts can formulate and articulate a practical, ethical, coherent programme to change the facts on the ground, ground that is teeming with abundance and possibilities. To strive for human liberation while protecting ecological integrity, we must end with the call from the outset. We must begin with the land.

Notes

1 Mark Fisher, *Capitalist Realism: Is There No Alternative?* (Winchester: Zer0 Books, 2009).
2 Beltran-Peña, Rosa, and D'Odorico, "Global Food Self-Sufficiency in the 21st Century," 1.
3 Stuart Mills, "Fully Automated Luxury Communism and Capitalist Realism," *Medium* website (13 July 2019): https://stuartmmills.medium.com/fully-automated-luxury-communism-and-capitalist-realism-33a62f8d1705.
4 The latter concerns are expressed in Kai Kornhuber, Corey Lesk, Carl F. Schleussner, Jonas Jägermeyr, Peter Pfleiderer, and Radley M. Horton, "Risks of Synchronized Low Yields are Underestimated in Climate and Crop Model Projections," *Nature Communications* 14, no. 3528 (2023): https://doi.org/10.1038/s41467-023-38906-7.
5 Gershuny, *Organic Revolutionary*, 49.
6 Ruth Levitas, *Utopia as Method: The Imaginary Reconstitution of Society* (Basingstoke: Palgrave Macmillan, 2013), 123–126.
7 DEFRA, "National Food Strategy: Independent Review. The Plan," 6.
8 World Wildlife Fund, "Land of Plenty," 9.
9 My rationale for this is explained in a previous effort drafted for Earth Strike, namely Bristol Industrial Workers of the World, *The Industrial Workers' Climate Plan: A Great Green Charter* (2019): https://ecology.iww.org/taxonomy/term/1897.

CULTURE, SOCIETY, & POLITICS

Contemporary culture has eliminated the concept and public figure of the intellectual. A cretinous anti-intellectualism presides, cheer-led by hacks in the pay of multinational corporations who reassure their bored readers that there is no need to rouse themselves from their stupor. Zer0 Books knows that another kind of discourse—intellectual without being academic, popular without being populist—is not only possible but already flourishing. Zer0 is convinced that in the unthinking, blandly consensual culture in which we live, critical and engaged theoretical reflection is more important
than ever before.
If you have enjoyed this book, why not tell other readers by posting a review on your preferred book site.
You may also wish to
subscribe to our Zer0 Books YouTube Channel.

Bestsellers from Zer0 Books include:

Poor but Sexy

Culture Clashes in Europe East and West
Agata Pyzik
How the East stayed East and the West stayed West.
Paperback:978-1-78099-394-2 ebook: 978-1-78099-395-9

An Anthropology of Nothing in Particular

Martin Demant Frederiksen
A journey into the social lives of meaninglessness.
Paperback: 978-1-78535-699-5 ebook: 978-1-78535-700-8

In the Dust of This Planet

Horror of Philosophy vol. 1
Eugene Thacker
In the first of a series of three books on the Horror of Philosophy, *In the Dust of This Planet* offers the genre of horror as a way of thinking about the unthinkable.
Paperback: 978-1-84694-676-9 ebook: 978-1-78099-010-1

The End of Oulipo?

An Attempt to Exhaust a Movement
Lauren Elkin, Veronica Esposito
Paperback: 978-1-78099-655-4 ebook: 978-1-78099-656-1

Capitalist Realism

Is There No Alternative?
Mark Fisher
An analysis of the ways in which capitalism has presented itself as the only realistic political-economic system.
Paperback: 978-1-84694-317-1 ebook: 978-1-78099-734-6

Rebel Rebel

Chris O'Leary
David Bowie: every single song. Everything you want to know, everything you didn't know.
Paperback: 978-1-78099-244-0 ebook: 978-1-78099-713-1

Cartographies of the Absolute

Alberto Toscano, Jeff Kinkle
An aesthetics of the economy for the twenty-first century.
Paperback: 978-1-78099-275-4 ebook: 978-1-78279-973-3

Malign Velocities

Accelerationism and Capitalism
Benjamin Noys
Long-listed for the Bread and Roses Prize 2015, *Malign Velocities* argues against the need for speed, tracking acceleration as the symptom of the ongoing crises of capitalism.
Paperback: 978-1-78279-300-7 ebook: 978-1-78279-299-4

Babbling Corpse

Vaporwave and the Commodification of Ghosts
Grafton Tanner
Paperback: 978-1-78279-759-3 ebook: 978-1-78279-760-9

New Work New Culture

Work we want and a culture that strengthens us
Frithjof Bergmann
A serious alternative for humankind and the planet.
Paperback: 978-1-78904-064-7 ebook: 978-1-78904-065-4

Romeo and Juliet in Palestine

Teaching Under Occupation
Tom Sperlinger
Life in the West Bank, the nature of pedagogy, and the role of a university under occupation.
Paperback: 978-1-78279-637-4 ebook: 978-1-78279-636-7

Color, Facture, Art and Design

Iona Singh
This materialist definition of fine art develops guidelines for architecture, design, cultural studies, and ultimately, social change.
Paperback: 978-1-78099-629-5 ebook: 978-1-78099-630-1

Sweetening the Pill

or How We Got Hooked on Hormonal Birth Control
Holly Grigg-Spall
Has contraception liberated or oppressed women?
Sweetening the Pill breaks the silence on the dark side of hormonal contraception.
Paperback: 978-1-78099-607-3 ebook: 978-1-78099-608-0

Why Are We the Good Guys?

Reclaiming Your Mind from the Delusions of Propaganda
David Cromwell
A provocative challenge to the standard ideology that Western power is a benevolent force in the world.
Paperback: 978-1-78099-365-2 ebook: 978-1-78099-366-9

The Writing on the Wall

On the Decomposition of Capitalism and its Critics
Anselm Jappe, Alastair Hemmens
A new approach to the meaning of social emancipation.
Paperback: 978-1-78535-581-3 ebook: 978-1-78535-582-0

Neglected or Misunderstood

The Radical Feminism of Shulamith Firestone
Victoria Margree
An interrogation of issues surrounding gender, biology, sexuality, work, and technology, and the ways in which our imaginations continue to be in thrall to ideologies of maternity and the nuclear family.
Paperback: 978-1-78535-539-4 ebook: 978-1-78535-540-0

How to Dismantle the NHS in 10 Easy Steps (Second Edition)
Youssef El-Gingihy

The story of how your NHS was sold off and why you will have to buy private health insurance soon. A new expanded second edition with chapters on junior doctors' strikes and government blueprints for US-style healthcare.
Paperback: 978-1-78904-178-1 ebook: 978-1-78904-179-8

Digesting Recipes

The Art of Culinary Notation
Susannah Worth

A recipe is an instruction, the imperative tone of the expert, but this constraint can offer its own kind of potential. A recipe need not be a domestic trap but might instead offer escape— something to fantasise about or aspire to.
Paperback: 978-1-78279-860-6 ebook: 978-1-78279-859-0

Most titles are published in paperback and as an ebook. Paperbacks are available in traditional bookshops. Both print and ebook formats are available online.
Follow us at:
https://www.facebook.com/ZeroBooks
https://twitter.com/Zer0Books
https://www.instagram.com/zero.books

For video content, author interviews, and more, please subscribe to our YouTube channel:

zer0repeater

Follow us on social media for book news, promotions, and more:

Facebook: ZeroBooks
Instagram: @zero.books
X: @Zer0Books
Tik Tok: @zer0repeater